AF734995

OECD Business and Finance Outlook 2021

AI IN BUSINESS AND FINANCE

OECD
BETTER POLICIES FOR BETTER LIVES

This work is published under the responsibility of the Secretary-General of the OECD. The opinions expressed and arguments employed herein do not necessarily reflect the official views of OECD member countries.

This document, as well as any data and map included herein, are without prejudice to the status of or sovereignty over any territory, to the delimitation of international frontiers and boundaries and to the name of any territory, city or area.

The statistical data for Israel are supplied by and under the responsibility of the relevant Israeli authorities. The use of such data by the OECD is without prejudice to the status of the Golan Heights, East Jerusalem and Israeli settlements in the West Bank under the terms of international law.

Please cite this publication as:
OECD (2021), *OECD Business and Finance Outlook 2021: AI in Business and Finance*, OECD Publishing, Paris, *https://doi.org/10.1787/ba682899-en*.

ISBN 978-92-64-64469-4 (print)
ISBN 978-92-64-76483-5 (pdf)

OECD Business and Finance Outlook
ISSN 2617-2569 (print)
ISSN 2617-2577 (online)

Photo credits: Cover © ipopba/iStock

Corrigenda to publications may be found on line at: *www.oecd.org/about/publishing/corrigenda.htm*.

© OECD 2021

The use of this work, whether digital or print, is governed by the Terms and Conditions to be found at *http://www.oecd.org/termsandconditions*.

Foreword

This is the seventh edition of the *OECD Business and Finance Outlook*, an annual publication that presents unique data and analysis on the trends, both positive and negative, that are shaping tomorrow's world of business, finance and investment.

Artificial Intelligence (AI) has progressed rapidly in recent years and is being applied in settings ranging from health care, to scientific research, to financial markets. It offers opportunities, amongst others, to reinforce financial stability, enhance market efficiency and support the implementation of public policy goals. These potential benefits need to be accompanied by appropriate governance frameworks and best practices to mitigate risks that may accompany the deployment of AI systems in both the public and private sphere. Using analysis from a wide range of perspectives, the 2021 Outlook examines the implications arising from the growing importance of AI-powered applications in finance, responsible business conduct, competition, foreign direct investment and regulatory oversight and supervision. It offers guidelines and a number of policy solutions to help policy makers achieve a balance between harvesting the opportunities offered by AI while also mitigating its risks.

The publication was prepared under the supervision of Antonio Gomes and Antonio Capobianco, supported by James Mancini and Cristina Volpin, with contributions from Cristina Volpin (executive summary), Karine Perset, Luis Aranda, Louise Hatem and Laura Galindo (Chapter 1), Iota Kaousar Nassr (Chapter 2), Rashad Abelson (Chapter 3), James Mancini, Sophie Flaherty and Takuya Ohno (Chapter 4), Emeline Denis (Chapter 5), and Joachim Pohl and Nicolas Rosselot (Chapter 6). The following colleagues from the Directorate for Financial and Enterprise provided comments and other contributions: Daniel Blume, Antonio Capobianco, Pedro Caro de Sousa, Mary Crane-Charef, Thomas Dannequin, Pamela Duffin, Laura Dunbabin, Renato Ferrandi, Sophie Flaherty, Oliver Garrett-Jones, Vitor Geromel, Tyler Gillard, Allan Jorgensen, Miles Larbey, Federica Maiorano, Ana Novik, Takuya Ohno, Robert Patalano, Baxter Roberts, Cristina Volpin, Paul Whittaker and Mamiko Yokoi-Arai.

This *Outlook* is unique among previous editions for having been prepared in close collaboration with the Directorate for Science, Technology and Innovation. This collaboration reflects the cross-sectoral nature of the OECD AI Principles and the OECD's commitment to work across policy disciplines and specific contexts towards the implementation of the Principles. Under the leadership of Director Andrew Wyckoff, colleagues from the Directorate for Science, Technology and Innovation worked closely with the authors throughout the process and provided extensive comments on all chapters: Brigitte Acoca, Luis Aranda, Laurent Bernat, Sarah Box, Mario Cervantes, Gallia Daor, Karine Perset, Dirk Pilat, Audrey Plonk and Jeremy West.

The chapters also benefited from comments by the OECD Economics Department, Directorate for Employment, Labour and Social Affairs, Directorate for Public Governance, and Trade and Agriculture Directorate.

Editorial

Artificial intelligence (AI) is transforming many aspects of our lives, including the way we provide and use financial services. AI-powered applications are now a familiar feature of the fast-evolving landscape of technological innovations in financial services (FinTech). Yet we have reached a critical juncture for the deployment of AI-powered FinTech. Policy makers and market participants must redouble their engagement on the rules needed to ensure trustworthy AI for trustworthy financial markets.

New technologies often pose risks and challenges alongside their potential benefits, and AI applications in the finance sector are no exception. **For all of their remarkable promise, AI applications can amplify existing risks in financial markets or give rise to new challenges and risks**. These concerns increasingly preoccupy policy makers as more financial firms turn to AI-powered FinTech and expand the scope of its uses. Growing complexity in AI models, and difficulty – or in some cases, impossibility – in explaining how these models produce certain outcomes, presents an important challenge for trust and accountability in AI applications. Complexity, and the need to train and manage AI models continually, can create skills dependencies for financial firms. Data management is another key challenge, as the quality of AI outcomes depends in large part on the quality of data inputs, which in turn need to be managed in line with privacy, confidentiality, cyber security, consumer protection and fairness considerations. Dependencies on third-party providers and outsourcing of AI models or datasets raise further issues related to governance and accountability.

There is growing awareness that existing financial regulations, based in many countries on a technology-neutral approach, may fall short of addressing systemic risks presented by wide-scale adoption of AI-based FinTech by financial firms. Some of these challenges are not unique to AI technologies. Others are intimately linked to singular characteristics of AI, especially the growing complexity, dynamic adaptability and autonomy of AI-based models and techniques. While many countries have adopted dedicated AI strategies at the national level, few have introduced concrete rules targeting the use of AI-powered algorithms and models, let alone rules that apply specifically to AI applications in the finance sector.

Today, many countries find themselves at an important crossroads in these policy fields. Financial regulators are considering whether and how to adapt existing rules or create new rules to keep pace with technological advances in AI applications. At this critical juncture, it is incumbent upon us all to recall certain pillars of good policymaking. Stakeholder engagement in an inclusive policy process is key. Public-private dialogues can help to identify mutually acceptable solutions that nurture innovation and experimentation in AI-based FinTech while also addressing shared risks and challenges to long-term market stability, competition and the primacy placed on consumer protection and trust. Governments must explore ways to incentivise firms to develop trustworthy AI, responsibly and transparently, thereby aligning broader public interests with business interests. A candid assessment of the suitability of existing rules and skill bases in the public sector will also be indispensable.

At the international level, the OECD AI Principles, adopted in May 2019, became the first international standard agreed by governments for the responsible stewardship of trustworthy AI. The OECD, together with international partners working to support financial markets and financial sustainability, must **reinforce**

efforts to facilitate multilateral engagement on implementing the OECD AI Principles in the context of financial markets and other business sectors. The Principles recall that:

- AI should benefit people and the planet by driving inclusive growth, sustainable development and well-being;
- AI systems should be designed in a way that respects the rule of law, human rights, democratic values and diversity, and they should include appropriate safeguards – for example, enabling human intervention where necessary – to ensure a fair and just society;
- there should be transparency and responsible disclosure around AI systems to ensure that people understand AI-based outcomes and can challenge them;
- AI systems must function in a robust, secure and safe way throughout their life cycles and potential risks should be continually assessed and managed; and
- organisations and individuals developing, deploying or operating AI systems should be held accountable for their proper functioning in line with the above principles.

With these reflections in mind, this year's *OECD Business and Finance Outlook on Artificial Intelligence* offers the OECD's latest contribution to a global dialogue on the uses, risks and rules needed for new technologies like AI in financial markets. It puts forward considerations for policy makers and market participants charting a course towards ensuring trustworthy AI for trustworthy financial markets. It is part of the OECD's ongoing commitment to promote international cooperation and collaboration to ensure that these technologies develop in a way that supports fair, orderly and transparent financial markets and, by extension, better lives for all.

Further impetus is needed, however, to apply these values-based principles to the specific challenges facing regulators, participants and consumers of AI-powered FinTech. The OECD stands ready to serve as a forum and knowledge hub for data and analysis, exchange of experiences, best-practice sharing, and advice on policies and standard-setting on these issues.

This year's *Outlook* forms part of broader OECD work to help policy makers better understand the digital transformation that is taking place and develop appropriate policies to help shape a positive digital future. This includes updating and revising many of our standards for business and markets to ensure that they remain fit for purpose and adequately address this digital transformation. These efforts ensure that OECD instruments reflect the needs and priorities of today and tomorrow, and support policy makers as they grapple with the myriad implications of digital transformation.

Dr. Mathilde Mesnard

Acting Director, OECD Directorate for Financial and Enterprise Affairs

Table of contents

Tables

Figures

Boxes

Follow OECD Publications on:

http://twitter.com/OECD_Pubs

http://www.facebook.com/OECDPublications

http://www.linkedin.com/groups/OECD-Publications-4645871

http://www.youtube.com/oecdilibrary

OECD Alerts *http://www.oecd.org/oecddirect/*

Abbreviations and acronyms

AI	Artificial Intelligence
AIDA	Artificial Intelligence and Data Analytics Grant
ALMA	automated alarm and market monitoring system
AML	anti-money laundering
API	application programming interface
ASIC	Australian Securities and Investment Commission
ATPCO	Airline Tariff Publishing Company
BCB	Central Bank of Brazil
BoE	Bank of England
BRIAS	Korea's Bid Rigging Indicator Analysis System
CADE	Brazil's Administrative Council for Economic Defense
CDO	Chief Data Officer
CFIUS	Committee on Foreign Investment in the United States
CJEU	Court of Justice of the European Union
CNBV	Mexico's National Banking and Securities Commission
COVID-19	Novel Coronavirus Disease of 2019
DLT	Distributed ledger technologies
DNFBP	Designated Non-Financial Businesses and Professions
DoJ	US Department of Justice
DeFi	decentralised finance
EC	European Commission
EU	European Union
FEAT	Fairness, Ethics, Accountability and Transparency
FinTech	Financial Technology
FIU	financial intelligence unit
FSB	Financial Stability Board
FTC	US Federal Trade Commission
GDPR	EU General Data Protection Regulation
HFT	high-frequency trading
InsurTech	Insurance Technology
IoT	Internet of Things
KFTC	Korean Fair Trade Commission
MAI	Australia's Market Analysis and Intelligence platform
MAS	Monetary Authority of Singapore
ML	machine learning

NLP	natural language processing
OECD	Organisation for Economic Co-operation and Development
OECD INFE	OECD and its International Network on Financial Education
OTC	over-the-counter
OECD WGB	OECD Working Group on Bribery
RBC	responsible business conduct
RegTech	regulatory technology
RFI	Request for Information
RPA	robotic process automation
RPM	resale price maintenance
R&D	research and development
RPA	robotic process automation
RWA	risk-weighted assets
SDGs	Sustainable Development Goals
SIC	Colombia's Superintendence of Industry and Commerce
Singapore FCA	Singapore Financial Conduct Authority
SME	Small and Medium Enterprise
SupTech	supervisory technology
TFEU	Treaty on the Functioning of the European Union
UK CMA	UK Competition and Markets Authority
UK FCA	UK Financial Conduct Authority
USACM	US Public Policy Council of the Association for Computing Machinery
US CFPB	US Consumer Financial Protection Bureau
VC	Venture Capital

Executive summary

Deployment of AI applications across the full spectrum of finance and business sectors has progressed rapidly in recent years such that these applications have become or are on their way to becoming mainstream. AI, i.e. machine-based systems able to make predictions, recommendations or decisions based on machine or human input for a given set of objectives, is being applied in digital platforms and in sectors ranging from health care to agriculture. It is also transforming financial services. In 2020 alone, financial markets witnessed a global spend of over USD 50 billion in AI, and a total investment in AI venture capital of over USD 4 billion worldwide, accompanied by a boom in the number of AI research publications and in the supply of AI job skills.

AI applications offer remarkable opportunities for businesses, investors, consumers and regulators. AI can facilitate transactions, enhance market efficiency, reinforce financial stability, promote greater financial inclusion and improve customer experience. Banks, traders, insurance firms and asset managers increasingly use AI to generate efficiencies by reducing friction costs and improving productivity levels. Increased automation and advances in "deep learning" can help financial service providers assess risk quickly and more accurately. Better forecasting of demand fluctuations through data analytics can help to avoid shortages and overproduction. Consumers also have increased access to financial services and support thanks to AI-powered online customer service tools like "chat-bots", credit scoring, "robo-advice" and claims management.

As AI applications become increasingly integrated into business and finance, the use of trustworthy AI becomes more important for ensuring trustworthy financial markets. Increasing complexity of AI-powered applications in the financial sector, as well as the functions supported by AI technologies, pose risks to fairness, transparency, and the stability of financial markets that current regulatory frameworks may not adequately address. Appropriate and transparent designs and uses of AI-powered applications are essential to ensuring these risks are managed, including risks to consumer protection and trust, as well as AI's ability to introduce systemic risk for the sector.

Explainability, transparency, accountability and robust data management practices are key to trustworthy AI in the financial sector. Explaining how AI algorithms reach decisions and other outcomes is an essential ingredient of fostering trust and accountability for AI applications. Outcomes of AI algorithms are often unexplainable, however, which presents a conundrum: the complexity of AI models that can hold the key to great advances in performance is also a crucial challenge for building trust and accountability. Transparency is another key determinant of trustworthy AI. Market participants should be able to know when AI is being used and how it is being developed and operated in order to promote accountability and help minimise the risks of unintended bias and discrimination in AI outcomes. Data quality and governance are also critical as the inappropriate use of data in AI-powered applications and the use of inadequate data can undermine trust in AI outcomes. Failing to foster these key qualities in AI systems could lead to the introduction of biases generating discriminatory and unfair results, market convergence and herding behaviour or the concentration of markets by dominant players, among other outcomes, which can all undermine market integrity and stability.

This edition of the OECD Business and Finance Outlook focuses on these four determinants of trustworthy AI in the financial sector. It examines these determinants in the key areas of finance, competition, responsible business conduct and foreign direct investment, as well as their impact on initiatives by regulators to deploy AI-powered tools to assist with supervisory, investigative and enforcement functions.

Explainability, transparency, accountability and robust data management practices are key components of the OECD AI Principles adopted in May 2019. Chapter 1 introduces these Principles and how they can be used to frame policy discussions on AI in the financial sector alongside two alternative and complementary frameworks – the AI system lifecycle and the OECD framework for the classification of AI systems.

Explainability poses a defining challenge for policy makers in the finance sector seeking to ensure that service providers use AI in ways that are consistent with promoting financial stability, financial consumer protection, market integrity and competition. Chapter 2 focuses on these issues. Difficulty in understanding how and why AI models produce their outputs can affect financial consumers in various ways, including making it harder to adjust their strategies in times of market stress. This chapter identifies recommendations for financial policy makers to support responsible AI innovation in the financial sector, while ensuring that investors and financial consumers are duly protected and that the markets around such products and services remain fair, orderly and transparent.

Robust data management practices can help to mitigate potential negative impacts of AI-powered applications on certain human rights. Chapter 3 highlights the importance of robust and secure AI systems for ensuring respect of human rights across a broad scope of applications in the financial sector, focusing on the rights to privacy, non-discrimination, fair trial and freedom of expression. It sets out practical guidance to help mitigate these risks and illustrates how OECD Due Diligence Guidance for Responsible Business Conduct can assist financial service providers in this regard.

Better accountability and less opacity in the design and operation of AI algorithms can help limit anticompetitive behaviour. Chapter 4 explores the implications of AI for competition policy. It examines the potential anticompetitive risks that AI applications could create or heighten. These include collusive practices, but also strategies by firms to abuse their market dominance to exclude competitors or harm consumers. Anticompetitive mergers may also pose concerns, for instance when they combine AI capacity and datasets. The chapter further discusses the detection, evidentiary and enforcement challenges related to AI that policy makers and competition authorities are starting to address.

AI-powered applications developed for the public sector also need to be explainable, transparent and robust. Chapter 5 analyses how regulators and other authorities are turning to AI applications to help them supervise markets, detect and enforce rule breaches and reduce the burdens on regulated entities. Supervisory technology (SupTech) tools and solutions face many similar challenges to private sector AI innovations, not least of all the need for quality data inputs, algorithm designs and outcomes that public officials understand, investment in skills and public-facing transparency regarding use and outcomes. Each of these factors must inform governments' SupTech strategies.

Governments also seek to strike a balance between transparency, openness and security imperatives in the context of policies to guard against possible impacts of foreign acquisitions of some AI applications. Chapter 6 analyses recent developments in policies to manage risk for essential security interests that may result from transfer of AI technologies to potentially malicious actors or hostile governments through foreign direct investments. This chapter also explores related security concerns arising from financing of research abroad as a parallel legal avenue to acquire know-how that is unavailable domestically without requiring the acquisition of established companies.

1 Trends and policy frameworks for AI in finance

Compared to many other sectors, AI is being diffused rapidly in the financial sector. This creates opportunities but also raises distinctive policy issues, particularly with respect to the use of personal data and security, fairness and explainability considerations.

This chapter introduces AI and its applications in finance and proposes three complementary frameworks to structure the AI policy debate in this sector to help policy makers assess the opportunities and challenges of AI diffusion in this sector. One approach assesses how each of the ten OECD AI Principles applies to this sector. A second approach considers the policy implications and stakeholders involved in each phase of the AI system lifecycle, from planning and design to operation and monitoring. A third approach looks at different types of AI systems using the OECD framework for the classification of AI systems to identity different policy issues, depending on the context, data, input and models used to perform different tasks.

The chapter concludes with a stocktaking of recent AI policies and regulations in the financial sector, highlighting policy efforts to design regulatory frameworks that promote innovation while mitigating risks.

Key messages

AI is diffusing apace in the financial sector as shown by live data on the OECD.AI Policy Observatory. R&D on AI in finance, led by the United States, the European Union and China, increased dramatically after 2000 and has soared again since 2019 after a slowdown in growth over 2014-2018. The demand for skills related to audit, regulatory compliance, and digital security reflects the increasingly important role played by AI in finance – particularly natural language processing – to help verify transactions, codify compliance rules and decrease banks' legal compliance costs. In 2020, AI-oriented start-ups in the financial and insurance industry ranked seventh in terms of the amount of venture capital (VC) they attracted, with total VC investment of over USD 4 billion worldwide concentrated in American AI start-ups.

As in many other sectors, AI creates opportunities for the financial sector but also raises distinctive policy issues, particularly with respect to the use of personal data but also considerations related to security, fairness and explainability. Three complementary frameworks can help structure policy discussions about AI in finance: the OECD AI Principles, the AI system lifecycle, and the different types of AI systems as characterised by the OECD framework for the classification of AI systems. As AI diffuses in the financial sector, these three approaches can help shape an inclusive, safe and innovation-friendly environment for AI adoption.

First, the five values-based principles and the five policy recommendations contained in the OECD AI Principles adopted in May 2019 identify core values and policies that should be prioritised for trustworthy AI in all industries, including finance. Salient policy considerations for the use of AI in finance pertain to inclusion and broadening access to financial services, while mitigating bias and digital security risks. Transparency and explainability of AI systems in finance are also key to allow people to understand and as appropriate, to challenge the outcomes of AI systems and to enable regulatory oversight.

Second, the AI system lifecycle helps assess policy considerations and identify the actors involved in each stage of the lifecycle – from planning and design to operation and monitoring. In a fraud detection system for example, the data collection phase requires that data collectors and processors comply with privacy and digital security standards and regulations, whereas the deployment phase concerns robustness, security and organisational change, including workforce reskilling and upskilling.

Third, different types of AI systems raise different policy considerations. The OECD framework for the classification of AI systems helps assess policy issues raised by different types of AI systems in the financial sector along four dimensions: the context in which the AI system is applied; the data and input the system leverages; the AI model; and the task and outcome that impact the AI system's context or environment. For example, credit scoring applications in the financial sector (context) that collect payments history and other personal data (data/input) to perform recommendation tasks (task/output) using a neural network (AI model) to determine whether a person is likely to default on a loan has different policy implications than trading systems. The latter consider user preferences and market data (data/input) to recommend and possibly execute stock orders (task/output) using both machine learning and rules-based system (AI model).

In addition, national AI strategies and policies have started to explicitly promote AI deployment in finance to build or leverage their country's comparative advantage. Certain countries foster AI deployment in the sector as a priority sector in their national AI strategies. Additionally, regulatory bodies are using a variety of instruments to leverage AI and AI-powered innovation in finance while mitigating its risks. These range from issuing guidance to establishing regulatory sandboxes and developing legal requirements for the development and deployment of high-risk AI systems in finance.

1.1. Introduction to AI in finance

Artificial Intelligence (AI) is a key set of technologies powering digital transformation with tremendous potential to improve productivity and innovation. AI systems are being deployed rapidly in the financial sector.

AI in the financial sector can help improve customer experiences, rapidly identify investment opportunities and possibly grant more credit at better conditions. Alongside these benefits for firms, customers and societies, AI can create new risks, or reinforce existing risks. These risks include entrenching bias; lack of explainability of financial decisions affecting an individual's well-being; introducing new forms of cyber-attacks; and automating jobs ahead of society adjusting to the changes. The myriad uses of AI technology calls for balanced policy approaches that can support AI development and adoption while mitigating risks.

AI differs from other technologies by the fact that it can "perceive and interact with its environment" and do so with "varying degrees of autonomy" (OECD, 2019[1]). Taking these distinctive features into account, this chapter provides an introduction to AI in finance and proposes three different approaches to frame the public policy debate so that businesses, institutions and societies can reap the benefits of AI.

1.2. Insights from OECD.AI on AI diffusion in the financial sector

AI is a general-purpose technology that is seeing rapid uptake in many industrial sectors, including transport, agriculture, marketing and advertising, healthcare, as well as finance and insurance. At the same time, digital technologies have enabled the tracking and monitoring of AI trends and developments across sectors in almost real time. The "Trends and data" pillar of the OECD.AI Policy Observatory provides a collection of timely indicators that can illustrate the uptake of AI technologies in different sectors, including business and finance. As illustrated in Figure 1.1, AI research publications in the financial sector increased dramatically after the year 2000, stabilising over the period 2015-2018 and booming again since 2019. It is led by the United States, the European Union and China.

Figure 1.1. Top countries in finance and insurance-related AI research

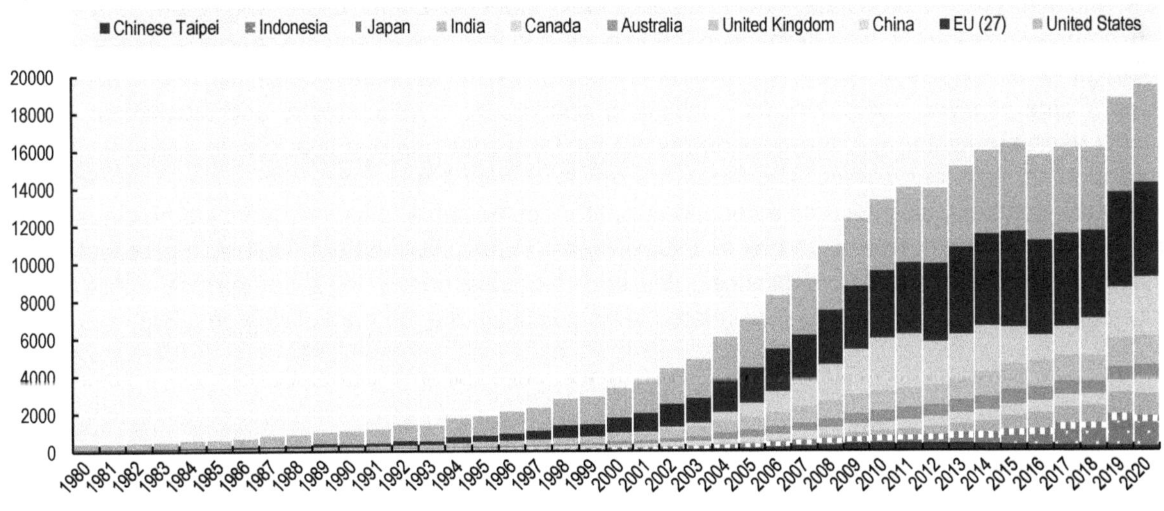

Note: all research publications are considered, including books, book chapters, conference proceedings, journal articles, and research repositories. Please see methodological note for more information.
Source: OECD.AI (2021), visualisations powered by JSI using data from Microsoft Academic Graph, version of 15/03/2021, accessed on 23/4/2021, www.oecd.ai.

Data on the supply and demand for AI skills can illustrate national industrial profiles, inform a country's digital strategy, and uncover educational and labour policy priorities. For instance, the supply of AI skills in a particular country and sector could be proxied by self-declared skills in LinkedIn profiles. On average, a higher proportion of people working in the financial sector in India, the United States and Canada declare being equipped with AI skills (Figure 1.2).

Figure 1.2. Relative AI skills diffusion in the financial sector by country

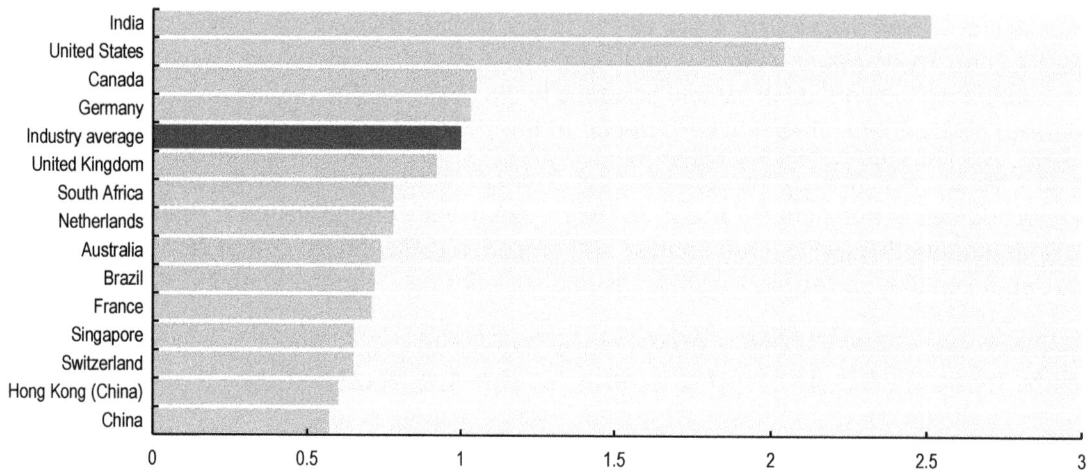

Note: Average from 2015 to 2020 for a selection of countries with 100 000 LinkedIn members or more. The value represents the ratio between a country's AI skills penetration and the average AI skills penetration of all countries in the sample for the selected industry, controlling for occupations. To ensure representativeness, only countries meeting LinkedIn's sample size thresholds for the selected industry are displayed. Please see methodological note for more information.
Source: OECD.AI (2021), visualisations powered by JSI using data from LinkedIn, version of 15/03/2021, accessed on 23/4/2021, www.oecd.ai.

Financial and AI skills coexist in different domains. Digital security is an example. Given the sensitivity of financial and insurance-related data – including personally identifiable information and health data – digital security competencies are in high demand in the finance and insurance sector. Analysis of digital security job postings for all sectors in 16 countries show the top competencies that companies are looking for in this area. Some of these competencies – including encryption, cryptocurrency and blockchain – have commonly been associated with the development of FinTech solutions and financial innovation. Others – such as algorithms, programming languages, swarm intelligence and fuzzy sets[1] – are related to AI. Together with competencies such as audit and regulatory compliance, digital security job postings reflect the increasingly important role played by AI technologies – particularly natural language processing – to help verify transactions, codify compliance rules and decrease banks' legal compliance costs. Digital security jobs illustrate that AI and finance-related skills coexist in the job market (Figure 1.3).

Figure 1.3. Digital security jobs illustrate the coexistence of FinTech and AI-related competencies in the labour market (2017-2021)

Note: snapshot skill demand in 16 countries for digital security job postings. The countries include Australia, Austria, Brazil, Canada, France, Germany, India, Italy, The Netherlands, New Zealand, Poland, Russia, Singapore, South Africa, United Kingdom and United States. The bigger the size of the word, the higher its importance to digital security jobs, as assigned by the algorithm used to process the job postings. Please see methodological note for more information.
Source: OECD.AI (2021), visualisations powered by JSI using data from LinkedIn, version of 15/03/2021, accessed on 23/4/2021, www.oecd.ai.

Another interesting vantage point by which to proxy AI development is that of venture capital (VC) investments. VC investments can provide some context on a country's entrepreneurial activity and sectoral specialisation. As shown in Figure 1.4a, VC investments in AI start-ups have seen a steep increase in the United States in recent years, and have resumed growth in China after declining in 2019. While the number of VC investments in AI start-ups has been consistently higher in the United States than in China – more than twice as many in 2020 – the median size of VC investments in Chinese start-ups has been considerably higher than in the United States since 2016 (Figure 1.4b). Multiple mega investments of more than USD 100 million in the Chinese mobility and autonomous vehicles industry – which is capital-intensive – support this finding.

In addition, AI technologies are being used in virtually all sectors of the economy, leading to a great diversity of systems. While the speed and scale of adoption varies across industries and firm sizes (OECD, 2019[2]), AI-powered applications have expanded beyond digital sectors to sectors like transportation, marketing, healthcare, finance and retail. As shown in Figure 1.5 a, the sum of venture capital investments in AI start-ups for all sectors has increased over twenty-eight fold between 2012 and 2020.[2]

The financial and insurance sector has consistently been within the top 10 industries in terms of the amount of VC investments in AI start-ups, with a total of over USD 4 billion worldwide in 2020 alone (Figure 1.5 a). That same year, almost 65% of VC investments in the financial and insurance sector went to American AI start-ups, following a dramatic increase in the past three years. In contrast, other countries have experienced a decline in VC investments in the financial and insurance sector, notably China (84% decrease from 2018 to 2020) and the United Kingdom (70% decrease since from 2019 to 2020) (Figure 1.5 b).

Figure 1.4. Venture capital investments in AI start-ups by country (USD millions)

a) Sum of venture capital investments

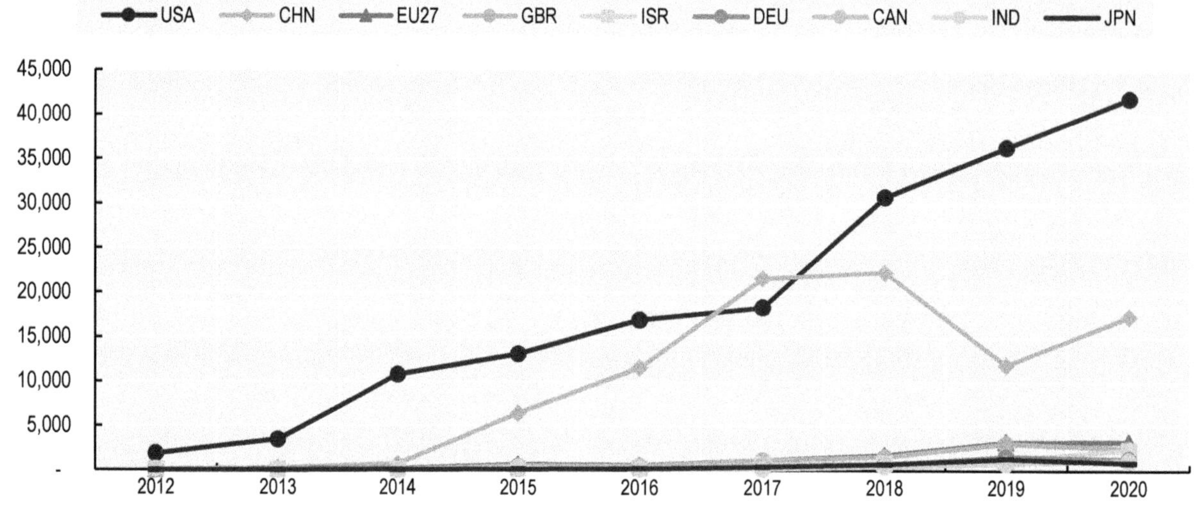

b) Median size of venture capital investments

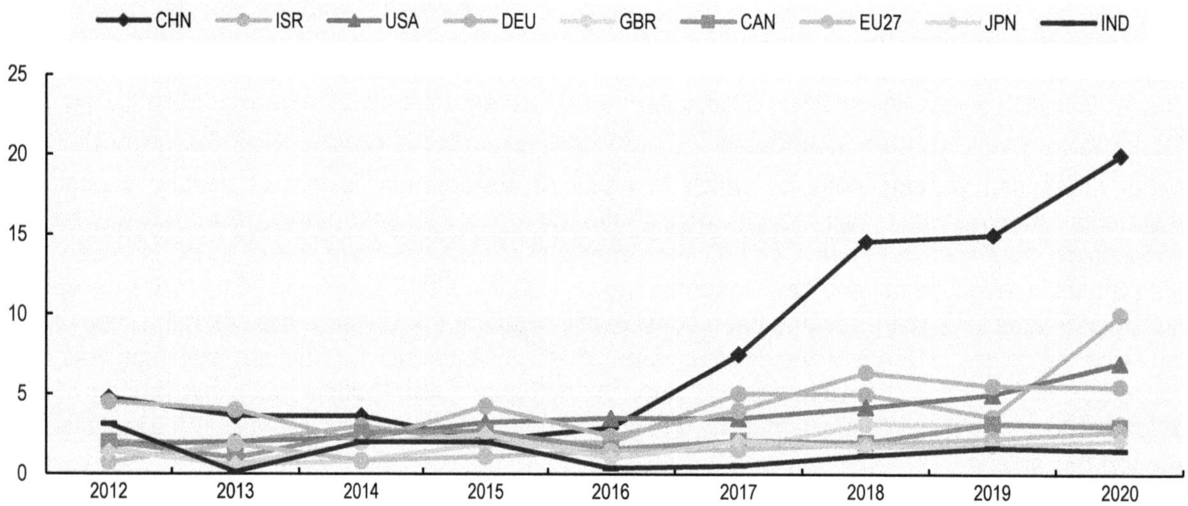

Note: an AI start-up is considered to be a private venture that researches and delivers AI services, software or hardware, and/or products and services that rely significantly on AI systems. Start-ups are identified as AI start-ups based on Preqin's manual categorisation, as well as on OECD automated analysis of the keywords contained in the description of the company's activity. Please see methodological note for more information.

Source: OECD.AI (2021), visualisations powered by JSI using data from Preqin, version of 15/03/2021, accessed on 23/4/2021, www.oecd.ai.

Recent large VC recipients for AI in the financial sector include US-based start-up Stripe, which develops and provides financial infrastructure solutions that enable companies to accept online payments, including a suite of modern tools for fraud detection and prevention based on machine learning techniques. VC recipients also included OakNorth UK, which operates an AI-integrated platform that provides online banking solutions such as personal saving accounts, loans, and business credit financing services.[3]

Figure 1.5. Sum of venture capital investments in AI start-ups (USD millions)

a) Sum of venture capital investments by sector

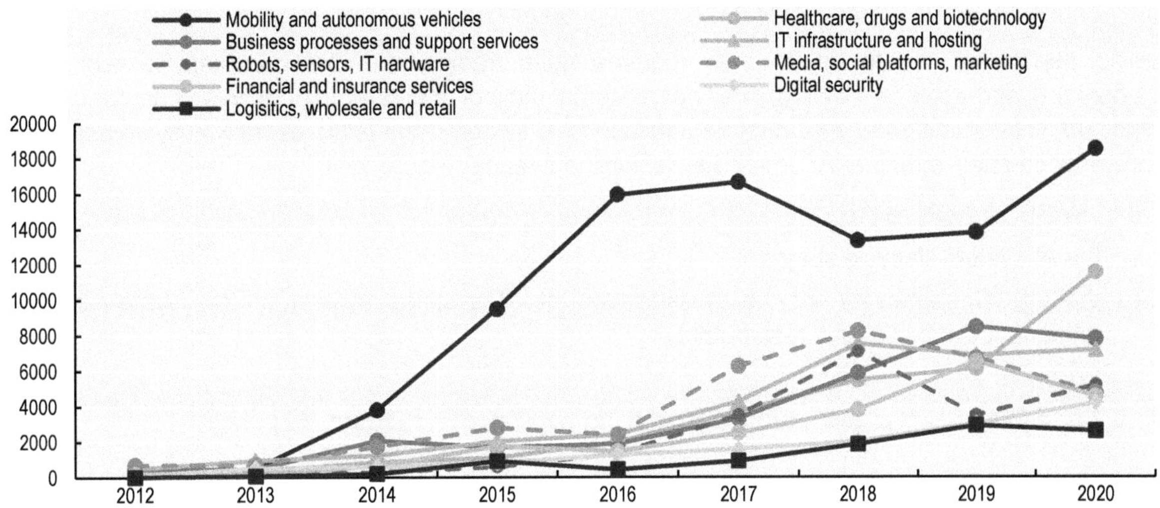

b) Sum of venture capital investments in the financial and insurance services sector by country

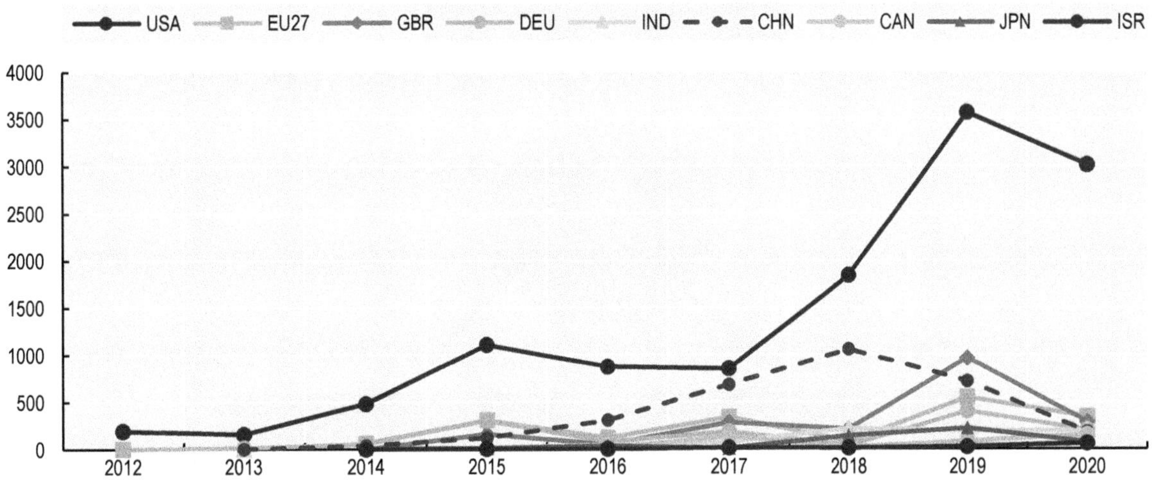

Note: an AI start-up is considered to be a private venture that researches and delivers AI services, software or hardware, and/or products and services that rely significantly on AI systems. Start-ups are identified as AI start-ups based on Preqin's manual categorisation, as well as on OECD automated analysis of the keywords contained in the description of the company's activity. The sectors were constructed by clustering 228 pre-defined Preqin industry labels into 20 larger categories. Please see methodological note for more information.
Source: OECD.AI (2021), visualisations powered by JSI using data from Preqin, version of 15/03/2021, accessed on 23/4/2021, www.oecd.ai.

1.3. Framing policy discussions on AI in finance

In view of its ability to perceive, learn from and interact with its environment with varying degrees of autonomy, AI promises substantial transformative benefits but also creates risks. As such, AI is a growing policy priority for all stakeholders (OECD, 2019[3]). While many countries already have dedicated AI strategies, AI remains a relatively new and challenging field for policy that requires adequate tools. One of the challenges faced by policy makers is to keep abreast of the rapid innovations taking place in the field.[4] AI techniques have been evolving and diversifying apace into what is now described as a "family of technologies" (European Commission, 2021). AI includes systems that use human-generated representations (symbolic models) but also ones that identify patterns and extract knowledge from data (machine learning models) or combine both (hybrid models). AI can also be used to perform a variety of tasks, from identifying and categorising data; to detecting patterns, outliers or anomalies; to predicting future behaviours and courses of action (OECD, forthcoming[4]).

Framing the policy debate on AI thus requires agile frameworks that can capture technological developments and apply to a wide diversity of systems, subject to different contexts and sector dynamics. To this end, this section provides a brief introduction to AI systems and explores how three complementary frameworks can help structure AI policy discussions in finance (Figure 1.6):

- the OECD AI Principles;
- the AI system lifecycle stages;
- the OECD framework for the classification of AI systems, based on the system's context; data/input; AI model; and task/output.

Figure 1.6. Schematic representation of analytical approaches to frame AI policy

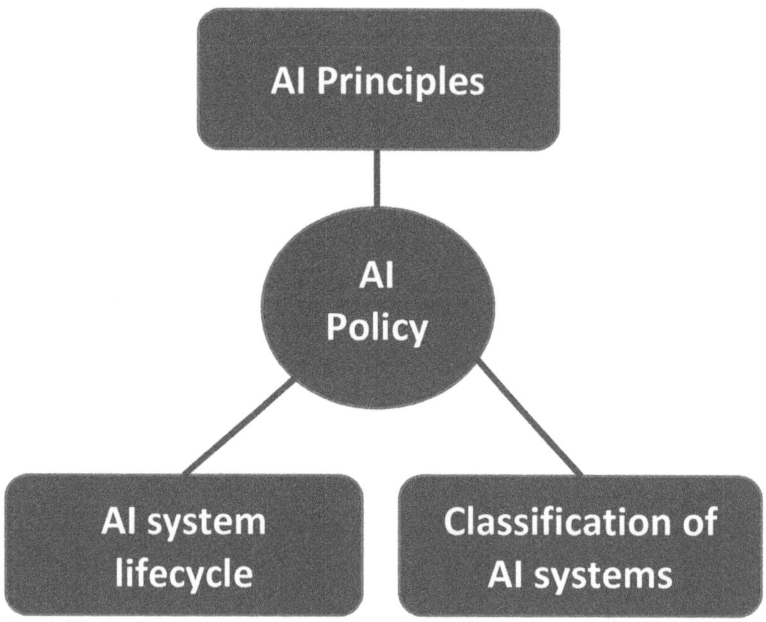

1.3.1. Defining AI, its different types and its lifecycle

In November 2018 the OECD and its group of experts on AI set out to characterise AI systems. The description aimed to be understandable, technically accurate, technology-neutral and applicable to short- and long-term time horizons. Importantly, it informed the development of the OECD AI Principles (OECD, 2019[3]). The resulting description of an AI system is broad enough to encompass many of the definitions of AI commonly used by the scientific, business and policy communities (Box 1.1).

Box 1.1. What is an AI system, building on the OECD AI Principles (2019)

An AI system is a machine-based system that is capable of influencing its environment by producing recommendations, predictions or other outcomes for a given set of objectives.[5] It uses machine and/or human-based inputs/data to: i) perceive environments; ii) abstract these perceptions into models through analysis in an automated manner (e.g. with machine learning), or manually; and iii) use the models to formulate options for outcomes.[6] AI systems are designed to operate with varying levels of autonomy (OECD, 2019[5])

Figure 1.7. Stylised conceptual view of an AI system (per OECD AI Principles)

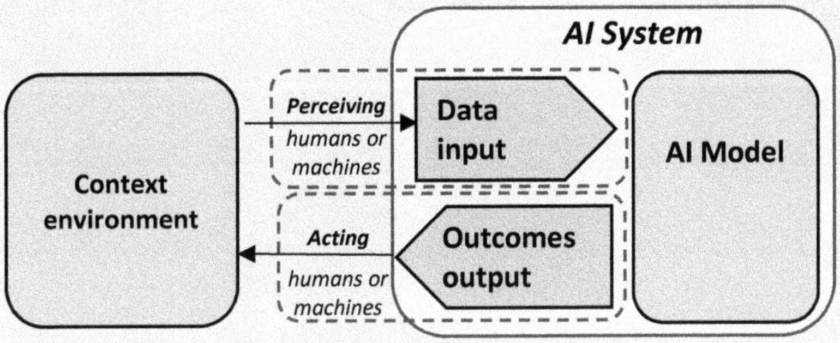

Source: (OECD, 2019[6])

As AI continues to diffuse apace, the diversity of AI systems increases: AI can power systems in different contexts (e.g. in different industries; for a variety of business functions; interacting with consumers or regulators; users that are AI experts or not), using different types of data (e.g. private or public data; structured or unstructured) and AI models (e.g. symbolic; probabilistic) to perform a range of tasks (e.g. forecasting; recognition; optimisation). These four dimensions, namely *i*) context, *ii*) data and input, *iii*) AI model *iv*) and task and output are the foundation of the OECD Framework for the Classification of AI Systems (OECD, forthcoming[4]). Recognising that different types of AI systems raise very different policy opportunities and challenges, the classification framework helps users to classify AI systems according to their potential impact on values and policy areas covered by the OECD AI Principles (see section 1.3.4).

These four dimensions of an AI system can be linked to the AI system lifecycle. The AI system lifecycle typically involves six specific phases: planning and design; data collection and processing; model building and interpretation; verification and validation; deployment; and operation and monitoring. Figure 1.8 illustrates how these phases can be mapped to the four dimensions of the classification framework. The AI system lifecycle phases often take place in an iterative manner and are not necessarily sequential. Importantly, the decision to retire an AI system from operation may occur at any point during the operation and monitoring phase.

Figure 1.8. Mapping the AI system lifecycle to the four classification dimensions of AI systems

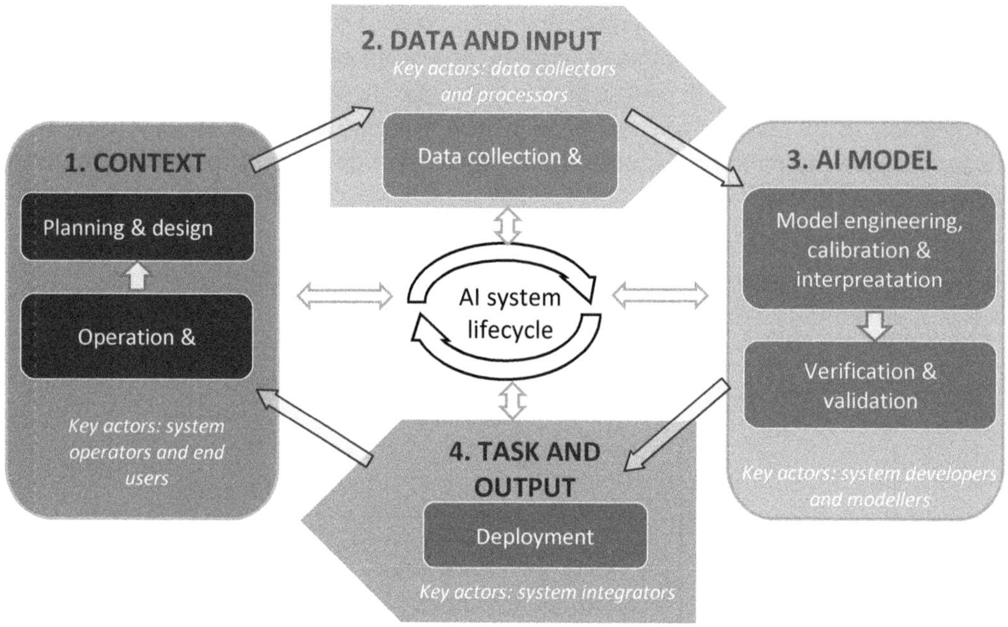

Source: (OECD, forthcoming[4])

Characteristics that make the AI system lifecycle unique – compared to traditional system development lifecycles – include that AI systems can interact with their (real or virtual) environment and "learn" to improve in a dynamic process. In addition, phases in the AI system lifecycle can be nonlinear and are capable of operating with varying degrees of autonomy (OECD, 2019[6]).

The OECD AI Principles, the AI system lifecycle and the OECD classification framework provide three relevant perspectives to assess the impacts of AI systems across different policy domains. In a context of high complexity and fast-changing technological trends, greater understanding of these impacts can set the course for informed AI policy design and implementation in the financial sector and beyond. Rather than taking a one-size-fits-all approach, policies may target specific principles, types of AI systems and/or activities in the AI system lifecycle to seize opportunities for innovation or to address risks.

1.3.2. Policy through the lens of the OECD AI Principles

An AI system differs from other computer systems by its ability to impact its environment with varying levels of autonomy (Box 1.1) and in some cases, to evolve and learn "in the field". AI creates significant economic and social opportunities by changing how people work, learn, interact and live but also distinctive challenges for policy, including risks to human rights and democratic values.

The OECD AI Principles were adopted in May 2019 as the first intergovernmental standard focusing on policy issues that are specific to AI. The Principles aim to be implementable and flexible enough to stand the test of time (OECD, 2019[3]). The Principles include five high-level values-based principles and five recommendations for national policies and international co-operation (Table 1.1). The Principles offer a framework to think through and core values and policies that enable the deployment and use of trustworthy AI.

The first five Principles propose values to guide trustworthy AI deployment. Chief among them are the promotion of sustainable and inclusive societies (Principle 1.1) and the respect of human rights and democratic values (Principle 1.2). While AI can be leveraged for social good and contribute to achieving the Sustainable Development Goals (SDGs) in areas such as education, health, transport, agriculture and environment, it also poses the risk of transferring biases from the analogue into the digital world or to fundamental rights and freedoms (OECD, 2019[2]). For instance, AI can raise issues related to individuals' right to privacy (e.g. AI systems inferring information about a person without consent) and individual self-determination (e.g. if users cannot opt out from using AI's input that influences their choices). This calls for transparent and explainable AI systems (Principle 1.3) and clear accountability standards (Principle 1.5, Chapter 3). Some AI systems could raise safety and security concerns (Principle 1.4): for example, connected products such as driverless cars need to be sufficiently secure to impede malicious attacks that would put the physical safety of their passengers at risk.

Table 1.1. The OECD AI Principles

		Principle	Excerpt
Values-based Principles	1.1	Inclusive growth, sustainable development and well-being	*Trustworthy AI has the potential to contribute to overall growth and prosperity for all – individuals, society, and planet – and advance global development objectives.*
	1.2	Human-centred values and fairness	*AI systems should be designed in a way that respects the rule of law, human rights, democratic values and diversity, and should include appropriate safeguards to ensure a fair and just society.*
	1.3	Transparency and explainability	*AI systems need transparency and responsible disclosure to ensure that people understand when they are engaging with them and can challenge outcomes.*
	1.4	Robustness, security and safety	*AI systems must function in a robust, secure and safe way throughout their lifetimes, and potential risks should be continually assessed and managed.*
	1.5	Accountability	*Organisations and individuals developing, deploying or operating AI systems should be held accountable for their proper functioning in line with the OECD's values-based principles for AI.*
Policy recommendations	**2.1**	Investing in R&D	*Governments should facilitate public and private investment in research & development to spur innovation in trustworthy AI.*
	2.2	Fostering a digital ecosystem for AI	*Governments should foster accessible AI ecosystems with digital infrastructure and technologies, and mechanisms to share data and knowledge.*
	2.3	Shaping an enabling policy environment	*Governments should create a policy environment that will open the way to deployment of trustworthy AI systems.*
	2.4	Building human capacity and preparing for labour market transformation	*Governments should equip people with the skills for AI and support workers to ensure a fair transition.*
	2.5	International cooperation	*Governments should co-operate across borders & sectors to share information, develop standards and work towards responsible stewardship of AI.*

Source: (OECD, 2019[3])

In addition to being grounded in specific values, fostering the development and deployment of trustworthy AI calls for the design and implementation of tailored policies in various areas. This includes encouraging private investment and directing public investment towards AI research (Principle 2.1); fostering the infrastructure and mechanisms needed for AI, including computational power and data trusts (Principle 2.2); and designing an enabling policy environment to encourage innovation and competition for trustworthy AI (Principle 2.3). Trustworthy AI also requires labour policies that protect workers and build human capacity (Principle 2.4) to ensure the workforce, including regulators (Chapter 5), has the necessary skills for the jobs of the future (OECD, 2019[3]). Finally, given the global nature of AI, designing effective AI policy requires international co-operation (Principle 2.5), including on aspects like competition policy (Chapter 4).

Different environments raise significantly different challenges and the relevance of each Principle varies from one industrial sector to the next.

In the context of financial services, AI contributes to inclusive growth, sustainable development and well-being (Principle 1.1) through applications such as financial technology lending that widen people's access to financial services and lower the costs faced by consumers (OECD, 2017[7]). At the same time, AI applications can raise fairness concerns if they exclude certain populations from essential financial services such as mortgage loans or pension plans (Principle 1.2).

Transparency and explainability (Principle 1.3) are key to trustworthy AI deployment in the financial sector: in customer-facing applications, transparency and explainability enable customers to understand and possibly challenge particular outcomes (Financial Conduct Authority, 2020[8]). Transparency focuses on disclosing when AI is being used; on enabling people to understand how an AI system is developed, trained, operates, and deployed; and on providing meaningful information and clarity about what information is provided and why. Explainability means enabling people affected by the outcome of an AI system to understand how it was arrived at (OECD, 2019[3]). Both transparency and explainability are critical to enable auditing and compliance. Albeit an area of ongoing research, certain types of AI models – such as machine learning neural networks that are abstract mathematical relationships between factors – may pose challenges for explainability as they can be extremely complex and difficult to understand and monitor (OECD, 2019[2]). They are commonly called "black box" systems.

Many financial services are considered to be critical infrastructure of which "the interruption or disruption would have serious consequences on: 1) the health, safety, and security of citizens; 2) the effective functioning of services essential to the economy and society, and of the government; or 3) economic and social prosperity more broadly" (OECD, 2019[2]); (OECD, 2019[9]). Critical infrastructure is accompanied by heightened risk considerations and ex ante regulations. In addition, financial services often process vast amounts of sensitive personal data. As such, ensuring the digital security, safety and robustness of AI systems (Principle 1.4) is particularly important in this sector. Clear accountability standards (Principle 1.5) for the developers and operators of AI systems in financial services are key to building trust in AI used in finance (Bank of England, 2019[10]).

Governments can foster trustworthy AI in finance by incentivising research that addresses societal considerations, such as widening access to financial services or improving system-wide risk management (Principle 2.1). At the same time, AI adoption in the financial sector requires infrastructure, including access to sufficient computational capacity, affordable high-speed broadband networks and services (Principles 2.2).

AI uptake in a highly-regulated sector such as finance could benefit from a policy environment that is flexible enough to keep up with technological and business model developments and promote innovation, yet remains safe and provides legal certainty (Principle 2.4). Regulatory sandboxes are increasingly being leveraged in the financial sector to this effect (see section 1.4.2). Labour market policies are also important to reskill and upskill finance practitioners, regulators and supervisors to adapt to new technologies and practices enabled by AI diffusion (Principle 2.4; see chapter 5).

Lastly, given the global nature of the financial sector (OECD, 2012[11]), international cooperation (Principle 2.5) can help set a level playing field for the safe deployment of AI and prevent systemic risk in the international financial system (European Banking Federation, 2019).

1.3.3. Policy through the lens of the AI system lifecycle

Another approach to consider policy implications posed by AI-enabled systems is to segment them by phase in the AI system lifecycle. AI applications in the financial sector include customer service chatbots, algorithmic financial planning, recommender systems for personalised financial products, automated check verification, and assessments for loan applications or insurance claims processing. Each of these AI system applications can be analysed using a lifecycle approach. For example, the following illustrates policy implications at each phase of the AI system lifecycle for AI-based fraud detection systems, which use machine learning on past transaction data to flag suspicious operations:

Planning and design: In fraud detection, banking professionals must weigh the financial loss of a fraudulent transaction against the eventual disruption to customers of inaccurately flagging a valid transaction. Implementation of an AI-enabled fraud detection system may require IT systems' compatibility and workforce readiness assessments. Transparency, explainability and accountability requirements may affect the choice of the model, as well as regulatory constraints and the availability of appropriate data. Additionally, the level of human involvement in the process should be determined.

These and other trade-offs should be addressed in the planning and design phase by clearly identifying the goals of the fraud detection system at the onset.

Data collection and processing: Generally, fraud detection systems collect vast amounts of data containing sensitive information, including personal and geolocation data. In order to mitigate risks to users, data collection, storage and processing must comply with privacy and digital security standards and regulation. The relevant criteria should be in place to ensure that data are of good quality – representative, complete, and with low levels of "noise" – and appropriate for fraud detection purposes.

Data quality and appropriateness have important policy implications to human rights and fairness, as well as to the robustness of fraud detection systems. The data collection and processing phase must include actions to detect and mitigate potential biases, for instance by ensuring that fraud predictions are not influenced by "protected characteristics" – such as race and gender – to avoid biased outcomes.

Model building and interpretation: Fraud can be detected using several different algorithmic approaches. For example, several fraud detection systems combine supervised and unsupervised machine learning to detect known and unknown – previously unseen – anomalies in their transactions, respectively. However, unsupervised machine learning techniques might pose a challenge to transparency and explainability by making it more difficult to understand the output of the fraud detection system. More complex models are in general more difficult to explain, although the relationship between complexity and explainability is not necessarily linear.

Fraud detection systems that iterate and evolve over time in response to new data – changing their behaviour in unforeseen ways while in production – may pose robustness, fairness and liability implications.

Verification and validation: Inaccurate fraud detection could lead to erroneous outcomes that range from blocking innocent clients' accounts to taking legal action against them. It is thus necessary to verify the accuracy and performance of the system against false positives and false negatives. This requires human-in-the-loop mechanisms to vet an AI system's outcome as well as rigorous testing and calibration of the algorithms, including assessing outcome variations when the relevant variables in the training data are modified. The system should be accurate and produce consistent outputs: two similar-looking fraud cases should result in similar outcomes.

Adversarial evaluations – a technique that tests the robustness of a model by intentionally feeding it with deceptive data – of the fraud detection system should also be conducted during the verification and validation phase to test the security of the system. Additionally, a fraud detection system's performance should be tested for bias.

Deployment: Deployment of the fraud detection system into live production entails implementing the system in a real-world setting. It involves checking its robustness, security and compatibility with legacy systems, as well as ensuring regulatory compliance and evaluating its impact on users. Deployment has organisational change implications, including workforce reskilling and upskilling.

Operation and monitoring: The level of autonomy with which the fraud detection system operates poses different policy considerations. On the one hand, high-autonomy fraud detection systems – with no human involvement – may put human rights and fundamental values at risk. They will also raise liability concerns. On the other hand, fraud detection systems may automate tasks that had previously been – or are currently being – executed by humans, impacting both job quantity and quality in the financial industry.

Additionally, fraud detection systems should be constantly monitored for fairness, security, transparency and explainability. Issues identified should be corrected by the AI actors involved at the relevant lifecycle phase (including data collectors, developers, modellers, and system integrators and operators). Retirement of a fraud detection system from operation should be possible at the operation and monitoring phase.

1.3.4. Policy through the lens of the OECD Framework for the classification of AI systems

Alongside the frameworks provided by the OECD AI Principles and the AI system lifecycle, AI policy considerations can be informed by the type of AI system considered, including the specific context in which it is applied (OECD, forthcoming[4]).

Given the multitude of AI systems and their rapid evolution, differentiating these systems according to characteristics that are relevant to policy can be challenging. In response, the OECD's Committee on Digital Economy Policy, through its OECD.AI Network of Experts, has developed a classification framework for AI systems (OECD, forthcoming[4]) to help policy makers differentiate various types of AI systems according to their potential impact on public policy in areas covered by the OECD AI Principles.

Figure 1.9. OECD framework to classify AI systems

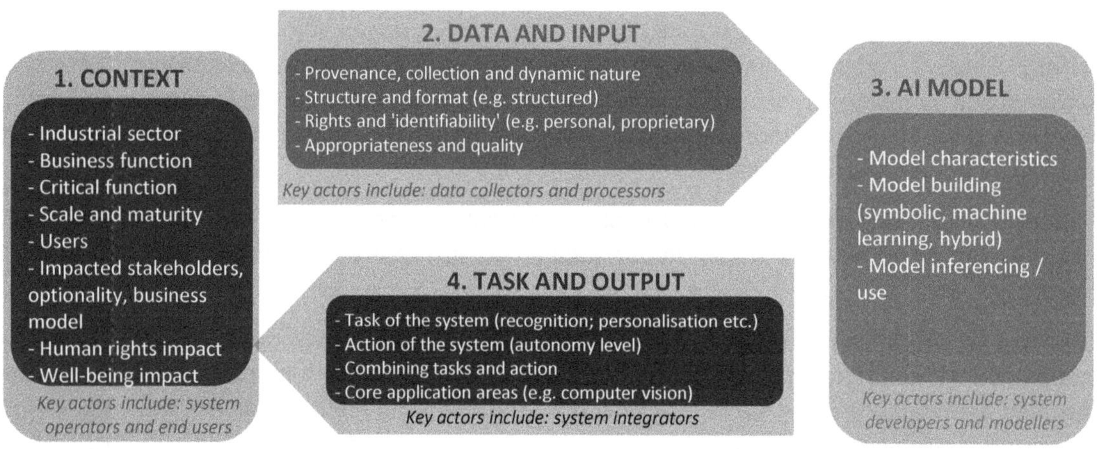

Note: key actors are illustrative, non-exhaustive and based on the work of the AI group of experts at the OECD (AIGO) on the different stages of the AI system lifecycle.
Source: based on the work of ONE AI and the AI system lifecycle work of AIGO (OECD, 2019[1]).

The Framework organises the different characteristics of AI systems across four key dimensions: the context in which a system operates; the data and input it uses; the AI model; and task and output performed (Figure 1.9). The Framework then links each of these characteristics, to relevant policy considerations. In doing so it seeks to create a user-friendly tool to help policy makers assess the opportunities and risks presented by specific system types to tailor regulation and policy accordingly.

First, the context in which the AI system is deployed is particularly relevant to policy, chiefly because the sector and business function are central parameters for policy design. An AI system deployed in finance has different policy considerations than a system deployed in healthcare. Within a given sector, the business function performed by a system provides further nuance: AI systems used to aid the hiring of financial professionals would pose fairness considerations, while systems used for compliance or information security raise issues around robustness and digital security. Other elements of context – such as the breadth of the system's deployment or the degree of AI expertise of its users – are also important elements to consider when assessing the potential risks or impact of an AI system (OECD, forthcoming[4]).

Second, identifying the type of data or input used by AI systems provides useful insights to design the appropriate policy response. For instance, structured or tabular data are easier to document and audit than unstructured data (e.g. free text, sound, images, and video). This relates to transparency and accountability concerns, both relevant to AI deployment in the financial sector. If used to train applications to set credit scores or risk premia, datasets that are not representative of an institution's existing and potential client base could be incompatible with fair access to essential financial services. As noted in chapter 2, the provenance of the data and the way they are collected can have specific privacy implications. Two common examples of sensitive data in the financial sector are observed: geolocation data collected with digital devices; and credit card transaction data.

Third, the type of AI model also bears consequences for policy: certain models are less transparent and explainable (e.g. neural networks that form mathematical relationships between factors that can be impossible for humans to understand) making compliance and auditing more complex (OECD, forthcoming[4]). In the context of financial services, the model type thus has implications for regulatory oversight and risk management. The AI model type also has implications for the robustness of the system: some machine learning models can fail in settings that are meaningfully different from those encountered in training (see chapter 2). To illustrate, AI-powered trading systems trained on long time series may not be able to perform well during one-off events, such as the COVID-19 outbreak that spread worldwide in 2020. This phenomenon – i.e. when a model's target variable changes over time in unforeseen ways – is known as "concept drift".

Lastly, the task(s) performed by an AI system imply(ies) different priorities for policy. For instance, AI systems that personalise financial offerings without letting users opt out can threaten individuals' right to self-determination or privacy (OECD, forthcoming[4]). By contrast, AI systems performing recognition tasks – such as biometric identifiers commonly used in FinTech applications – may raise concerns in relation to privacy, robustness and security in case of adversarial attacks. As in other sectors, the level of autonomy of AI systems deployed in the financial sector will have direct implications on job quantity, quality and security by assisting humans with certain tasks or replacing humans in certain tasks through automation (e.g. in fraud detection, trading or customer service).

1.4. National policies to seize opportunities and mitigate risks of AI in the financial sector

Countries are at different stages of their national AI strategies and policies. Canada, Finland, Japan were among the first to develop national AI strategies, setting targets and allocating budgets in 2017. Denmark, France, Germany, Korea, and the United States followed suit in 2018 and 2019. In 2020, countries continued to announce national AI strategies, including Bulgaria, Egypt, Hungary, Poland, and Spain. Brazil launched its national AI strategy in 2021. Several countries are in the consultation and development processes, such as Argentina, Chile, and Mexico (OECD, 2021[12]).

Policies relating to AI in finance include *i*) policies that promote the financial sector as a strategic area of focus in a country's national AI strategy and support the use of AI systems in this sector; and *ii*) new regulations and guidance to address risks associated with the deployment of AI systems in the financial sector, including the provision of experimentation environments to foster innovation while securing consumer safeguards.

Building on the OECD.AI Policy Observatory's database[7] of national AI strategies and policies, this section provides an overview of how national AI strategies and policies seek to foster trustworthy AI in the financial sector.

1.4.1. Several national AI policies promote AI development and deployment in the finance sector

National AI strategies and policies outline how countries plan to invest in AI to build or leverage their comparative advantage. Countries tend to prioritise a handful of economic sectors, including transportation, energy, health and agriculture (OECD, 2021[12]). Other service-oriented sectors, such as the financial sector, are also starting to be featured in national AI policies.

A few countries in which the financial sector accounts for a large share of GDP – including the United Kingdom, the United States, and Singapore – have articulated their ambition to promote the deployment and use of AI in the provision of financial services to maintain or increase their national competitiveness in this area. For example, the United Kingdom has invested in the use of AI in the financial services sector through the Next Generation Services Industrial Strategy Challenge. The challenge provides GBP 20 million (EUR 23 million) to create a network of collaborative Innovation Research Centres that develop AI and data-driven technologies in sectors such as accountancy, finance, insurance, and legal industries (UKRI, 2021[13]).

Singapore launched the Artificial Intelligence and Data Analytics Grant (AIDA) as part of the Financial Sector Technology and Innovation scheme under the Financial Sector Development Fund, to strengthen support for large-scale innovation projects, and build a stronger pipeline of Singaporean talent in FinTech. (MAS, 2019[14]). In August 2020, the Monetary Authority of Singapore (MAS) announced that it will commit SGD 250 million (EUR 153 million) until 2023 to accelerate technology and innovation-driven growth in the financial sector (MAS, 2020[15]). MAS will raise the maximum funding quantum for all qualifying AI projects under the AIDA Grant from SGD 1 million to SGD 1.5 million (EUR 922 000), to provide greater impetus for financial institutions to implement ground-breaking and innovative AI solutions.

In the United States, the Department of the Treasury is pursuing policies that promote the adoption of innovative tools such as AI and machine learning to empower people to make more informed decisions about their short-term and long-term financial goals (U.S. Department of the Treasury, 2018[16]).

1.4.2. Regulators are promoting safe and secure innovation while addressing specific challenges raised by the deployment of AI systems in financial services

Regulatory agencies are increasingly seeking ways to address the risks associated with the deployment of AI systems in the financial sector. These include risks to consumers' financial inclusion and stability. They also include risks relating to privacy; unlawful discrimination; unfair, deceptive or abusive acts or practices; and the security and reliability of financial institutions.

National and international regulatory approaches to address these risks are at an early stage. To date, financial regulators have responded to AI developments in various ways: *i)* mapping and gathering information on financial institutions' use of AI; *ii)* responding to developments in the financial (FinTech) and insurance (InsurTech) technology ecosystems by providing supervisory clarity and guidance for financial institutions and businesses using AI; *iii)* establishing regulatory sandboxes and innovation hubs to spur innovation in the financial sector (OECD, 2020[17]); and *iv)* developing specific regulations for the use of high-risk AI systems in the financial sector (see Figure 1.10). Additionally, some financial regulators are starting to use AI technologies for regulatory oversight and supervision (e.g. SupTech, see Chapter 5).

Figure 1.10. Current regulatory approaches to AI deployment in the financial sector

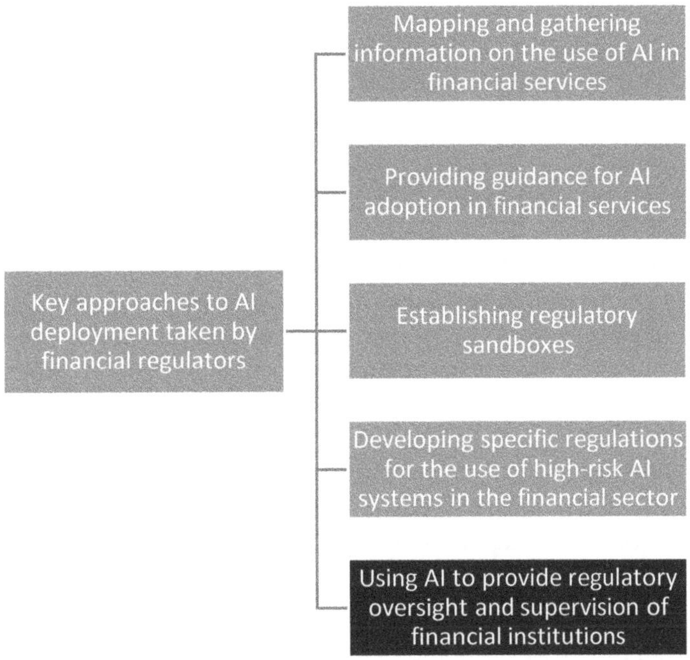

Note: This diagram summarises some of the most common approaches taken by regulators when addressing the risk associated with the deployment of AI systems in the financial sector, including the use of AI to support their regulatory activities. To this end, chapter 5 looks at how digital technologies and AI in particular offer new tools to regulatory oversight and supervision (SupTech).

Box 1.2 discusses a selection of national AI regulatory approaches seeking to address risks and challenges related to the use of AI systems in the financial services sector.

Box 1.2. A selection of AI regulatory approaches in the financial sector

- The **United Kingdom**'s Bank of England (BoE) and Financial Conduct Authority (FCA) jointly surveyed 300 financial institutions including banks, credit brokers, investment managers to better understand the current use of machine learning in UK financial services (Bank of England and FCA, 2019[18]). The BoE and the FCA established an Artificial Intelligence Public-Private Forum – with representatives from the public and private sectors – to explore how AI technologies can positively impact innovation for consumers and markets while considering deployment constraints (FCA, 2021[19]).

  The United Kingdom's FCA also established the world's first regulatory sandbox for FinTech in 2015. The sandbox seeks to provide financial firms with: a) the ability to test products and services in a controlled environment; b) reduced time-to-market at potentially lower costs; c) support in identifying appropriate consumer protection safeguards to build into new products and services; and d) better access to finance (FCA, 2021[20]). This model has been replicated in more than 50 countries (BIS, 2020[21]). In 2020, the FCA partnered with The Alan Turing Institute to better understand the practical challenges of AI transparency and explainability in the financial sector.

- In the **United States**, regulators are seeking input on AI use in financial services. On 31 March 2021, five United States federal agencies – including the Federal Reserve Board and the Consumer Financial Protection Bureau (CFPB) – published a Request for Information ("RFI") seeking comments on the use of AI by financial institutions (US Federal Register, 2021[22]). The goal is to better understand the use of AI systems, their governance and controls, as well as challenges in developing, implementing, and managing the technology. The RFI also solicits respondents' views "to assist in determining whether any clarifications from the agencies would be helpful for financial institutions' use of AI in a safe manner." (US Federal Register, 2021[22]).

  While no AI-specific federal legislation has been enacted to date, federal regulators, including the US Federal Trade Commission (FTC), have signalled that they will not wait to implement enforcement actions. The FTC has issued two blog posts to provide business guidance on how to ensure that businesses using AI do not violate the FTC Act's prohibition on unfair or deceptive business practices, the Fair Credit Reporting Act, or the Equal Credit Opportunity Act. The first blog post, published on 8 April 2020, emphasised that the use of AI tools should be transparent, explainable, fair, empirically sound, and foster accountability (FTC, 2020[23]). The second blog post, published on 19 April 2021, provided additional business guidance regarding the importance of fairness, transparency, and accountability in AI (FTC, 2021[24]). It also noted some recent examples of FTC enforcement actions that involved data or AI, and signalled that the FTC will take enforcement action when business use of AI violates the consumer protection laws. The statement expressly notes that "the sale or use of – for example – racially biased algorithms" falls within the scope of prohibition for unfair or deceptive business practices.

  Further, the CFPB plans to boost financial innovation through its Policy on the Compliance Assistance Sandbox, in which companies can obtain a safe harbour for testing innovative products and services for a limited period while sharing data with the CFPB (CFPB, 2021[25]).

- In 2018, the Monetary Authority of **Singapore** (MAS) released a set of principles – co-created with the financial industry and other relevant stakeholders – to promote Fairness, Ethics, Accountability and Transparency (FEAT) in the use of AI and data analytics in the financial sector.[8] The FEAT principles were released as part of Singapore's National AI Strategy to build a progressive and trusted environment for AI adoption in this sector. They seek to provide a baseline to strengthen internal governance of AI applications and foster the use and management of data in financial institutions (MAS, 2018[26]).

  The MAS convened a consortium of financial services institutions and technology partners to create guidelines and tools that support the implementation of the FEAT principles by leveraging the experience of relevant industry players.

- In **Norway**, the Data Protection Authority's regulatory sandbox for AI aims to promote the development of ethical and responsible AI solutions in different sectors, including finance and insurance (Datatilsynet, 2021[27]).

- In 2019, the Financial Supervisory Authority of **Denmark** published a regulatory note regarding good practices to consider when using supervised machine learning in financial services (DFSA, 2019[28]).

In April 2021, the European Commission (EC) published a legislative proposal for a Coordinated European approach to address the human and ethical implications of AI. The draft legislation follows a horizontal and risk-based regulatory approach that differentiates between uses of AI that create *i)* minimal risk; *ii)* low risk; *iii)* high risk; and *iv)* unacceptable risk, for which the EC proposes a strict ban. With regards to the financial sector, the legislative proposal identifies that "AI systems [that are] used to evaluate the credit score or creditworthiness of natural persons should be classified as high-risk AI systems since they determine those persons' access to financial resources or essential services such as housing, electricity, and telecommunication services". The EC legislative proposal requires that high-risk AI systems – including credit-scoring algorithms – abide by a risk management system, be continuously maintained and documented throughout their lifetime and enable interpretability of their outcomes and human oversight. The proposal also encourages European countries to establish AI regulatory sandboxes to facilitate the development and testing of innovative AI systems under strict regulatory oversight (European Commission, 2021[29]).

At a global level, national regulators take part in the Global Financial Innovation Network (GFIN), a "global sandbox" initiative led by theUK's FCA to help those firms which operate across more than one country to co-ordinate with different regulators and enable cross-border testing among sandboxes. The GFIN, which includes more than 50 financial authorities, central banks and international organisations, reflects the widespread desire to provide FinTech firms with an environment to test new technologies, including AI. Despite these efforts, there is still a lack of harmonised criteria – for instance, on what constitutes innovativeness or "genuine innovation" – and further cohesion is needed in terms of a common set of legal standards (Muñoz Ferrandis, 2021[30]).

References

Bank of England (2019), *Managing Machines: the governance of artificial intelligence*, https://www.bankofengland.co.uk/-/media/boe/files/speech/2019/managing-machines-the-governance-of-artificial-intelligence-speech-by-james-proudman.pdf?la=en&hash=8052013DC3D6849F91045212445955245003AD7D. [10]

Bank of England and FCA (2019), *Machine learning in UK financial services*, https://www.bankofengland.co.uk/-/media/boe/files/report/2019/machine-learning-in-uk-financial-services.pdf?la=en&hash=F8CA6EE7A5A9E0CB182F5D568E033F0EB2D21246. [18]

BIS (2020), *Inside the regulatory sandbox: effects on fintech funding*, https://www.bis.org/publ/work901.htm (accessed on 15 May 2021). [21]

CFPB (2021), *Innovation at the Bureau*, https://www.consumerfinance.gov/rules-policy/innovation/. [25]

Datatilsynet (2021), *Sandbox for responsible artificial intelligence*, https://www.datatilsynet.no/en/regulations-and-tools/sandbox-for-artificial-intelligence/. [27]

DFSA (2019), *Recommendations when using supervised machine learning*, https://www.dfsa.dk/Supervision/Fintech/Machine_learning_recommendations. [28]

European Banking Federation (2019), *EBF position paper on AI in the banking*, https://www.ebf.eu/wp-content/uploads/2020/03/EBF-AI-paper-_final-.pdf. [33]

European Commission (2021), "Proposal for a Regulation of the European Parliament and of the Council laying down Harmonised Rules on Artificial Intelligence and amending certain Union Legislative Acts (Artificial Intelligence Act)", *COM(2021) 206*, https://digital-strategy.ec.europa.eu/en/library/proposal-regulation-european-approach-artificial-intelligence. [29]

FCA (2021), *Artificial Intelligence Public-Private Forum - Second meeting (Minutes)*, https://www.bankofengland.co.uk/-/media/boe/files/minutes/2021/aippf-minutes-february-2021.pdf?la=en&hash=9D5EA2D09F4D3B8527768345D472D9253906ADA1 (accessed on 6 May 2021). [19]

FCA (2021), *Regulatory sandbox*, https://www.fca.org.uk/firms/innovation/regulatory-sandbox. [20]

Financial Conduct Authority (2020), "AI transparency in financial services - why, what, who, when?", *Insight*, https://www.fca.org.uk/insight/ai-transparency-financial-services-why-what-who-and-when. [8]

Financial Stability Board (2017), *Artificial intelligence and machine learning in financial services: Market developments and financial stability implications*, https://www.fsb.org/wp-content/uploads/P011117.pdf. [34]

FSB (2020), *BigTech Firms in Finance in Emerging Market and Developing Economies*, http://www.fsb.org/emailalert (accessed on 12 January 2021). [31]

FTC (2021), "Aiming for truth, fairness, and equity in your company's use of AI", *Business Blog, Elisa Jillson*, https://www.ftc.gov/news-events/blogs/business-blog/2021/04/aiming-truth-fairness-equity-your-companys-use-ai. [24]

FTC (2020), *Using Artificial Intelligence and Algorithms*, https://www.ftc.gov/news-events/blogs/business-blog/2020/04/using-artificial-intelligence-algorithms. [23]

MAS (2021), *Veritas Initiative Addresses Implementation Challenges in the Responsible Use of Artificial Intelligence and Data Analytics*, https://www.mas.gov.sg/news/media-releases/2021/veritas-initiative-addresses-implementation-challenges (accessed on 6 May 2021). [36]

MAS (2020), *MAS Commits S$250 Million to Accelerate Innovation and Technology Adoption in Financial Sector*, https://www.mas.gov.sg/news/media-releases/2020/mas-commits-s$250-million-to-accelerate-innovation-and-technology-adoption-in-financial-sector (accessed on 18 May 2021). [15]

MAS (2019), *Artificial Intelligence and Data Anlytics Grant*, https://www.mas.gov.sg/schemes-and-initiatives/Artificial-Intelligence-and-Data-Analytics-AIDA-Grant (accessed on 6 May 2021). [14]

MAS (2018), *Principles to Promote Fairness, Ethics, Accountability and Transparency (FEAT) in the Use of Artificial Intelligence and Data Analytics in Singapore's Financial Sector*, https://www.mas.gov.sg/-/media/MAS/News-and-Publications/Monographs-and-Information-Papers/FEAT-Principles-Updated-7-Feb-19.pdf (accessed on 6 May 2021). [26]

Muñoz Ferrandis, C. (2021), *Fintech Sandboxes and Regulatory Interoperability*, https://law.stanford.edu/2021/04/14/fintech-sandboxes-and-regulatory-interoperability/ (accessed on 6 May 2021). [30]

OECD (2021), *State of Implementation of the OECD AI Principles: Insights from National AI Policies*, https://one.oecd.org/document/DSTI/CDEP(2020)15/REV1/en/pdf. [12]

OECD (2020), *The Impact of Big Data and Artificial Intelligence (AI) in the Insurance Sector*. [17]

OECD (2019), *Artificial Intelligence in Society*, OECD Publishing, Paris, https://dx.doi.org/10.1787/eedfee77-en. [2]

OECD (2019), *Measuring the Digital Transformation: A Roadmap for the Future*, OECD Publishing, https://doi.org/10.1787/9789264311992-en. [5]

OECD (2019), "Recommendation of the Council on Artificial Intelligence", https://legalinstruments.oecd.org/en/instruments/OECD-LEGAL-0449. [3]

OECD (2019), *Recommendation of the Council on Digital Security of Critical Activities*, OECD, https://legalinstruments.oecd.org/en/instruments/OECD-LEGAL-0456. [9]

OECD (2019), *Scoping the OECD AI Principles*, OECD Publishing, https://doi.org/10.1787/d62f618a-en. [1]

OECD (2019), "Scoping the OECD AI Principles: Deliberations of the Expert Group on Artificial Intelligence at the OECD (AIGO)", in OECD Digital Economy Papers, No. 291, https://doi.org/10.1787/d62f618a-en. [6]

OECD (2018), "AI: Intelligent machines, smart policies: Conference summary", *OECD Digital Economy Papers*, No. 270, OECD Publishing, Paris, https://dx.doi.org/10.1787/f1a650d9-en. [35]

OECD (2017), *How's Life? 2017: Measuring Well-being*, OECD Publishing, Paris, https://dx.doi.org/10.1787/how_life-2017-en. [7]

OECD (2017), *The Next Production Revolution: Implications for Governments and Business*, OECD Publishing, https://dx.doi.org/10.1787/9789264271036-en. [32]

OECD (2012), *Systemic Financial Risk*, OECD Reviews of Risk Management Policies, OECD Publishing, Paris, https://dx.doi.org/10.1787/9789264167711-en. [11]

OECD (forthcoming), *OECD Framework for the Classification of AI systems - Preliminary findings*, OECD Publishing, Paris. [4]

OECD (forthcoming), *Venture Capital Investments in Artificial Intelligence: Analysing trends in VC in AI companies from 2012 through 2020*, Digital Economy Paper Series, OECD Publishing, Paris. [39]

OECD.AI (2021), "Database of national AI strategies - Singapore", *Powered by EC/OECD (2021), STIP Compass database*, https://www.oecd.ai/dashboards/policy-initiatives/2019-data-policyInitiatives-24572. [37]

Prudential Regulation Authority (2018), *The Prudential Regulation Authority's approach to banking supervision*, https://www.bankofengland.co.uk/-/media/boe/files/prudential-regulation/approach/banking-approach-2018.pdf?la=en&hash=3445FD6B39A2576ACCE8B4F9692B05EE04D0CFE3. [38]

U.S. Department of the Treasury (2018), *A Financial System that Creates Economic Opportunities*, https://home.treasury.gov/sites/default/files/2018-07/A-Financial-System-that-Creates-Economic-Opportunities---Nonbank-Financi....pdf (accessed on 6 May 2021). [16]

UKRI (2021), *Next generation services challenge*, https://www.ukri.org/our-work/our-main-funds/industrial-strategy-challenge-fund/artificial-intelligence-and-data-economy/next-generation-services-challenge/#:~:text=This%20challenge%20supports%20the%20UK's,80%25%20of%20the%20UK%20economy. (accessed on 6 May 2021). [13]

US Federal Register (2021), *Request for Information and Comment on Financial Institutions' Use of Artificial Intelligence, Including Machine Learning*, https://www.federalregister.gov/documents/2021/03/31/2021-06607/request-for-information-and-comment-on-financial-institutions-use-of-artificial-intelligence. [22]

Notes

[1] Fuzzy set theory permits the gradual assessment of the membership of elements in a set, in contrast to classical set theory where the membership of elements in a set is assessed in binary terms, e.g. an element either belongs or does not belong to the set. By allowing for intermediate possibilities – which is similar to how humans make decisions – fuzzy sets provide additional flexibility. Fuzzy sets are commonly used in AI applications, including natural language processing and expert systems.

[2] Contrastingly, sectors like the media, business support and healthcare are particularly dynamic in terms of number of deals made (OECD, forthcoming[39]).

[3] "Top start-ups per country and industry" visualisation, accessible at https://oecd.ai/data-from-partners.

[4] For instance, recent patent data show that AI-related inventions have accelerated since 2010 and continue to grow at a much faster pace than is observed on average across all patent domains (OECD, 2019[5]).

[5] The OECD AI Principles say "or decisions", which the expert group decided should be excluded to clarify that an AI system does not make an actual decision, which is the remit of human creators and outside the scope of the AI system.

[6] The characterisation of an AI system has been adapted by replacing the term 'interpret' with 'use' to avoid confusion with the term 'model interpretability.'

[7] For more information, please visit www.oecd.ai/dashboards.

[8] OECD.AI (2021), "Database of national AI strategies - Singapore", Powered by EC/OECD (2021), STIP Compass database, https://www.oecd.ai/dashboards/policy-initiatives/2019-data-policyInitiatives-24572.

2 AI in finance

Artificial intelligence (AI) is increasingly deployed by financial services providers across industries within the financial sector. It has the potential to transform business models and markets for trading, credit and blockchain-based finance, generate efficiencies, reduce friction and enhance the product offerings. With this potential comes the concern that AI could also amplify risks already present in financial markets, or give rise to new challenges and risks. This is becoming more of a preoccupation amidst the high growth of AI applications in finance. This chapter examines how policy makers can support responsible AI innovation in the financial sector, while ensuring that investors and financial consumers are duly protected and that the markets around such products and services remain fair, orderly and transparent. The chapter reviews benefits and challenges associated with data management; explainability and the robustness and resilience of machine learning models and their governance. It suggests policy recommendations to mitigate such risks and promote the safe development of AI use cases in finance.

2.1. Introduction

The adoption of artificial intelligence (AI)[1] systems and techniques in finance has grown substantially, enabled by the abundance of available data and the increase in the affordability of computing capacity. This trend is expected to persist and some estimates forecast that global spending on AI will double over the period 2020-24, growing from USD50.1bn in 2020 to more than USD110bn in 2024 (IDC, 2020[1]).

AI is increasingly deployed by financial services providers across industries within the financial sector: in retail and corporate banking (tailored products, chat-bots for client service, credit scoring and credit underwriting decision-making, credit loss forecasting, anti-money laundering (AML), fraud monitoring and detection, customer service, natural language processing (NLP) for sentiment analysis); asset management (robo-advice, management of portfolio strategies, risk management); trading (AI-driven algorithmic trading, automated execution, process optimisation, back-office); insurance (robo-advice, claims management). Importantly, AI is also being deployed in RegTech and SupTech applications by financial authorities and the public sector (see Chapter 5).

The deployment of AI techniques in finance can generate efficiencies by reducing friction costs (e.g. commissions and fees related to transaction execution) and improving productivity levels, which in turn leads to higher profitability. In particular, the use of automation and technology-enabled cost reduction allows for capacity reallocation, spending effectiveness and improved transparency in decision-making. AI applications for financial service provision can also enhance the quality of services and products offered to financial consumers, increase the tailoring and personalisation of such products and diversify the product offering. The use of AI mechanisms can unlock insights from data to inform investment strategies, while it can also potentially enhance financial inclusion by allowing for the analysis of creditworthiness of clients with limited credit history (e.g. thin file SMEs).

At the same time, the use of AI could amplify risks already present in financial markets, or give rise to new challenges and risks (OECD, 2021[2]). This aspect is becoming more of a preoccupation as the deployment of AI in finance is expected to further grow in importance and ubiquitous-ness. The inappropriate use of data or the use of poor quality data could create or perpetuate biases and lead to discriminatory and unfair results at the expense of financial consumers, for example, by unintentionally replicating or enhancing existing biases in practices or data. The use of the same models or datasets can lead to convergence and herding behaviour, increasing volatility and amplifying liquidity shortages in times of market stress. Growing dependencies on third party providers and outsourcing of AI models or datasets raise issues around governance and accountability, while concentration issues and dependence on few large dominant players may also arise, given the important investment required for the deployment of AI techniques is based on in-house capabilities rather than outsourcing. Existing model governance frameworks may be insufficiently addressing risks associated with AI, while the absence of clear accountability frameworks may give rise to market integrity and compliance risks. Novel risks arise from the difficulty in understanding how AI-based models generate results, what is generally referred to as 'explainability', and the lack of explainability can give rise to incompatibilities with existing regulatory and supervisory requirements. The increased use of AI in finance could also lead to potential increased interconnectedness in the markets, while a number of operational risks related to such techniques could pose threat to the resilience of the financial system in times of stress.

Against this backdrop, this chapter examines how policy makers can support responsible AI innovation in the financial sector, while ensuring that investors and financial consumers are duly protected, and the markets around such products and services remain fair, orderly and transparent. The chapter reviews the potential transformative effect of AI on certain financial market activities, key benefits, emerging challenges and risks from the use of such techniques, and discusses associated policy implications.

Section one provides an overview of the use of AI in certain parts of the financial markets, and examines how the deployment of AI techniques could affect the business models of specific financial market activity:

asset management, trading, credit intermediation and blockchain-based financial services. It highlights the expected benefits and potential unintended consequences of AI use-cases in these areas of finance, and examines how risks stemming from AI interact with existing risks.

Section two reviews some of the main challenges emerging from the deployment of AI in finance. It focuses on data-related issues, the lack of explainability of AI-based systems; robustness and resilience of AI models and governance considerations.

Section three offers policy implications from the increased deployment of AI in finance, and policy considerations that support the use of AI in finance while addressing emerging risks. It provides policy recommendations that can assist policy makers in supporting AI innovation in finance, while sharpening their existing arsenal of defences against risks emerging from, or exacerbated by, the use of AI.

2.2. AI and financial activity use-cases

AI is increasingly adopted by financial firms trying to benefit from the abundance of available big data datasets and the growing affordability of computing capacity, both of which are basic ingredients of machine learning (ML) models. Financial service providers use these models to identify signals and capture underlying relationships in data in a way that is beyond the ability of humans. However, the use-cases of AI in finance are not restricted to ML models for decision-making and expand throughout the spectrum of financial market activities (Figure 2.1). Research published in 2018 by Autonomous NEXT estimates that implementing AI has the potential to cut operating costs in the financial services industry by 22% by 2030.

This section looks at how AI and big data can influence the business models and activities of financial firms in the areas of asset management and investing; trading; lending; and blockchain applications in finance.

Figure 2.1. Examples of AI applications in financial market activities

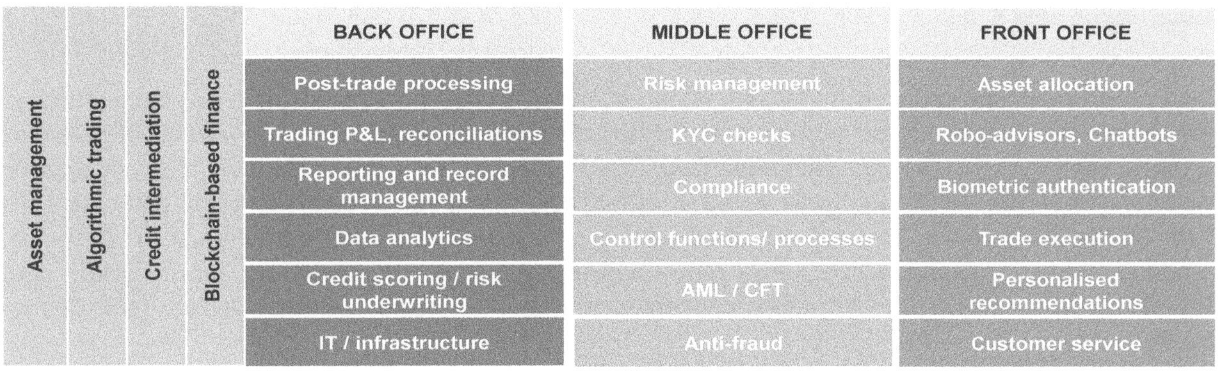

2.2.1. Asset management[2] and the buy-side

Asset managers and the buy-side of the market have used AI for a number of years already, mainly for portfolio allocation, but also to strengthen risk management and back-office operations. The use of AI techniques has the potential to create efficiencies at the operational workflow level by reducing back-office costs of investment managers, automating reconciliations and increasing the speed of operations, ultimately reducing friction (direct and indirect transaction costs) and enhancing overall performance by reducing noise (irrelevant features and information) in decision-making (Blackrock, 2019[3]) (Deloitte, 2019[4]). AI is also used by asset managers and other institutional investors to enhance risk management, as ML allow for the cost-effective monitoring of thousands of risk parameters on a daily basis, and for the simulation of portfolio performance under thousands of market/economic scenarios.

The main use-case of AI in asset management is for the generation of strategies that influence decision-making around portfolio allocation, and relies on the use of big data and ML models trained on such datasets. Information has historically been at the core of the asset management industry and the investment community as a whole, and data has been the cornerstone of many investment strategies before the advent of AI (e.g. fundamental analysis, quantitative strategies or sentiment analysis). The abundance of vast amounts of raw or unstructured data, coupled with the predictive power of ML models, provides a new informational edge to investors who use AI to digest such vast datasets and unlock insights that then inform their strategies at very short timeframes.

Figure 2.2. Use of AI techniques by hedge funds (H1 2018)

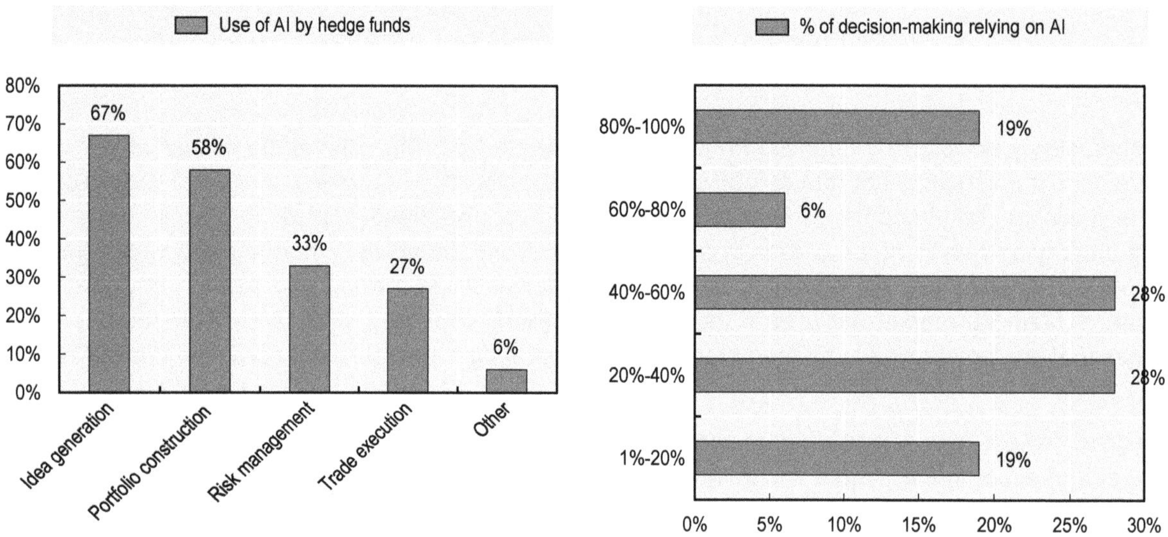

Note: based on Industrial research by Barclays, as of July 2018.
Source: (BarclayHedge, 2018[5]).

Given the investment required by firms for the deployment of AI strategies, there is potential risk of concentration in a small number of large financial services firms, as bigger and more powerful players may outpace some of their smaller rivals (Financial Times, 2020[6]). Such investment is not constrained in monetary resources required to be invested in AI technologies but also relates to talent and staff skills involved in such techniques. Such risk of concentration is somewhat curbed by the use of third-party vendors; however, such practice raises other challenges related to governance, accountability and dependencies on third parties (including concentration risk when outsourcing is involved) (see Section 2.3.5).

Importantly, the use of the same AI algorithms or models by a large number of market participants could lead to increased homogeneity in the market, leading to herding behaviour and one-way markets, and giving rise to new sources of vulnerabilities. This, in turn, translates into increased volatility in times of stress, exacerbated through the simultaneous execution of large sales or purchases by many market participants, creating bouts of illiquidity and affecting the stability of the system in times of market stress.

2.2.2. Algorithmic Trading

AI in trading is used for core aspects of trading strategies, as well as at the back-office for risk management purposes. Traders can use AI to identify and define trading strategies; make decisions based on predictions provided by AI-driven models; execute transactions without human intervention; but also manage liquidity, enhance risk management, better organise order flows and streamline execution. When used for risk management purposes, AI tools allow traders to track their risk exposure and adjust or exit positions depending on predefined objectives and environmental parameters, without (or with minimal) human intervention. In terms of order flow management, traders can better control fees and/or liquidity allocation to different pockets of brokers (e.g. regional market-preferences, currency determinations or other parameters of an order handling) (Bloomberg, 2019[7]).

Strategies based on deep neural networks can provide the best order placement and execution style that can minimise market impact (JPMorgan, 2019[8]). Deep neural networks mimic the human brain through a set of algorithms designed to recognise patterns, and are less dependent on human intervention to function and learn (IBM, 2020[9]). Traders can execute large orders with minimum market impact by optimising size, duration and order size of trades in a dynamic manner based on market conditions. The use of such techniques can be beneficial for market makers in enhancing the management of their inventory, reducing the cost of their balance sheet.

AI tools and big data are augmenting the capabilities of traders to perform sentiment analysis so as to identify themes, trends, patterns in data and trading signals based on which they devise trading strategies. While non-financial information has long been used by traders to understand and predict stock price impact, the use of AI techniques such as NLP brings such analysis to a different level. Text mining and analysis of non-financial big data (such as social media posts or satellite data) with AI allows for automated data analysis at a scale that exceeds human capabilities. Considering the interconnectedness of asset classes and geographic regions in today's financial markets, the use of AI improves significantly the predictive capacity of algorithms used for trading strategies.

The most disruptive potential of AI in trading comes from the use of AI techniques such as evolutionary computation, deep learning and probabilistic logic for the identification of trading strategies and their automated execution without human intervention. Although algorithmic trading has been around for some time (see Figure 2.4), AI-powered algorithms add a layer of development and complexity to traditional algorithmic trading, evolving into fully automated, computer-programmed algorithms that learn from the data input used and rely less on human intervention. Contrary to systematic trading, reinforcement learning allows the model to adjust to changing market conditions, when traditional systematic strategies would take longer to adjust parameters due to the heavy human involvement.

Figure 2.3. Historical evolution of trading and AI

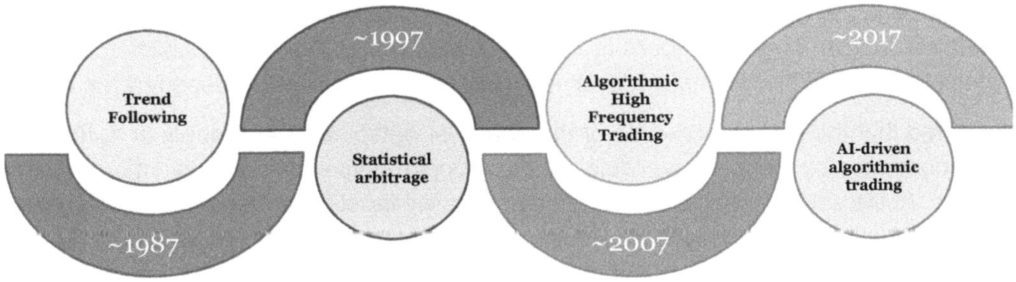

What is more, the use of ML models shifts the analysis towards prediction and real-time trend analysis instead of conventional back-testing strategies based on historical data, for example through the use of 'walk forward' tests[3] instead of back testing.[4] Such tests predict and adapt to trends in real time to reduce over-fitting in back tests based on historical data and trends (Liew, 2020[10]), and overcome the limitation of predictions based on historical data when previously identified trends break down.

While conventional algorithms have been used to detect 'high informational events' and provide speed of execution (e.g. in high frequency trading or HFT), more advanced forms of AI-based algorithms are currently being used to identify signals from 'low informational value' events in flow-based trading.[5] Such events consist of harder to identify events that are difficult to extract value from. As such, rather than provide speed of execution to front-run trades, AI at this stage is being used to extract signal from noise in data and convert this information into trade decisions. As AI techniques develop, however, it is expected that these algos will allow for the amplification of 'traditional' algorithm capabilities particularly at the execution phase. AI could serve the entire chain of action around a trade, from picking up signal, to devising strategies, and automatically executing them without any human intervention, with implications for financial markets.

AI algorithms, HFT and potential unintended consequences

The application of AI techniques in algorithmic and high-frequency trading (HFT) trading can increase market volatility and create bouts of illiquidity or even flash crashes, with possible implications for the stability of the market and for liquidity conditions particularly during periods of acute stress. Although HFT is an important source of liquidity for the markets under normal market conditions, improving market efficiency, any disruption in their operation can lead to the opposite results with liquidity being pulled out of the market, amplifying stress in the market and potentially affecting market resilience.

The possible simultaneous execution of large sales or purchases by traders using the similar AI-based models could give rise to new sources of vulnerabilities (FSB, 2017[11]). Indeed, some algo-HFT strategies appear to have contributed to extreme market volatility, reduced liquidity and exacerbated flash crashes that have occurred with growing frequency over the past several years (OECD, 2019[12]) . In addition, the use of 'off-the-shelf' algorithms by a large part of the market could prompt herding behaviour, convergence and one-way markets, further amplifying volatility risks, pro-cyclicality, and unexpected changes in the market both in terms of scale and in terms of direction. In the absence of market makers willing to act as shock-absorbers by taking on the opposite side of transactions, such herding behaviour may lead to bouts of illiquidity, particularly in times of stress when liquidity is most important.

At the single trader level, the lack of explainability of ML models used to devise trading strategies makes it difficult to understand what drives the decision and adjust the strategy as needed in times of poor performance. Given that AI-based models do not follow linear processes (input A caused trading strategy B to be executed) which can be traced and interpreted, users cannot decompose the decision/model output into its underlying drivers to adjust or correct it. Similarly, in times of over-performance, users are unable to understand why the successful trading decision was made, and therefore cannot identify whether such performance is due to the model's superiority and ability to capture underlying relationships in the data or to other unrelated factors. That said, there is no formal requirement for explainability for human-initiated trading strategies, although the rational underpinning these can be easily expressed by the trader involved.

It should be noted that the massive take-up of third-party or outsourced AI models or datasets by traders could benefit consumers by reducing available arbitrage opportunities, driving down margins and reducing bid-ask spreads. At the same time, the use of the same or similar standardised models by a large number of traders could lead to convergence in strategies and could contribute to amplification of stress in the markets, as discussed above. Such convergence could also increase the risk of cyber-attacks, as it becomes easier for cyber-criminals to influence agents acting in the same way rather than autonomous agents with distinct behaviour (ACPR, 2018[13]).

Box 2.1. Safeguarding mechanisms built in trading systems

A number of defences are available to traders wishing to mitigate some of the unintended consequences of AI-driven algorithmic trading, such as automated control mechanisms, referred to as 'kill switches'. These mechanisms are the ultimate line of defence of traders, and instantly switch off the model and replace technology with human handling when the algorithm goes beyond the risk system and do not behave in accordance with the intended purpose. In Canada, for instance, firms are required to have built-in 'override' functionalities that automatically disengage the operation of the system or allows the firm to do so remotely, should need be (IIROC, 2012[14]).

Kill switches and other similar control mechanisms need to be tested and monitored themselves, to ensure that firms can rely on them in case of need. Nevertheless, such mechanisms could be considered suboptimal from a policy perspective, as they switch off the operation of the systems when it is most needed in times of stress, giving rise to operational vulnerabilities.

In the UK, for example, firm are expected to have manual and automated controls that stop trading or prevent user access, and with manual intervention required to restart trading (referred to as 'kill-switch' controls) (Bank of England, 2018[15]). A firm, at a minimum, is expected to: (a) have a governance process around the use of kill-switch controls; (b) detail the action to be taken in respect of outstanding and placed orders when kill-switch controls are activated; and (c) periodically assess kill-switch controls to ensure that they operate as intended. This includes an assessment of the speed at which the procedure can be affected (Bank of England, 2018[15]).Safeguards are also built in pre-trading risk management systems, aiming to prevent and stop potential misuse of AI-based systems. Defences could also be applied at the exchange level where the trading is executed, and could include automatic cancellation of orders when the AI system is switched off for some reason and methods that provide resistance to sophisticated manipulation enabled by technology. Circuit breakers, currently triggered by massive drops between trades, could perhaps be adjusted to also identify and be triggered by large numbers of smaller trades performed by AI-driven systems, with the same effect.

What is more, the deployment of AI by traders could amplify the interconnectedness of financial markets and institutions in unexpected ways, potentially increasing correlations and dependencies of previously unrelated variables (FSB, 2017[11]). The scaling up of the use of algorithms that generate uncorrelated profits or returns may generate correlation in unrelated variables if their use reaches a sufficiently important scale. It can also amplify network effects, such as unexpected changes in the scale and direction of market moves.

Potential consequences of the use of AI in trading are also observed in the competition field (see Chapter 4). Traders may intentionally add to the general lack of transparency and explainability in proprietary ML models so as to retain their competitive edge. This, in turn, can raise issues related to the supervision of ML models and algorithms. In addition, the use of algorithms in trading can also make collusive outcomes easier to sustain and more likely to be observed in digital markets (OECD, 2017[16]). AI-driven systems may exacerbate illegal practices aiming to manipulate the markets, such as 'spoofing'[6], by making it more difficult for supervisors to identify such practices if collusion among machines is in place.

Similar considerations apply to trading desks of central banks, which aim to provide temporary market liquidity in times of market stress or to provide insurance against temporary deviations from an explicit target. As outliers could move the market into states with significant systematic risk or even systemic risk, a certain level of human intervention in AI-based automated systems could be necessary in order to manage such risks and introduce adequate safeguards.

2.2.3. Credit intermediation and assessment of creditworthiness

AI is being used by banks and fintech lenders in a variety of back-office and client-facing use-cases. Chat-bots powered by AI are deployed in client on-boarding and customer service, AI techniques are used for KYC, AML/CFT checks, ML models help recognise abnormal transactions and identify suspicious and/or fraudulent activity, while AI is also used for risk management purposes. When it comes to credit risk management of loan portfolios, ML models used to predict corporate defaults have been shown to produce superior results compared to standard statistical models (e.g. logic regressions) when limited information is available (Bank of Italy, 2019[17]). AI-based systems can also help analyse the degree of interconnectedness between borrowers, allowing for better risk management of lending portfolios.

The AI use case with the most transformational effect on credit intermediation is the assessment of creditworthiness of prospective borrowers for credit underwriting. Advanced AI-based analytics models can increase the speed and reduce the cost of underwriting through automation and associated efficiencies. More importantly, credit scoring models powered by big data and AI allow for the analysis of creditworthiness of clients with limited credit history or insufficient collateral, referred to as 'thin-files' through a combination of conventional credit information with big data not intuitively related to creditworthiness (e.g. social media data, digital footprints, and transactional data accessible through Open Banking initiatives).

The use of AI and big data has the potential to promote greater financial inclusion by enabling the extension of credit to unbanked parts of the population or to underbanked clients, such as near-prime customers or SMEs. This is particularly important for those SMEs that are viable but unable to provide historical performance data or pledge tangible collateral and who have historically faced financing gaps in some economies. Ultimately, the use of AI could support the growth of the real economy by alleviating financing constraints to SMEs. Nevertheless, it should be noted that AI-based credit scoring models remain untested over longer credit cycles or in case of a market downturn.

Risks of bias and disparate impact in credit outcomes

The use of ML models and big data for credit underwriting raises risks of disparate impact in credit outcomes and the potential for discriminatory or unfair lending (US Treasury, 2016[18]).[7] Biased, unfair or discriminatory lending decisions can stem from the inadequate or inappropriate use of data or the use of poor quality or unsuitable data, as well as the lack of transparency or explainability of AI-based models. Similar to all models using data, the risk of 'garbage in, garbage out' exists in ML-based models for risk scoring. Inadequate data may include poorly labelled or inaccurate data, data that reflects underlying human prejudices, or incomplete data (S&P, 2019[19]). A neutral machine learning model that is trained with inadequate data, risks producing inaccurate results even when fed with 'good' data. Equally, a neural network[8] trained on high-quality data, which is fed inadequate data, will produce a questionable output, despite the well-trained underlying algorithm.

The difficulty in comprehending, following or replicating the decision-making process, referred to as lack of explainability, raises important challenges in lending, while making it harder to detect inappropriate use of data or the use of unsuitable data by the model. Such lack of transparency is particularly pertinent in lending decisions, as lenders are accountable for their decisions and must be able to explain the basis for denials of credit extension. The lack of explainability also means that lenders have limited ability to explain how a credit decision has been made, while consumers have little chance to understand what steps they should take to improve their credit rating or seek redress for potential discrimination. Importantly, the lack of explainability makes discrimination in credit allocation even harder to find (Brookings, 2020[20]).

Biased or discriminatory outcomes of AI credit rating models can be unintentional: well-intentioned but poorly designed and controlled models can inadvertently generate biased conclusions, discriminate against protected classes of people (e.g. based on race, sex, religion) or reinforce existing biases. Algorithms may combine facially neutral data points and treat them as proxies for immutable characteristics such as race or gender, thereby circumventing existing non-discrimination laws (Hurley, 2017[21]). For example, while a credit officer may be diligent not to include gender-based variants as input to the model, the model can infer the gender based on transaction activity, and use such knowledge in the assessment of creditworthiness. Biases may also be inherent in the data used as variables and, given that the model trains itself on such data, it may perpetuate historical biases incorporated in the data used to train it.

Safeguarding mechanisms to mitigate risks of disparate treatment and bias

Developed economies have regulations in place to ensure that specific types of data are not being used in the credit risk analysis (e.g. US regulation around race data or zip code data, protected category data in the United Kingdom). Regulation promoting anti-discrimination principles, such as the US fair lending laws, exists in many jurisdictions, and regulators are globally considering the risk of potential bias and discrimination risk that AI/ML and algorithms can pose (White & Case, 2017[22]).

In some jurisdictions, comparative evidence of disparate treatment, such as lower average credit limits for members of protected groups than for members of other groups, is considered discrimination regardless of whether there was intent to discriminate. Potential mitigants against such risks are the existence of auditing mechanisms that sense check the results of the model against baseline datasets; testing of such scoring systems to ensure their fairness and accuracy (Citron and Pasquale, 2014[23]); disclosure to the customer and opt-in procedures; and governance frameworks for AI-enabled products and services and assignment of accountability to the human parameter of the project, to name a few (see Section 1.4).

Box 2.2. AI and Big Data in financial services provided by BigTech in certain jurisdictions

The use of AI by BigTech is amplifying the use of massive datasets of customer information that is already leveraged by such firms to provide tailored financial services, and intensifies ensuing risks particularly in certain jurisdictions where BigTech is very active in financial service provision (e.g. China). Such risks are associated with data privacy considerations and concerns around the collection, storage and use of personal data for commercial gain and which could disadvantage customers through discriminatory practices related to credit (or other services) availability and pricing. Financial consumers risk receiving discriminatory product offering, pricing or advice, while the lack of explainability of AI-based techniques makes it increasingly difficult for supervisors to access and audit the activities provided by such firms.

AI techniques could further strengthen the ability of BigTech to provide novel and customised services, reinforcing their competitive advantage over traditional financial services firms and potentially allowing BigTech to dominate in certain parts of the market. The data advantage of BigTech could in theory allow them to build monopolistic positions, both in relation to client acquisition (for example through effective price discrimination) and through the introduction of high barriers to entry for smaller players.

Excessive market concentration and the dependence of the market on a few large firms could have possible systemic implications depending on their scale and scope (FSB, 2017[11]). A related risk of potential anti-competitive behaviours and market concentration is associated with the technological aspect of the service provision by BigTech (e.g. cloud computing service providers) and the possible emergence of a small number of key players in markets for AI solutions and/or services incorporating AI technologies, evidence of which is already observed in some parts of the world (ACPR, 2018[13]).

At the end of 2020, the European Union and the UK published regulatory proposals, the Digital Markets Act, that seek to establish an ex ante framework to govern 'Gatekeeper' digital platforms such as BigTech, aiming to mitigate some of the above risks and ensure fair and open digital markets (European Commission, 2020[24]). Some of the obligations proposed include the requirement for such Gatekeepers to provide business users with access to the data generated by their activities and provide data portability, while prohibiting them from using data obtained from business users to compete with these business users (to address dual role risks). The proposal also provides for solutions addressing self-preferencing, parity and ranking requirements to ensure no favourable treatment to the services offered by the Gatekeeper itself against those of third parties.

2.2.4. AI in blockchain[9]-based financial services

Distributed ledger technologies (DLT) are increasingly being used in finance, supported by their purported benefits of speed, efficiency and transparency, driven by automation and disintermediation (OECD, 2020[25]). Major applications of DLTs in financial services include issuance and post-trade/clearing and settlement of securities; payments; central bank digital currencies and fiat-backed stablecoins; and the tokenisation of assets more broadly. Merging AI models, criticised for their opaque and 'black box' nature, with blockchain technologies, known for their transparency, sounds counter-intuitive in the first instance.

Although a convergence of AI and DLTs in blockchain-based finance is promoted by the industry as a way to yield better results in such systems, this is not observed in practice at this stage. Increased automation amplifies efficiencies claimed by DLT-based systems, however, the actual level of AI implementation in DLT-based projects does not appear to be sufficiently large at this stage to justify claims of convergence between the two technologies. Instead, what is currently observed is the use of specific AI applications in blockchain-based systems (e.g. for the curation of data to the blockchain) or the use of DLT systems for the purposes of AI models (e.g. for data storage and sharing).

DLT solutions are used for the data management aspect of AI techniques, benefiting from the immutable and trust-less characteristics of the blockchain, while also allowing for the sharing of confidential information on a zero-knowledge basis without breaching confidentiality and privacy requirements. In the future, the use of DLTs in AI mechanisms is expected to allow users of such systems to monetise their data used by AI-driven systems through the use of Internet of Things (IoT) applications, for instance.

The implementation of AI applications in blockchain systems is currently concentrated in use-cases related to risk management, detection of fraud and compliance processes, including through the introduction of automated restrictions to a network. AI can be used to reduce (but not eliminate) security susceptibilities and help protect against compromising of the network, for example in payment applications, by identifying irregular activities for instance.. Similarly, AI applications can improve on-boarding processes on a network (e.g. biometrics for AI identification), as well as AML/CFT checks in the provision of any kind of DLT-based financial services. AI applications can also provide wallet-address analysis results that can be used for regulatory compliance purposes or for an internal risk-based assessment of transaction parties (Ziqi Chen et al., 2020[26]).

AI could also be used to improve the functioning of third party off-chain nodes, such as so-called 'Oracles'[10], nodes feeding external data into the network. The use of Oracles in DLT networks carries the risk of erroneous or inadequate data feeds into the network by underperforming or malicious third-party off-chain nodes (OECD, 2020[25]). As the responsibility of data curation shifts from third party nodes to independent, automated AI-powered systems that are more difficult to manipulate, the robustness of information recording and sharing could be strengthened. In a hypothetical scenario, the use of AI could further increase disintermediation by bringing AI inference directly on-chain, which would render Oracles redundant. In theory, it could act as a safeguard by testing the veracity of the data provided by the Oracles and prevent Oracle manipulation. Nevertheless, the introduction of AI in DLT-based networks does not necessarily resolve the 'garbage in, garbage out' conundrum as the problem of poor quality or inadequate data inputs is a challenge observed equally in AI-based applications.

Using AI to augment the capabilities of smart contracts

The largest potential of AI in DLT-based finance lies in its use in smart contracts[11], with practical implications around their governance and risk management and with numerous hypothetical (and yet untested) effects on roles and processes of DLT-based networks. Smart contracts rely on simple software code and have existed long before the advent of AI. Currently, most smart contracts used in a material way do not have ties to AI techniques. As such, many of the suggested benefits from the use of AI in DLT systems remains theoretical, and industry claims around convergence of AI and DLTs functionalities in marketed products should be treated with caution.

That said, some AI use-cases are proving helpful in augmenting smart contract capabilities, particularly when it comes to risk management and the identification of flaws in the code of the smart contract. AI techniques such as NLP[12] are already being tested for use in the analysis of patterns in smart contract execution so as to detect fraudulent activity and enhance the security of the network. Importantly, AI can test the code in ways that human code reviewers cannot, both in terms of speed and in terms of level of detail. Given that code is the underlying basis of any smart contract, flawless coding is fundamental for the robustness of smart contracts.

Box 2.4. AI and decentralised finance (DeFi)

Smart contracts are at the core of the decentralised finance (DeFi) market, which is based on a user-to-smart contract or smart-contract to smart-contract transaction model. User accounts in DeFi applications interact with smart contracts by submitting transactions that execute a function defined on the smart contract.

Smart contracts facilitate the disintermediation from which DLT-based networks can benefit, and are one of the major source of efficiencies that such networks claim to offer. They allow for the full automation of actions such as payments or transfer of assets upon triggering of certain conditions, which are pre-defined and registered in the code.

AI integration in blockchains could in theory support decentralised applications in the DeFi space through use-cases that could increase automation and efficiencies in the provision of certain financial services. Indicatively, the introduction of AI models can support the third-party private sector provision of customised recommendations across products and services; credit scoring based on users' online data; investment advisory services and trading based on financial data; as well as other reinforcement learning[13] applications on blockchain-based processes (Ziqi Chen et al., 2020[26]). Researchers suggest that, in the future, AI could also be integrated for forecasting and automating in 'self-learned' smart contracts, similar to models applying reinforcement learning AI techniques (Almasoud et al., 2020[27]). In other words, AI can be used to extract and process information of real-time systems and feed such information into smart contracts. As in other blockchain-based financial applications, the deployment of AI in DeFi augments the capabilities of the DLT use-case by providing additional functionalities; however, it is not expected to radically affect any of the business models involved in DeFi applications.

The use of AI to build fully autonomous chains would raise important challenges and risks to its users and the wider ecosystem. In such environments, AI contracts rather than humans execute decisions and operate the systems and there is no human intervention in the decision-making or operation of the system. In addition, the introduction of automated mechanisms that switch off the model instantaneously (such as kill switches) is very difficult in such networks, not least because of the decentralised nature of the network.

In theory, using AI in smart contracts could further enhance their automation, by increasing their autonomy and allowing the underlying code to be dynamically adjusted according to market conditions. The use of NLP could improve the analytical reach of smart contracts that are linked to traditional contracts, legislation and court decisions, going even further in analysing the intent of the parties involved (The Technolawgist, 2020[28]). It should be noted, however, that such applications of AI for smart contracts are purely theoretical at this stage and remain to be tested in real-life examples.

Operational challenges relating to compatibility and interoperability of conventional infrastructure with DLT-based one and AI technologies remain to be resolved for such applications to come to life. In particular, AI techniques such as deep learning require significant amounts of computational resources, which may pose an obstacle to performing well on the Blockchain (Hackernoon, 2020[29]). It has been argued that at this stage of development of the infrastructure, storing data off chain would be a better option for real time recommendation engines to prevent latency and reduce costs (Almasoud et al., 2020[27]). Challenges also exist with regards to the legal status of smart contracts, as these are still not considered to be legal contracts in most jurisdictions (OECD, 2020[25]). Until it is clarified whether contract law applies to smart contracts, enforceability and financial protection issues will persist.

Box 2.3. Innovation in infrastructure

The provision of infrastructure systems and services like transportation, energy, water and waste management are at the heart of meeting significant challenges facing societies such as demographics, migration, urbanisation, water scarcity and climate change. Modernising existing infrastructure stock, while conceiving and building infrastructure to address these challenges and providing a basis for economic growth and development is essential to meet future needs.

The role of technology and innovation in achieving these policy objectives is an important topic for policy makers. For example, embracing new technologies that enable drastic reductions in greenhouse gas (GHG) emissions when building and operating infrastructure will be a crucial element to net zero emissions. This could be from the type of cement that is used to installation of energy efficient charging stations for electric vehicles. Governments, in cooperation with diverse stakeholders, could benefit from sharing good practices related to technology and innovation in infrastructure, while also setting supportive policy frameworks to harness the benefits while mitigating risks.

The G20 Riyadh Infratech Agenda, endorsed by Leaders in 2020, provides high-level policy guidance for national authorities and the international community to advance the adoption of new and existing technologies in infrastructure. This work highlights the important role technology can play in helping countries make well-informed decisions and achieve more efficient financial outlays, by mobilising private sector investment, by enhancing service delivery and by achieving environmental, social and economic benefits.

While infratech can include a number of technologies, AI and ML applications are of note, particularly as digital technologies become more integrated into structures, changing the nature of infrastructure from simple hard assets to dynamic information systems (G20 Saudi Arabia, 2020[30]). For example, AI can be a powerful tool to optimise windmill operations and safety, analyse traffic patterns in transportation, and improve operations in energy grids.

Source: (G20 Saudi Arabia, 2020[30]).

2.3. Emerging risks and challenges from the deployment of AI in finance

As the use of AI in finance grows in size and spectrum, a number of challenges and risks associated with such techniques are being identified and deserve further consideration by policy makers. This section examines some of these challenges, and touches upon potential risk mitigation tools. Challenges discussed relate to data management and use; risk of bias and discrimination; explainability; robustness and resilience of AI models; governance and accountability in AI systems; regulatory considerations; employment risks and skills.

2.3.1. Data management, privacy/confidentiality and concentration risks

Data is the cornerstone of any AI application, but the inappropriate use of data in AI-powered applications or the use of inadequate data introduces an important source of non-financial risk to firms using AI techniques. Such risk relates to the veracity of the data used; challenges around data privacy and confidentiality; fairness considerations and potential concentration and broader competition issues.

The quality of the data used by AI models is fundamental to their appropriate functioning, however, when it comes to big data, there is some uncertainty around of the level of truthfulness, or veracity, of big data (IBM, 2020[31]). Together with characteristics such as exhaustivity (how wide the scope is) and extensionality (how easy is it to add or change fields), veracity is key for the use of big data in finance, as it may prove difficult for users of AI-powered systems to assess whether the dataset used is complete and can be trusted. Correct labelling and structuring of big data is another pre-requisite for ML models to be able to successfully identify what a signal is, distinguish signal from noise and recognise patterns in data (S&P, 2019[19]). Different methods are being developed to reduce the existence of irrelevant features or 'noise' in datasets and improve ML model performance, such as the creation of artificial or 'synthetic' datasets generated and employed for the purposes of ML modelling. These can be extremely useful for model testing and validation purposes in case the existing datasets lack scale or diversity (see Section 1.3.4).

Synthetic datasets can also allow financial firms to secure non-disclosive computation to protect consumer privacy, another of the important challenges of data use in AI, by creating anonymous datasets that comply with privacy requirements. Traditional data anonymisation approaches do not provide rigorous privacy guarantees, as ML models have the power to make inferences in big datasets. The use of big data by AI-powered models could expand the universe of data that is considered sensitive, as such models can become highly proficient in identifying users individually (US Treasury, 2018[32]). Facial recognition technology or data around the customer profile can be used by the model to identify users or infer other characteristics, such as gender, when joined up with other information.

Data privacy can be safeguarded through the use of 'notification and consent' practices, which may not necessarily be the norm in ML models. For example, when observed data is not provided by the customer (e.g. geolocation data or credit card transaction data) notification and consent protections are difficult to implement. The same holds when it comes to tracking of online activity with advanced modes of tracking, or to data sharing by third party providers. In addition, to the extent that consumers are not necessarily educated on how their data is handled and where it is being used, their data may be used without their understanding and well informed consent (US Treasury, 2018[32]).

Additional concerns are raised around data connectivity and the economics of data used by ML models in finance. Given the critical importance of the ability to aggregate, store, process, and transmit data across borders for financial sector development, the importance of appropriate data governance safeguards and rules is becoming increasingly important (Hardoon, 2020[33]). At the same time, the economics of data use are being redefined: A small number of alternative dataset players have emerged, exploiting the surge in demand for datasets that inform AI techniques, with limited visibility and overseeing over their activity at this stage. Increased compliance costs of regulations aiming to protect consumers may further redefine the economics of the use of big data for financial market providers and, by consequence, their approach in the use of AI and big data.

Access to customer data by firms that fall outside the regulatory perimeter, such as BigTech, raises risks of concentrations and dependencies on a few large players. Unequal access to data and potential dominance in the sourcing of big data by few big BigTech in particular, could reduce the capacity of smaller players to compete in the market for AI-based products/services. The strength and nature of the competitive advantages created by advances in AI could potentially harm the operations of efficient and competitive markets if consumers' ability to make informed decisions is constrained by high concentrations amongst market providers (US Treasury, 2018[32]).

Box 2.4. Financial Consumer Protection and AI: OECD Policy responses to protect and support financial consumers

The OECD has undertaken significant work in the area of digitalisation to understand and address the benefits, risks and potential policy responses for protecting and supporting financial consumers. The OECD has done this via its leading global policy work on financial education and financial consumer protection.

Financial education

The OECD and its International Network on Financial Education (OECD INFE) developed research and policy tools to empower consumers with respect to the increasing digitalisation of retail financial services, including the implications of a greater application of AI to financial services.

The G20/OECD INFE Policy Guidance on Digitalisation and Financial Literacy, developed by the OECD/INFE in the framework of Argentina's G20 Presidency provides non-binding policy directions to policy makers and other relevant stakeholders and is aimed at identifying and promoting effective initiatives that enhance digital and financial literacy of consumers and entrepreneurs, supporting their evaluation and dissemination, and promoting a responsible and beneficial development of digitalisation.

The Policy Guidance supports the development of core competencies on digital financial literacy to build trust and promote a safe use of digital financial services, protect consumers from digital crime and misselling, and support those at risk of over-reliance on digital credit.

The Guidance takes into account the increasing use of algorithms in determining decisions about credit or insurance, and how this can extend provision but also lead to new forms of exclusion for sectors of the population, and identifies core competencies to empower consumers to counter new kinds of digital exclusion. These competencies include:

- Awareness of the different types of financial products and services delivered through digital means for personal or business purposes, including their benefits and risks.
- Knowledge of consumer rights and obligations in the digital world.
- Encourage consumers to know where to check, when possible, that a digital financial service provider is authorised by the relevant national financial authorities.
- Prompting consumers to appropriately manage their digital footprint to the extent possible, avoid engaging in risky behaviours involving their personal data, and understand the consequences of sharing or disclosing personal data.

It invites policy makers to foster behaviours that can protect consumers and entrepreneurs from any negative consequences of these developments, and to prompt them in particular to:

- Appropriately manage their digital footprint to the extent possible and avoid engaging in risky behaviours involving their personal data, and understand the consequences of sharing personal identification numbers, account or personal information whether digitally or through other channels.
- Assess the kind of information that is requested by (financial) service providers to decide whether it is relevant and understand how it may be stored and used.
- Policy aimed at financial service providers would also benefit consumers, so the onus of financial literacy is not entirely on the consumer.

The G20 OECD INFE Policy Guidance has been complemented by specific work conducted by the OECD/INFE on personal data and financial literacy and on the implications of artificial intelligence and machine learning for retail consumers. This work led to the release in 2020 of the report Personal Data Use in Financial Services and the Role of Financial Education: A consumer-centric analysis. The report reviews the risks and benefits brought by the technological innovations that have increased the capacity to capture, store, combine and analyse customer data, presents consumer attitudes to data sharing, and suggests policy options to support consumer awareness with respect to personal data use.

It encourages financial education policy makers to cooperate with the authorities in charge of personal data protection frameworks and it identifies additional elements pertaining to personal data to complement the core competencies identified in the G20 OECD INFE Policy Guidance note. It notably calls on policy makers to increase awareness among consumers of the analytical possibilities of big data and of their rights over personal data, for them to take steps to manage digital footprints and protect their data online.

The report invites policy makers to take a targeted approach and address the needs of the least technologically-savvy, who are most at risk given their low familiarity with online transactions, and of the groups willing to share more personal information in exchange for personalised products and service, such as younger generations.

Financial consumer protection

The G20/OECD High Level Principles on Financial Consumer Protection (the Principles) are designed to assist G20, OECD and FSB jurisdictions as well as all other interested economies to enhance financial consumer protection. The Principles are administered by the G20/OECD Task Force on Financial Consumer Protection which has developed guidance for policy makers and oversight authorities to apply the Principles in the context of an increasingly digital environment.[1]

Key financial consumer protection policy responses relating to selected Principles

Principle 2: Oversight Bodies

Technological developments present a range of challenges and opportunities for oversight bodies responsible for supervising and enforcing financial consumer protection laws. These include balancing the development of FinTech innovations while ensuring the appropriate level of consumer protection; and ensuring the adequacy of supervisory tools, resources and capabilities to oversee digital financial services. As set out in the G20/OECD Policy Guidance on Financial Consumer Protection Approaches in the Digital Age, oversight bodies can seek to address these challenges and opportunities in a number of ways, including:

- Ensure that regulatory and supervisory resources, tools and methods are appropriate and adapted to the digital environment, which includes having access to data and exploring the use of technology to assist in market supervision.
- Ensure they have adequate knowledge of the financial services market, including by engaging with businesses, industry representatives and consumers to understand new digital products and services and identify market trends and issues.
- Ensure capability to deal effectively with technological innovation issues while ensuring appropriate consumer protections are maintained, for example, through regulatory sandboxes, innovation hubs, dedicated regulatory guidance or support for new entrants etc.

Principle 4: Disclosure & Transparency

New types of disclosure challenges emerge in the context of digitalisation, associated with complex interfaces, limited space in digital devices or opaque terms, changes to consumer behaviour in an online or mobile setting, conditions and fees, especially regarding complex digital products. Set out in the G20/OECD Policy Guidance on Financial Consumer Protection Approaches in the Digital Age, to address these challenges, oversight bodies responsible for financial consumer protection can seek to:

- Ensure that disclosure and transparency requirements are applicable and adequate to the provision of information through all channels relevant to digital financial services and covering all relevant stages of the product lifecycle.
- Support consumer communications that are clear and simple to understand regardless of the channel of communication.
- Embed an understanding of consumer decision-making and the impact of behavioural biases in the development of policies to ensure a customer-centric approach.
- Encourage financial services providers to test digital disclosure approaches to ensure their effectiveness and recognise that there may be consumers in the target audience for the product or service who are not digitally literate.

Principle 7: Protection of Consumer Assets

AI is underpinned by the explosion in recent times in the generation, collection, storage, sharing and use of personal and transactional data. Protection of consumer assets is a fundamental part of an overall financial consumer protection framework and includes covering fraudulent or unauthorised payments, segregation of consumer assets and procedures for protecting and recovering unclaimed assets. As outlined in the Financial Consumer Protection Policy Approaches in the Digital Age Protecting consumers' assets, data and privacy policy makers and oversight bodies responsible for financial consumer protection can seek to:

- Ensure they have the necessary technological capacity and supervisory tools to mitigate digital security risks and react to such risks where the financial assets of a consumer are at risk.
- Work collaboratively with industry, stakeholders, other regulatory and supervisory authorities and foreign counterparts to share information and understand emerging trends relating to digital financial risks.
- Ensure that financial services providers are required to continuously assess the digital security risk to the services they provide and adopt appropriate security measures to reduce the risks.

Principle 8: Protection of Consumer Data & Privacy

Consumers' financial and personal information should be protected through appropriate control and protection mechanisms. These mechanisms should define the purposes for which the data may be collected, processed, held, used and disclosed (especially to third parties). Also outlined in the Financial Consumer Protection Policy Approaches in the Digital Age Protecting consumers' assets, data and privacy, policy makers and oversight bodies responsible for financial consumer protection should:

- Ensure that the legal, regulatory and supervisory framework for financial consumer protection has appropriate safeguards and measures relating to the protection of consumer data and privacy, including a definition of "personal data".
- Liaise with data protection authorities to ensure understanding and application of data protection laws and regulations to financial services providers.

Ensure financial services providers have robust and transparent governance, accountability, risk management and control systems relating to use of digital capabilities (particularly AI, algorithms and machine learning technology).

1. The Task Force is currently conducting a strategic Review of the Principles to identify new or emerging developments in financial consumer protection policies or approaches over the last 10 years that may warrant updates to the Principles to ensure they are fully up to date. The Review will include considering digital developments and their impacts on the provision of financial services to consumers.

2.3.2. *Algorithmic bias and discrimination in AI*

Depending on how they are used, AI algorithms have the potential to help avoid discrimination based on human interactions, or intensify biases, unfair treatment and discrimination in financial services. The risk of unintended bias and discrimination of parts of the population is very much linked to the misuse of data and to the use of inappropriate data by ML model (e.g. in credit underwriting, see Section 1.2.3). AI applications can potentially compound existing biases found in the data; models trained with biased data will perpetuate biases; and the identification of spurious correlations may add another layer of such risk of unfair treatment (US Treasury, 2018[32]). Biased or discriminatory outcomes of ML models are not necessarily intentional and can even occur with strong quality, well-labelled data, through inference and proxies, or given the fact that correlations between sensitive and 'non-sensitive' variables may be difficult to detect in vast databases (Goodman and Flaxman, 2016[34]).

Careful design, diligent auditing and testing of ML models can further assist in avoiding potential biases. Inadequately designed and controlled AI/ML models carry a risk of exacerbating or reinforcing existing biases while at the same time making discrimination even harder to observe (Klein, 2020[35]). Auditing mechanisms of the model and the algorithm that sense check the results of the model against baseline datasets can help ensure that there is no unfair treatment or discrimination by the technology. Ideally, users and supervisors should be able to test scoring systems to ensure their fairness and accuracy (Citron and Pasquale, 2014[23]). Tests can also be run based on whether protected classes can be inferred from other attributes in the data, and a number of techniques can be applied to identify and/or rectify discrimination in ML models (Feldman et al., 2015[36]).

The human parameter is critical both at the data input stage and at the query input stage and a degree of scepticism in the evaluation of the model results can be critical in minimising the risks of biased model decision-making. Human intervention is necessary so as to identify and correct for biases built into the data or in the model design, and to explain the output of the model, although the extent to which all this is feasible remains an open question, particularly given the lack of interpretability or explainability of advanced ML models. Human judgement is also important so as to avoid interpreting meaningless correlations observed from patterns as causal relationships, resulting in false or biased decision-making.

2.3.3. *The explainability conundrum*

The difficulty in decomposing the output of a ML model into the underlying drivers of its decision, referred to as explainability, is the most pressing challenge in AI-based models used in finance. In addition to the inherent complexity of AI-based models, market participants may intentionally conceal the mechanics of their AI models to protect their intellectual property, further obscuring the techniques. The gap in technical literacy of most end-user consumers, coupled with the mismatch between the complexity characterising AI models and the demands of human-scale reasoning further aggravates the problem (Burrell, 2016[37]).

In the most advanced AI techniques, even if the underlying mathematical principles of such models can be explained, they still lack 'explicit declarative knowledge' (Holzinger, 2018[38]). This makes them incompatible with existing regulation that may require algorithms to be fully understood and explainable throughout their lifecycle (IOSCO, 2020[39]). Similarly, the lack of explainability is incompatible with regulations granting citizens a 'right to explanation' for decisions made by algorithms and information on the logic involved, such as the EU's General Data Protection Regulation (GDPR)[14] applied in credit decisions or insurance pricing, for instance. Another example is the potential use of ML in the calculation of regulatory requirements (e.g. risk-weighted assets (RWA) for credit risk), where the existing rules require that the model be explainable or at least subject to human oversight and judgement (e.g. Basel Framework for Calculation of RWA for credit risk – Use of models 36.33).

Lack of interpretability of AI and ML algorithms could become a macro-level risk if not appropriately supervised by micro prudential supervisors, as it becomes difficult for both firms and supervisors to predict how models will affect markets (FSB, 2017[11]). In the absence of an understanding of the detailed mechanics underlying a model, users have limited room to predict how their models affect market conditions, and whether they contribute to market shocks. Users are also unable to adjust their strategies in time of poor performance or in times of stress, leading to potential episodes of exacerbated market volatility and bouts of illiquidity during periods of acute stress, aggravating flash crash type of events (see Section 1.2.2). Risks of market manipulation or tacit collusions are also present in non-explainable AI models.

Interestingly, AI applications risk being held to a higher standard and thus subjected to a more onerous explainability requirement as compared to other technologies or complex mathematical models in finance, with negative repercussions for innovation (Hardoon, 2020[33]). The objective of the explainability analysis at committee level should focus on the underlying risks that the model might be exposing the firm to, and whether these are manageable, instead of its underlying mathematical promise. A minimum level of explainability would still need to be ensured for a model committee to be able to analyse the model brought to the committee and be comfortable with its deployment.

Given the trade-off between explainability and performance of the model, financial services providers need to strike the right balance between explainability of the model and accuracy/performance. It should also be highlighted that there is no need for a single principle or one-size-fits-all approach for explaining ML models, and explainability will depend to a large extent on the context (Brainard, 2020[40]) (Hardoon, 2020[33]). Importantly, ensuring the explainability of the model does not by itself guarantee that the model is reliable (Brainard, 2020[40]). Contextual alignment of explainability with the audience needs to be coupled with a shift of the focus towards 'explainability of the risk', i.e. understanding the resulting risk exposure from the use of the model instead of the methodology underlying such model. Recent guidance issued by the UK Information Commissioner's Office suggests using five contextual factors to help in assessing the type of explanation needed: domain, impact, data used, urgency, and audience (UK Information Commissioner's Office, 2020[41]).

Improving the explainability levels of AI applications can contribute to maintaining the level of trust by financial consumers and regulators/supervisors, particularly in critical financial services (FSB, 2017[11]). Research suggests that explainability that is 'human-meaningful' can significantly affect the users' perception of a system's accuracy, independent of the actual accuracy observed (Nourani et al., 2020[42]). When less human-meaningful explanations are provided, the accuracy of the technique that does not operate on human-understandable rationale is less likely to be accurately judged by the users.

Auditability and disclosure of AI techniques used by financial service providers

The opacity of algorithm-based systems could be addressed through transparency requirements, ensuring that clear information is provided as to the AI system's capabilities and limitations (European Commission, 2020[43]). Separate disclosure should inform consumers about the use of AI system in the delivery of a product and their interaction with an AI system instead of a human being (e.g. robo-advisors), to allow customers to make conscious choices among competing products. Suitability requirements, such as the ones applicable to the sale of investment products, might help firms better assess whether the prospective clients have a solid understanding of how the use of AI affects the delivery of the product/service. To date, there is no commonly accepted practice as to the level of disclosure that should be provided to investors and financial consumers and potential proportionality in such information.

In the absence of explainability about the model workings, financial service providers find it hard to document the model process of AI-enabled models used for supervisory purposes (Bank of England and FCA, 2020[44]). Some jurisdictions have proposed a two-pronged approach to AI model supervision: (i) analytical: combining analysis of the source code and of the data with methods (if possible based on standards) for documenting AI algorithms, predictive models and datasets; and (ii) empirical: leveraging methods providing explanations for an individual decision or for the overall algorithm's behaviour, and relying on two techniques for testing an algorithm as a black box: challenger models (to compare against the model under test) and benchmarking datasets, both curated by the auditor (ACPR, 2020[45]).

Documentation of the logic behind the algorithm, to the extent feasible, is being used by some regulators as a way to ensure that the outcomes produced by the model are explainable, traceable and repeatable (FSRA, 2019[46]). The EU, for instance, is considering requirements around disclosure documentation of programming and training methodologies, processes and techniques used to build, test, and validate AI systems, including documentation on the algorithm (what the model shall optimise for, which weights are designed to certain parameters at the outset etc.) (European Commission, 2020[43]). The US Public Policy Council of the Association for Computing Machinery (USACM) has proposed a set of principles targeting inter alia transparency and auditability in the use of algorithms, suggesting that models, data, algos and decisions be recorded so as to be available for audit where harm is suspected (ACM US Public Policy Council, 2017[47]). The Federal Reserve's guidance for model risk management includes also documentation of model development and validation that is sufficiently detailed to allow parties unfamiliar with a model to understand how the model operates, its limitations and key assumptions (Federal Reserve, 2011[48]).

2.3.4. Training, validation and testing of AI models to promote their robustness and resilience

Appropriate training of ML models is fundamental for their performance, and the datasets used for that purpose need to be large enough to capture non-linear relationships and tail events in the data. This, however, is hard to achieve in practice, given that tail events are rare and the dataset may not be robust enough for optimal outcomes. The inability of the industry to train models on datasets that include tail events is creating a significant vulnerability for the financial system, weakening the reliability of such models in times of unpredicted crisis and rendering AI a tool that can be used only when market conditions are stable.

The validation of ML models using different datasets than the ones used to train the model, helps assess the accuracy of the model, optimise its parameters, and mitigate the risk of over-fitting. The latter occurs when a trained model performs extremely well on the samples used for training but performs poorly on new unknown samples, i.e. the model does not generalise well (Xu and Goodacre, 2018[49]). Validation sets contain samples with known provenance, but these classifications are not known to the model, therefore, predictions on the validation set allow the operator to assess model accuracy. Based on the errors on the validation set, the optimal model parameters set is determined using the one with the lowest validation error (Xu and Goodacre, 2018[49]). Validation processes go beyond the simple back testing of a model using historical data to examine ex-post its predictive capabilities, and ensure that the model's outcomes are reproducible.

Synthetic datasets and alternative data are being artificially generated to serve as test sets for validation, used to confirm that the model is being used and performs as intended. Synthetic databases provide an interesting alternative given that they can provide inexhaustible amounts of simulated data, and a potentially cheaper way of improving the predictive power and enhancing the robustness of ML models, especially where real data is scarce and expensive. Some regulators require, in some instances, the evaluation of the results produced by AI models in test scenarios set by the supervisory authorities (e.g. Germany) (IOSCO, 2020[39]).

Box 2.5. AI and tail risk: learnings from the COVID-19 pandemic

In spite of the dynamic nature of AI models and their evolution through learning from new data, they may not be able to perform under idiosyncratic one-time events not reflected in the data used to train the model, such as the COVID-19 pandemic. Evidence based on a survey conducted in UK banks suggest that around 35% of banks experienced a negative impact on ML model performance during the pandemic (Bholat, Gharbawi and Thew, 2020[50]). This is likely because the pandemic has created major movements in macroeconomic variables, such as rising unemployment and mortgage forbearance, which required ML (as well as traditional) models to be recalibrated.

Tail and unforeseen events, such as the recent pandemic, give rise to discontinuity in the datasets, which in turn creates model drift that undermine the models' predictive capacity. Tail events cause unexpected changes in the behaviour of the target variable that the model is looking to predict, and previously undocumented changes to the data structure and underlying patterns of the dataset used by the model, both caused by a shift in market dynamics during such events. These are naturally not captured by the initial dataset on which the model was trained and are likely to result in performance degradation.

Synthetic datasets generated to train the models could going forward incorporate tail events of the same nature, in addition to data from the COVID-19 period, with a view to retrain and redeploy redundant models. Ongoing testing of models with (synthetic) validation datasets that incorporate extreme scenarios and continuous monitoring for model drifts is therefore of paramount importance to mitigate risks encountered in times of stress.

Ongoing monitoring and validation of models throughout their life is foundational for the appropriate risk management of any type of model (Federal Reserve, 2011[48]) and is the most effective way to identify and address 'model drift'. Model drift comes in the form of concept drifts or data drifts: Concept drifts describe situations where the statistical properties of the target variable studied by the model change, which changes the very concept of what the model is trying to predict (Widmer, 1996[51]). For example, the definition of fraud or the way it shows up in the data could evolve over time with new ways of conducting illegal activity, such a change would result in concept drift. Data drifts occur when statistical properties of the input data change, affecting the model's predictive power. The major shift of consumer attitudes and preferences towards e-commerce and digital banking is a good example of such data drifts not captured by the initial dataset on which the model was trained and result in performance degradation.

2.3.5. Governance of AI systems and accountability

Solid governance arrangements and clear accountability mechanisms are indispensable, particularly as AI models are increasingly deployed in high-value decision-making use-cases (e.g. credit allocation). Organisations and individuals developing, deploying or operating AI systems should be held accountable for their proper functioning (OECD, 2019[52]). Importantly, intended outcomes for consumers would need to be incorporated in any governance framework, together with an assessment of whether and how such outcomes are reached using AI technologies.

In advanced deep learning models, issues may arise concerning the ultimate control of the model, as AI could unintentionally behave in a way that is contrary to consumer interests (e.g. biased results in credit underwriting). In addition, the autonomous behaviour of some AI systems during their life cycle may entail important product changes having an impact on safety, which may require a new risk assessment (European Commission, 2020[43]). Human oversight from the product design and throughout the lifecycle of the AI products and systems may be needed as a safeguard (European Commission, 2020[43]).

Currently, financial market participants rely on existing governance and oversight arrangements for the use of AI techniques, as AI-based algorithms are not considered to be fundamentally different from conventional ones (IOSCO, 2020[39]). Model governance best practices have been adopted by financial firms since the emergence of traditional statistical models for credit and other consumer finance decisions. In accordance with such best practices, financial service providers must ensure that models are built using appropriate datasets; that certain data is not used in the models; that data that is a proxy for a protected class is not used; that models are rigorously tested and validated (sometimes by independent validators); and that when models are used in production, the production input data is consistent with the data used to build the model. Documentation and audit trails are also held around deployment decisions, design, and production processes.

The increasing use of complex AI-based techniques and ML models will warrant the adjustment, and possible upgrade, of existing governance and oversight arrangements to accommodate for the complexities of AI techniques. Explicit governance frameworks that designate clear lines of responsibility for the development and overseeing of AI-based systems throughout their lifecycle, from development to deployment, will further strengthen existing arrangements for operations related to AI. Internal governance frameworks could include minimum standards or best practice guidelines and approaches for the implementation of such guidelines (Bank of England and FCA, 2020[44]).

Currently existing model governance frameworks have yet to address how to handle AI models in finance, which exist only ephemerally, and change very frequently, although the need for such remains debatable in some jurisdictions. Model governance frameworks should provide that models must be monitored to ensure they do not produce results that constitute comparative evidence of disparate treatment. However, there are challenges to testing that premise: since many ML models are non-deterministic, there is no guarantee that even with the same input data the same model will be produced.

Box 2.6. Governance considerations when outsourcing and third party providers are involved

Possible risks of concentration of certain third-party providers may rise in terms of data collection and management (e.g. dataset providers) or in the area of technology (e.g. third party model providers) and infrastructure (e.g. cloud providers) provision. AI models and techniques are being commoditised through cloud adoption, and the risk of dependency on providers of outsourced solutions raises new challenges for competitive dynamics and potential oligopolistic market structures in such services.

In addition to concentration and dependency risks, the outsourcing of AI techniques or enabling technologies and infrastructure raises challenges in terms of accountability. Governance arrangements and contractual modalities are important in managing risks related to outsourcing, similar to those applying in any other type of services. Finance providers need to have the skills necessary to audit and perform due diligence over the services provided by third parties. Over-reliance on outsourcing may also give rise to increased risk of disruption of service with potential systemic impact in the markets. Similar to other types of models, contingency and security plans need to be in place, as needed (in particular related to whether the model is critical or not), to allow business to function as usual if any vulnerability materialises.

The ease of use of standardised, off-the-shelf AI tools may encourage non-regulated entities to provide investment advisory or other services without proper certification/licensing in a non-compliant way. Such regulatory arbitrage is also happening with mainly BigTech entities making use of datasets they have access to from their primary activity.

2.3.6. Other sources of risks in AI use-cases in finance: regulatory considerations, employment and skills

Although many countries have dedicated AI strategies (OECD, 2019[52]), a very small number of jurisdictions have current requirements that are specifically targeting AI-based algorithms and models. In most cases, regulation and supervision of ML applications are based on overarching requirements for systems and controls (IOSCO, 2020[39]). These consist primarily of rigorous testing of the algorithms used before they are deployed in the market, and continuous monitoring of their performance throughout their lifecycle.

The technology-neutral approach that is being applied by most jurisdictions to regulate financial market products (in relation to risk management, governance, and controls over the use of algorithms) may be challenged by the rising complexity of some innovative use-cases in finance. Given the depth of technological advances in AI areas such as deep learning, existing financial sector regulatory regimes could fall short in addressing the systemic risks posed by a potential broad adoption of such techniques in finance (Gensler and Bailey, 2020[53]). The complex nature of AI could give rise to potential incompatibilities with existing financial rules and regulations (e.g. due to the lack of explainability, see Section 1.3.3).[15]

Industry participants note a potential risk of fragmentation of the regulatory landscape with respect to AI at the national, international and sectoral level, and the need for more consistency to ensure that these techniques can function across borders (Bank of England and FCA, 2020[44]). In addition to existing regulation that is applicable to AI models and systems, a multitude of published AI principles, guidance, and best practice have been developed in recent years although views differ over their practical value and the difficulty of translating such principles into effective practical guidance (e.g. through real life examples) (Bank of England and FCA, 2020[44]).

Employment and skills

The widespread adoption of AI and ML by the financial industry may give rise to some employment challenges and needs to upgrade skills, both for market participants and for policy makers alike. Demand for employees with applicable skills in AI methods, advanced mathematics, software engineering and data science is rising, while the application of such technologies may result in potentially significant job losses across the industry (Noonan, 1998[54]) (US Treasury, 2018[32]). Such loss of jobs replaced by machines may result in an over-reliance in fully automated AI systems, which could, in turn, lead to increased risk of disruption of service with potential systemic impact in the markets. If markets dependent on such systems face technical or other disruptions, financial service providers need to ensure that from a human resources perspective, they are ready to substitute the automated AI systems with well-trained humans acting as a human safety net and capable of ensuring there is no disruption in the markets.

Skills and technical expertise becomes increasingly important for regulators and supervisors who need to keep pace with the technology and enhance the skills necessary to effectively supervise AI-based applications in finance. Enforcement authorities need to be technically capable of inspecting AI-based systems and empowered to intervene when required (European Commission, 2020[43]). The upskilling of policy makers will also allow them to expand their own use of AI in RegTech and SupTech, an important area of application of innovation in the official sector (see Chapter 5).

AI in finance should be seen as a technology that augments human capabilities instead of replacing them. It could be argued that a combination of 'man and machine', where AI informs human judgment rather than replaces it (decision *aid* instead of decision *maker*), could allow for the benefits of the technology to materialise, while maintaining safeguards of accountability and control as to the ultimate decision-making. At the current stage of maturity of AI solutions, and to ensure that vulnerabilities and risks arising from the use of AI-driven techniques are minimised, some level of human supervision of AI-techniques is still necessary. The identification of converging points, where human and AI are integrated, will be critical for the practical implementation of such a combined 'man and machine' approach ('human in the loop').

2.4. Policy considerations

AI use-cases in finance have potential to deliver significant benefits to financial consumers and market participants, by improving the quality of services offered and producing efficiencies to financial firms, reducing friction and transaction costs. At the same time, the deployment of AI in finance gives rise to new challenges, while it could also amplify pre-existing risks in financial markets (OECD, 2021[2]).

Policy makers and regulators have a role in ensuring that the use of AI in finance is consistent with promoting financial stability, protecting financial consumers, and promoting market integrity and competition. Emerging risks from the deployment of AI techniques need to be identified and mitigated to support and promote the use of responsible AI without stifling innovation. Existing regulatory and supervisory requirements may need to be clarified and sometimes adjusted to address some of the perceived incompatibilities of existing arrangements with AI applications.

One such source of potential incompatibility with existing laws and regulations is associated with the lack of explainability in AI, and more efforts are needed to overcome these both at the policy and industry levels. The difficulty in understanding how and why AI models produce their outputs and the ensuing inability of users to adjust their strategies in times of stress may lead to exacerbated market volatility and bouts of illiquidity during periods of market stress, and to flash crashes. Risks related to pro-cyclicality, convergence, and increased market volatility through simultaneous purchases and sales of large quantities can further amplify systemic risks. Overcoming or improving the explainability conundrum will help promote trust of users and supervisors around AI applications.

The application of regulatory and supervisory requirements on AI techniques could be looked at under a contextual and proportional framework, depending on the criticality of the application and the potential impact on the consumer involved (OECD, 2021[2]). In particular, policy makers may need to sharpen their existing arsenal of defences against risks emerging from, or exacerbated by, the use of AI, in a number of areas:

- **Sharpen the policy focus on better data governance by financial firms, aiming to reinforce consumer protection across AI use-cases in finance.** Some of the most important risks raised in AI use-cases in finance relate to data management: data privacy, confidentiality, concentration of data and possible impact on the competitive dynamics of the market, but also risk of data drifts. The importance of data is undisputed when it comes to training, testing and validation of ML models, but also when defining their capacity to retain their predictive powers in tail events. Policy makers could consider the introduction of specific requirements or best practices for data management in AI-based techniques. These could touch upon data quality, adequacy of the datasets used depending on the intended use of the AI model, as well as tools to monitor and correct for conceptual drifts. When it comes to databases purchased by third party providers, additional vigilance may be required by financial firms and only databases approved for use and compliant with data governance requirements should be permitted. Requirements for additional transparency over the use of personal data and opt-out options for the use of personal data could also be considered by authorities.
- **Promote practices that will help overcome risk of unintended bias and discrimination.** In addition to efforts around data quality, safeguards could be put in place to provide assurance about the robustness of the model when it comes to avoiding potential biases. Appropriate sense checking of model results against baseline datasets and other tests based on whether protected classes can be inferred from other attributes in the data are two examples of best practices to

mitigate risks of discrimination. The validation of the appropriateness of variables used by the model could reduce a source of potential biases.

- **Consider disclosure requirements around the use of AI techniques in finance when these have an impact on the customer outcome.** Financial consumers should be informed about the use of AI techniques in the delivery of a product, as well as potential interaction with an AI system instead of a human being, to be able to make conscious choices among competing products. Clear information around the AI system's capabilities and limitations may need to be included in such disclosure. Suitability requirements for AI-driven financial services, similar to the ones applicable to the sale of investment products, could be considered by authorities for the sounder assessment of prospective clients' understanding of the impact on AI in the delivery of the product. Policy makers might consider mandating that financial services providers use active disclosure (e.g. giving potential customers information and explanation directly, having a dedicated question line or FAQ) as opposed to simply passive disclosure to ensure maximum understanding by consumers.
- **Strengthen model governance and accountability mechanisms.** Policy makers should consider requiring clear and explicit governance frameworks and attribution of accountability to the human element to help build trust in AI-driven systems. Designation of clear lines of responsibility for the development and overseeing of AI-based systems throughout their lifecycle, from development to deployment, may need to be put in place by financial services providers so as to strengthen existing arrangements for operations related to AI, particularly when third party providers and outsourcing are involved. Currently applicable frameworks for model governance may need to be adjusted for AI, and although audit trails of processes are helpful for model oversight, the supervisory focus could be shifted from documentation of the development process to model behaviour and outcomes. Supervisors may also wish to look into more technical ways of managing risk, such as adversarial model stress testing or outcome-based metrics (Gensler and Bailey, 2020[53]).
- **Consider requirements for firms to provide confidence around the robustness and resilience of AI models:** The provision of increased assurance by financial firms around the robustness and resilience of AI models is fundamental as policy makers seek to guard against build-up of systemic risks, and will help AI applications in finance gain trust. The performance of models needs to be tested in extreme market conditions, to prevent systemic risks and vulnerabilities that may arise in times of stress. The introduction of automatic control mechanisms (such as kill switches) that trigger alerts or switch off models in times of stress could further assist in mitigating risks, although they expose the firm to new operational risks and could amplify market stress. Back-up plans, models and processes should be in place to ensure business continuity in case the models fails or acts in unexpected ways. Further, regulators could consider add-on or minimum buffers if banks were to determine risk weights or capital based on AI algorithms (Gensler and Bailey, 2020[53]). The importance of cybersecurity should also be considered for the generation of robust technological AI systems and the importance of cyber resilience for financial services.
- **Consider the introduction or reinforcement of frameworks for appropriate training, retraining and rigorous testing of AI models**. Such processes help ensure that ML model-based decisioning is operating as intended and in compliance with applicable rules and regulations. Datasets used for training must be large enough to capture non-linear relationships and tail events in the data, even if synthetic, so as to improve model reliability in times of unprecedented crisis.
- **Promote the ongoing monitoring and validation of AI models as the most effective way to improve model resilience, prevent, and address model drifts**. Best practices around standardised procedures for continuous monitoring and validation throughout the lifetime of a model could assist in improving model resilience, and identify whether the model necessitates

adjustment, redevelopment, or replacement. Model validation processes may need to be separated from model development ones and documented as best possible for supervisory purposes. The frequency of testing and validation may need to be defined depending on the complexity of the model and the materiality of the decisions made by such model.

- **Place emphasis in human primacy in decision making for higher-value use-cases (e.g. lending).** Appropriate emphasis could be placed on human primacy in decision making when it comes to higher-value use-cases (e.g. lending decisions) which have a significant impact on consumers. Authorities could consider the introduction of processes that can allow customers to challenge the outcome of AI models and seek redress, such as the ones introduced by GDPR (right of individuals 'to obtain human intervention' and to contest the decision made by an algorithm (EU, 2016[55])). Public communication by the official sector that clearly sets expectations could further build confidence in AI applications in finance.
- **Deploy resources to keep pace with advances in technology, investing in research and in the upscaling of skills for financial sector participants and policy makers alike.** Given the increasing technical complexity of AI, investment in research could allow some of the issues around explainability and unintended consequences of AI techniques to be resolved. Investment in skills for both finance sector participants and policy makers would allow them to follow advancements in technology and maintain a multidisciplinary dialogue at operational, regulatory and supervisory level. Enforcement authorities in particular will need to be technically capable of inspecting AI-based systems and empowered to intervene when required, but also to enjoy the benefits of this technology by deploying AI in RegTech/SupTech applications.
- **Promote multidisciplinary dialogue between policy makers and the industry at national and international level, including whether the application of existing rules is sufficient to cater for emerging risks linked to the innovative nature of such technologies.** Software engineers, data scientists, modelers, operational and front office executives from the industry as well as academics and supervisors need to engage in a continuous dialogue and exchange to promote a better understanding of the opportunities and limitations of AI's use in finance. Given the ease of cross-border provision of financial services, dialogue between the different stakeholders involved should be fostered and maintained at domestic and global levels. There is a role for multilateral organisations in facilitating such dialogue and sharing best practices among countries.
- **Oversee financial industry use of AI so as to indirectly foster trust in AI:** The role of policy makers is important in supporting innovation in the sector while ensuring that financial consumers and investors are duly protected and the markets around such products and services remain fair, orderly and transparent. Efforts to mitigate emerging risks could help instil trust and confidence and promote the adoption of such innovative techniques.

References

ACM US Public Policy Council (2017), *Principles for Algorithmic Transparency and Accountability*, https://www.acm.org/binaries/content/assets/public-policy/2017_usacm_statement_algorithms.pdf. [47]

ACPR (2020), *Governance of Artificial Intelligence in Finance*, https://acpr.banque-france.fr/sites/default/files/medias/documents/20200612_ai_governance_finance.pdf. [45]

ACPR (2018), *Artificial intelligence: challenges for the financial sector*, https://acpr.banque-france.fr/sites/default/files/medias/documents/2018_12_20_intelligence_artificielle_en.pdf. [13]

Almasoud, A. et al. (2020), *Toward a self-learned Smart Contracts*, https://www.researchgate.net/publication/330009052_Toward_a_self-learned_Smart_Contracts. [27]

Bank of England (2018), "Algorithmic trading - Supervisory statement SS5/18", https://www.bankofengland.co.uk/-/media/boe/files/prudential-regulation/supervisory-statement/2018/ss518. [15]

Bank of England and FCA (2020), *Minutes: Artificial Intelligence Public-Private Forum-First meeting*, https://www.bankofengland.co.uk/minutes/2020/artificial-intelligence-public-private-forum-minutes. [44]

Bank of Italy (2019), *Corporate default forecasting with machine learning*, https://www.bancaditalia.it/pubblicazioni/temi-discussione/2019/2019-1256/en_Tema_1256.pdf?language_id=1. [17]

BarclayHedge (2018), *BarclayHedge Survey: Majority of Hedge Fund Pros Use AI/Machine Learning in Investment Strategies.*, https://www.barclayhedge.com/insider/barclayhedge-survey-majority-of-hedge-fund-pros-use-ai-machine-learning-in-investment-strategies. [5]

Bholat, D., M. Gharbawi and O. Thew (2020), *The impact of Covid on machine learning and data science in UK banking | Bank of England*, Bank of England Quarterly Bulletin Q4 2020, https://www.bankofengland.co.uk/quarterly-bulletin/2020/2020-q4/the-impact-of-covid-on-machine-learning-and-data-science-in-uk-banking. [50]

Blackrock (2019), *Artificial intelligence and machine learning in asset management Background*, https://www.blackrock.com/corporate/literature/whitepaper/viewpoint-artificial-intelligence-machine-learning-asset-management-october-2019.pdf. [3]

Bloomberg (2019), *What's an "Algo Wheel?" And why should you care? | Bloomberg Professional Services*, https://www.bloomberg.com/professional/blog/whats-algo-wheel-care/. [7]

Brainard (2020), *Speech by Governor Brainard on supporting responsible use of AI and equitable outcomes in financial services - Federal Reserve Board*, https://www.federalreserve.gov/newsevents/speech/brainard20210112a.htm. [40]

Brookings (2020), *Reducing bias in AI-based financial services*, https://www.brookings.edu/research/reducing-bias-in-ai-based-financial-services/. [20]

Burrell, J. (2016), "How the machine 'thinks': Understanding opacity in machine learning algorithms", http://dx.doi.org/10.1177/2053951715622512. [37]

Citron, D. and F. Pasquale (2014), "The Scored Society: Due Process for Automated Predictions", https://papers.ssrn.com/abstract=2376209. [23]

Deloitte (2019), *Artificial intelligence The next frontier for investment management firms*. [4]

EU (2016), *EUR-Lex - 32016R0679 - EN - EUR-Lex*, https://eur-lex.europa.eu/eli/reg/2016/679/oj. [55]

European Commission (2020), *Digital Services Act*, https://ec.europa.eu/digital-single-market/en/digital-services-act-package. [24]

European Commission (2020), *On Artificial Intelligence - A European Approach To Excellence and Trust White Paper on Artificial Intelligence*, https://ec.europa.eu/commission/sites/beta-political/files/political-guidelines-next-commission_en.pdf. [43]

Federal Reserve (2011), *The Fed - Supervisory Letter SR 11-7 on guidance on Model Risk Management -- April 4, 2011*, https://www.federalreserve.gov/supervisionreg/srletters/sr1107.htm. [48]

Feldman, M. et al. (2015), *Certifying and removing disparate impact*, Association for Computing Machinery, New York, NY, USA, http://dx.doi.org/10.1145/2783258.2783311. [36]

Financial Times (2020), *Hedge funds: no market for small firms | Financial Times*, https://www.ft.com/content/d94760ec-56c4-4051-965d-1fe2b35e4d71. [6]

FSB (2017), *Artificial Intelligence and Machine Learning In Financial Services Market Developments and Financial Stability Implications*, https://www.fsb.org/wp-content/uploads/P011117.pdf. [11]

FSRA (2019), *Supplementary Guidance-Authorisation of Digital Investment Management ("Robo-advisory") Activities.* [46]

G20 Saudi Arabia (2020), *G20 Riyadh InfraTech Agenda*, https://cdn.gihub.org/umbraco/media/3008/g20-riyadh-infratech-agenda.pdf. [30]

Gensler, G. and L. Bailey (2020), "Deep Learning and Financial Stability", *SSRN Electronic Journal*, http://dx.doi.org/10.2139/ssrn.3723132. [53]

Goodman, B. and S. Flaxman (2016), *European Union regulations on algorithmic decision-making and a ``right to explanation''*, http://dx.doi.org/10.1609/aimag.v38i3.2741. [34]

Hackernoon (2020), *Running Artificial Intelligence on the Blockchain | Hacker Noon*, https://hackernoon.com/running-artificial-intelligence-on-the-blockchain-77490d37e616. [29]

Hardoon, D. (2020), *Contextual Explainability*, https://davidroihardoon.com/blog/f/contextual-explainability?blogcategory=Explainability (accessed on 15 March 2021). [33]

Holzinger, A. (2018), "From Machine Learning to Explainable AI", https://www.researchgate.net/profile/Andreas_Holzinger/publication/328309811_From_Machine_Learning_to_Explainable_AI/links/5c3cd032a6fdccd6b5ac71e6/From-Machine-Learning-to-Explainable-AI.pdf. [38]

Hurley, M. (2017), *Credit scoring in the era of big data*, Yale Journal of Law and Technology, https://yjolt.org/sites/default/files/hurley_18yjolt136_jz_proofedits_final_7aug16_clean_0.pdf. [21]

IBM (2020), *AI vs. Machine Learning vs. Deep Learning vs. Neural Networks: What's the Difference? | IBM*, https://www.ibm.com/cloud/blog/ai-vs-machine-learning-vs-deep-learning-vs-neural-networks. [9]

IBM (2020), *The Four V's of Big Data | IBM Big Data & Analytics Hub*, https://www.ibmbigdatahub.com/infographic/four-vs-big-data. [31]

IDC (2020), *Worldwide Spending on Artificial Intelligence Is Expected to Double in Four Years, Reaching $110 Billion in 2024, According to New IDC Spending Guide*, https://www.idc.com/getdoc.jsp?containerId=prUS46794720. [1]

IIROC (2012), *Rules Notice Guidance Note Guidance Respecting Electronic Trading*, https://www.iiroc.ca/news-and-publications/notices-and-guidance/guidance-respecting-electronic-trading. [14]

IOSCO (2020), "The use of artificial intelligence and machine learning by market intermediaries and asset managers Consultation Report INTERNATIONAL ORGANIZATION OF SECURITIES COMMISSIONS", http://www.iosco.org (accessed on 14 September 2021). [39]

JPMorgan (2019), *Machine Learning in FX*, https://www.jpmorgan.com/solutions/cib/markets/machine-learning-fx. [8]

Klein, A. (2020), *Reducing bias in AI-based financial services*, Brookings, https://www.brookings.edu/research/reducing-bias-in-ai-based-financial-services/. [35]

Liew, L. (2020), *What is a Walk-Forward Optimization and How to Run It? - AlgoTrading101 Blog*, Algotrading101, https://algotrading101.com/learn/walk-forward-optimization/. [10]

Noonan (1998), *AI in banking: the reality behind the hype | Financial Times*, Financial Times, https://www.ft.com/content/b497a134-2d21-11e8-a34a-7e7563b0b0f4. [54]

Nourani, M. et al. (2020), *The Effects of Meaningful and Meaningless Explanations on Trust and Perceived System Accuracy in Intelligent Systems*, http://www.aaai.org. [42]

OECD (2021), *Artificial Intelligence, Machine Learning and Big Data in Finance: Opportunities, Challenges and Implications for Policy Makers*, https://www.oecd.org/finance/financial-markets/Artificial-intelligence-machine-learning-big-data-in-finance.pdf. [2]

OECD (2020), *The Tokenisation of Assets and Potential Implications for Financial Markets*, OECD Paris, https://www.oecd.org/finance/The-Tokenisation-of-Assets-and-Potential-Implications-for-Financial-Markets.htm. [25]

OECD (2019), *Artificial Intelligence in Society*, OECD Publishing, Paris, https://dx.doi.org/10.1787/eedfee77-en. [52]

OECD (2019), *OECD Business and Finance Outlook 2019: Strengthening Trust in Business*, OECD Publishing, Paris, https://doi.org/10.1787/af784794-en. [12]

OECD (2017), *Algorithms and Collusion: Competition Policy In the Digital Age*, https://www.oecd.org/daf/competition/Algorithms-and-colllusion-competition-policy-in-the-digital-age.pdf. [16]

S&P (2019), *Avoiding Garbage in Machine Learning*, https://www.spglobal.com/en/research-insights/articles/avoiding-garbage-in-machine-learning-shell. [19]

The Technolawgist (2020), *Does the future of smart contracts depend on artificial intelligence? - The Technolawgist*, https://www.thetechnolawgist.com/2020/12/07/does-the-future-of-smart-contracts-depend-on-artificial-intelligence/. [28]

UK Information Commissioner's Office (2020), *What are the contextual factors?*, https://ico.org.uk/for-organisations/guide-to-data-protection/key-data-protection-themes/explaining-decisions-made-with-artificial-intelligence/part-1-the-basics-of-explaining-ai/what-are-the-contextual-factors/. [41]

US Treasury (2018), *A Financial System That Creates Economic Opportunities Nonbank Financials, Fintech, and Innovation Report to President Donald J. Trump Executive Order 13772 on Core Principles for Regulating the United States Financial System Counselor to the Secretary*, https://home.treasury.gov/sites/default/files/2018-08/A-Financial-System-that-Creates-Economic-Opportunities---Nonbank-Financials-Fintech-and-Innovation.pdf. [32]

US Treasury (2016), *Opportunities and Challenges in Online Marketplace Lending*, https://www.treasury.gov/connect/blog/Pages/Opportunities-and-Challenges-in-Online-Marketplace-Lending.aspx. [18]

White & Case (2017), *Algorithms and bias: What lenders need to know*, https://www.jdsupra.com/legalnews/algorithms-and-bias-what-lenders-need-67308/. [22]

Widmer, G. (1996), *Learning in the Presence of Concept Drift and Hidden Contexts*. [51]

Xu, Y. and R. Goodacre (2018), "On Splitting Training and Validation Set: A Comparative Study of Cross-Validation, Bootstrap and Systematic Sampling for Estimating the Generalization Performance of Supervised Learning", *Journal of Analysis and Testing*, Vol. 2/3, pp. 249-262, http://dx.doi.org/10.1007/s41664-018-0068-2. [49]

Ziqi Chen et al. (2020), *Cortex Blockchain Whitepaper*, https://www.cortexlabs.ai/cortex-blockchain. [26]

Notes

[1] The use of the term AI in this note includes AI and its applications through ML models and the use of big data.

[2] For the purposes of this section, asset managers include traditional and alternative asset managers (hedge funds).

[3] Walk forward optimisation is a process for testing a trading strategy by finding its optimal trading parameters in a certain time period (called the in-sample or training data) and checking the performance of those parameters in the following time period (called the out-of-sample or testing data) (Liew, 2020[10]).

[4] Such tools can also be used in high frequency trading to the extent that investors use them to place trades ahead of competition.

[5] As opposed to value-based trade, which focuses on fundamentals.

[6] Spoofing is an illegal market manipulation practice that involves placing bids to buy or offers to sell securities or commodities with the intent of cancelling the bids or offers prior to the deal's execution. It is designed to create a false sense of investor demand in the market, thereby manipulating the behaviour and actions of other market participants and allowing the spoofer to profit from these changes by reacting to the fluctuations.

[7] It should be noted, however, that the risk of discrimination and unfair bias exists equally in traditional, manual credit rating mechanisms, where the human parameter could allow for conscious or unconscious biases.

[8] Inspired by the functionality of human brains where hundreds of billions of interconnected neurons process information in parallel, neural networks are composed of basic units somewhat analogous to human neurons, with units linked to each other by connections whose strength is modifiable as a result of a learning process or algorithm. Deep learning neural networks are modelling the way neurons interact in the brain with many ('deep') layers of simulated interconnectedness (OECD, 2021[2]).

[9] Blockchain and distributed ledger technologies are terms used interchangeably in this Chapter.

[10] Oracles feed external data into the blockchain. They can be external service providers in the form of an API endpoint, or actual nodes of the chain. They respond to queries of the network with specific data points that they bring from sources external to the network.

[11] Smart contracts are distributed applications written as code on Blockchain ledgers, automatically executed upon reaching pre-defined trigger events written in the code (OECD, 2020[25]).

[12] Natural Language Processing (NLP), a subset of AI, is the ability of a computer program to understand human language as it is spoken and written (referred to as natural language).

[13] Reinforcement learning involves the learning of the algorithm through interaction and feedback. It is based on neural networks and may be applied to unstructured data like images or voice.

[14] In cases of credit decisions, this also includes information on factors, including personal data that have influenced the applicant's credit scoring. In certain jurisdictions, such as Poland, information should also be provided to the applicant on measures that the applicant can take to improve their creditworthiness.

[15] Regulatory sandboxes specifically targeting AI applications could be a way to understand some of these potential incompatibilities, as was the case in Colombia.

3 Human rights due diligence through responsible AI

While the benefits and opportunities of AI seem boundless, certain applications of AI risk causing intentional or unintentional harms. It is critical to ground conversations on AI development in international standards on responsible business conduct, a foundation of sustainable economic development. International standards set out recommendations to help companies identify and address the negative impacts their operations and products may have on people and the environment. This chapter focuses on potential human rights impacts of AI and how companies developing and using AI can apply OECD guidance on human rights due diligence. It also examines how existing legislation, both on human rights and on AI, deals with this issue.

3.1. Introduction

The ability of AI to quickly analyse enormous amounts of data, recognise patterns, build upon existing knowledge, and build predictive models make it an invaluable tool for economic and social development. AI is being applied, for example, in healthcare for drug development, patient monitoring, and epidemiology; in law enforcement to detect financial crime, to combat kidnapping and human trafficking, to identify situations of bonded or child labour, and analyse crime scenes; and in local government administration to improve welfare distribution, to predict infrastructure maintenance requirements and direct traffic flows to reduce road congestion. While the benefits and opportunities of AI seem boundless, it is critical to ground conversations in in international standards on responsible business conduct (RBC), a foundation of sustainable economic development, as well as the OECD AI Principle on "robustness, security and safety". To maximise the positive impact of AI, companies and governments also need to understand and prevent risks of harm that the technology can cause.

Key message

To maximise the positive impact of AI, companies and governments also need to understand and prevent risks of harm. The OECD Guidelines for Multinational Enterprises and OECD Due Diligence Guidance for Responsible Business Conduct provide government-backed frameworks, aligned with international standards on business and human rights that companies can implement to better identify and address risks of harm.

This chapter broadly lays out how certain applications of AI risk causing intentional or unintentional harms, and how companies developing, selling and using AI can apply OECD recommendations to help prevent and mitigate negative impacts. The chapter also summarises current national, international, business-led, and multi-stakeholder initiatives helping to tackle some of these issues.

Since its inception, the OECD has been committed to utilising the power of international business and new technology as a driving force for sustainable economic, environmental and social development. In parallel to acknowledging and encouraging this, the OECD also recognises that business activities can result in adverse impacts related to workers, human rights, the environment, bribery, consumers and corporate governance. This is why the OECD Guidelines for Multinational Enterprises (the OECD Guidelines) were first adopted in 1976.[1]

The OECD Guidelines go beyond the traditional, philanthropic Corporate Social Responsibility (CSR) approach by setting out government-backed recommendations for business to proactively address potential harms they may cause, contribute to, or are directly linked to. The OECD Guidelines specifically recommend that companies carry out due diligence to identify and address any adverse impacts associated with their operations, their supply chains or other business relationships.

On technology specifically, the OECD Guidelines call on companies to support science and technological innovation in the countries where they operate.[2] Companies are encouraged to do this through establishing partnerships with local research institutions (such as universities), hiring and training local staff to work with new technologies and to sell or license new tech on reasonable terms and with due consideration to the long term development effects on the host country.

The OECD Guidelines are also a commitment by governments to provide an enabling environment for RBC. Governments can enable RBC in several ways including: Regulating – establishing and enforcing an adequate legal framework that protects the public interest and underpins RBC, and monitoring business performance and compliance with regulatory frameworks; Facilitating – clearly communicating expectations on what constitutes RBC, providing guidance with respect to specific practices and enabling companies to meet those expectations; and Co-operating – working with stakeholders in the business community, worker organisations, civil society, general public, across internal government structures, as well as other governments to create synergies and establish coherence with regard to RBC.

The OECD Guidelines are aligned with the United Nations Guiding Principles on Business and Human Rights and the International Labour Organisation Tripartite Declaration of Principles Concerning Multinational Enterprises. In addition, certain RBC expectations outlined in the OECD Guidelines (e.g. on addressing environmental degradation in business activities) are also referenced in global frameworks such as the G20 agenda, the Sustainable Development Goals, and the Paris Climate Accord.

3.2. Overview of human rights impacts of AI

AI's impacts on RBC are manifold given the positive and negative potential of the technology and far reaching effects. Given the potential breadth of its application and use, AI promises to advance the protection and fulfilment of human rights, as well as allowing people with disabilities to overcome hurdles to living a more independent life. Examples include using AI to facilitate more personalised education to individuals with learning disabilities, assisting visually impaired people to navigate electronic devices, and shedding light on discrimination (OECD, 2019[11]). Likewise, as described in Section 3.5 below, AI is being used to support supply chain management in a way to make human rights due diligence far more efficient for companies.

Beyond impacts to the financial markets and competitive practices (which all concern RBC, but are covered in more detail in other chapters and other OECD publications), AI has had an observed negative impact on human rights and labour rights across a broad scope of applications. This includes the following use-cases, which were selected for illustrative purposes and are not an exhaustive list. It should also be noted that the issues themselves are not mutually exclusive (e.g. applications that could affect rights to privacy may also impact freedom of expression and in some cases, the right to life and freedom from cruel and degrading treatment).

Figure 3.1. Examples of AI impacts on human rights enumerated in the Universal Declaration of Human Rights

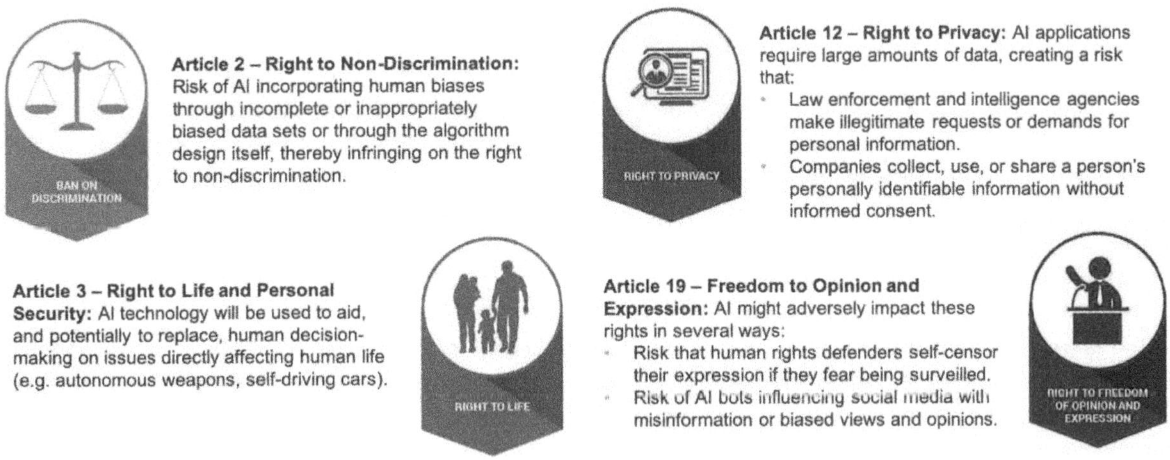

Source: Adapted from OECD (2019) briefing paper on RBC & AI, https://mneguidelines.oecd.org/RBC-and-artificial-intelligence.pdf.

3.2.1. Right to privacy[3]

As billions of smartphones, laptops, cameras, and other devices collect data and analyse it using increasingly powerful and sophisticated software, users of that data are able to build more accurate profiles of individuals, that can be monetised, used to track and predict movements and purchases, or ultimately used to manipulate the individual. Much of the privacy-sensitive data analysis, such as search algorithms, recommendation engines, and advertising software, is driven by AI. While existing consumer privacy and consent laws restrict access to some information, AI powered analysis can still create highly accurate behaviour predictions based on existing publicly available data. As AI improves, it magnifies the ability to exploit personal information in ways that can intrude on privacy rights and other human rights by raising analysis of personal information to new levels (Kerry, 2020[2]).

AI applications for facial recognition provide a salient example. Drawing from the thousands of images of an individual available on social media and government databases (such as driver's licenses and passports), AI-powered surveillance cameras can recognise individuals and match their images with broader sets of data on the individual. This type of technology is already being deployed for police use in some countries, and risks being used by authoritarian regimes to oppress political dissidents and minority populations.

A 2016 study found that half of US adults are already in police facial recognition databases across the country (Bedoya, 2016[3]). Though advocates point to the positive aspects of the technology to find missing persons and identify victims of crime, there have also been accusations of misuse, such as targeting political activists for arrest during larger protests against police violence (Vincent, 2020[4]). In other contexts, reports have emerged of surveillance and facial recognition being used to track ethnic minorities based on physical appearance, while keeping records of their movements for search and review (Mozur, 2019[5]).

Owing to concerns over privacy and misuse, multiple major cities in the United States have adopted bans on the technology. California, New Hampshire, and Oregon all have enacted legislation banning use of facial recognition technology with police body cameras (Kerry, 2020[2]). Following the Black Lives Matter protests in the United States in 2020, IBM, Amazon, and Microsoft, restricted or suspended sales of their facial recognition products.

In Europe, the General Data Protection Regulation (GDPR) prohibits the processing of biometric data for the purpose of uniquely identifying a natural person, data concerning health, data concerning a natural person's sex life or sexual orientation and the processing of data revealing racial or ethnic origins.[4] GDPR rules on AI more broadly are discussed in the section below on data use legislation (1.4.4). EU officials had originally considered a blanket ban on facial recognition in public spaces, but have instead left it to member states to impose the ban after strong opposition from some members. Additionally, in April 2021, the European Commission proposed new rules and actions on the development of trustworthy AI, where facial recognition is considered to be a high-risk application and is only allowed in specific cases (European Commission, 2021[6]).

3.2.2. Right to non-discrimination[5]

Human biases are often present in non-automated systems of reviewing data (e.g. reviewing job applications) and automated AI systems can, in theory, help correct or compensate for some of those biases. However, AI systems can also be intentionally or unintentionally biased themselves. Biases present in AI systems can include those that relate to model design (e.g. deciding which variables to consider) and pre-existing biases in the data (e.g. only male applicants in a data pool of CVs). The initial design of a programme may omit important aspects of an issue or reflect the biases of designers which can mean that decisions are improperly influenced by data on ethnicity, sex, age when hiring or firing, offering loans, or even in criminal proceedings. The decision-making generated by these systems might be perceived incorrectly as inherently fair and neutral. In a phenomenon sometimes referred to as 'mathwashing', using AI-generated numbers to represent complex social realities can make findings seem factual and precise when they are not (European Commission, 2021[7]).

Concerns of discrimination arise when individual variables in algorithms indirectly serve as proxies for protected or undisclosed information such as race, sexual orientation, gender or age. An algorithm may lead users to discriminate against a group which correlates with the proxy variable in question.

The direct impacts of this are obvious when applied to something like filtering job applications. For example, Amazon's failed experiment with a hiring algorithm replicated the company's existing disproportionately male workforce (Destin, 2018[8]). In that situation, computer models were trained to vet job applicants by observing patterns in successful applications submitted to the company over a 10-year period. Most came from men. As a result, the algorithm taught itself to penalise women candidates by correlating less preferable applications with the word "women" when it appeared in phrases in applications like "women's college", "women in business club" or "women's basketball team".

Another striking but less obvious impact is observed in search engines discriminating when providing search results. Due to a number of the factors taken into account, search engines rank advertisements of smaller companies that are registered in less affluent neighbourhoods lower than those of large entities, which may put them at a commercial disadvantage and perpetuate economic inequality (Council of Europe Committee of Experts on Internet Intermediaries, 2018[9]). Different users of the search engine are also provided with different results based on their profiles, resulting in differential pricing. In a related example, a Harvard study found that names linked with black Americans were 25% more likely to have results that prompted the searcher to click on a link to search criminal record history which is certain to have detrimental effects when potential employers, loan officers, etc., use those search engines. (Sweeny, 2013[10]).

When applied to contexts of crime prevention and predictive policing, discriminatory AI decision support can result in serious infringements on other rights such as presumption of innocence, the right to be informed promptly of the cause and nature of an accusation, the right to a fair hearing and the right to defend oneself in person. Such examples include the use of AI systems to support identifying potential terrorists based on content they post online, to determine if an individual poses a flight risk, to suggest the length of a prison sentence or whether an individual should be granted parole (Council of Europe Committee of Experts on Internet Intermediaries, 2018[9]). AI learning in such applications is based on current police databases, which often reflect and reinforce existing racial and cultural biases present in communities. Existing databases may be biased or incomplete, or even when complete, AI systems may fail to apply a presumption of innocence when recommending an action to be taken based on probabilities.

3.2.3. Right to fair trial and due process[6]

When investigators enter a crime scene or initiate an investigation, they are often presented with an enormous amount of very detailed information. AI systems are being used to help investigators analyse and process that information to filter out only the most useful, timely evidence (Baraniuk, 2019[11]). Applications range from analysing thousands of photographs on a phone to reconstructing the faces of murder victims based on small fragments of genetic information. The extreme efficiency that comes with higher computing power can have positive impacts on police ability to resolve crimes and catch suspects. AI is also being used to help law enforcement in the financial sector through what is called 'SupTech' or supervisory technology (see Chapter 5). This could help regulators analyse large amounts of financial data to spot risks of fraud, market manipulation or anti-competitive practices.

AI is also being applied in the courts to reduce the burdens of judges and magistrates. For example, the Estonian Ministry of Justice are asking AI firms to design a "robot judge" that could adjudicate small claims disputes of less than €7000 (Niiler, 2018[12]). In some parts of the United States, AI systems are used to help recommend criminal sentences. This trend is increasing across different countries to handle the notoriously overwhelmed legal dockets of judges, prosecutors and public defenders. Likewise, AI systems are being used to help provide limited forms of legal aid to individuals who might not be able to afford it (Chouhan, 2019[13]). For example, an app developed by a university student in the United States in 2018 uses AI systems to fight parking tickets by automatically filling up appeals forms based on interactions with users (Walter, 2019[14]). The same technology is being deployed more broadly to help users fill out complicated government applications or to act as a screener for potential clients at law firms.

There is a some fear, however, that decision support systems based on AI are inappropriately used and that they are perceived as being more "objective", even when this is not the case. Questions also arise when legal decisions are made based on difficult (or impossible) to explain algorithms (e.g. obtaining an arrest or search warrant). Deep Learning Algorithms are able to rework the rules on the basis for which they were programmed and may make decisions that are incomprehensible to the AI actors designing and developing it (Floridi, Mittelstadt and Watcher, 2017[15]) (Gasparri, 2019[16]). In criminal law, evidence obtained illegally is inadmissible at trial. If the party against whom evidence is introduced during a trial cannot dispute its accuracy and reliability, the question then arises as to whether evidence gathered through a system not subject to criticism, because the inaccessibility of the source code or other characteristics of the software, is legally permissible. This also raises broader questions about who bears responsibility for AI decision-making, which some legislation is attempting to addresses (see discussion on the European General Data Protection Regulation and the European Commission proposal for an AI regulation in section 1.4.1 of this chapter) and which is discussed in the OECD AI Principle on transparency and explainability.

3.2.4. Freedom of expression[7]

Content moderation and content curation are often automated procedures, with AI deciding on which content is taken down or to whom it is disseminated. This can be very helpful for managing massive amounts of information uploaded onto a website, particularly for quickly flagging and removing clearly prohibited content (i.e. child pornography, illegal weapons sales, snuff videos, etc.). Questions and questions arise when automating these features with regard to political content, including extremist views. Without a transparent, clearly explainable decision-making process, arbitrary silencing of views can pose risks for state capture of online platforms that violate freedom of expression under the guise of moderation of extremist content or fake news. Google, Youtube, and Facebook have developed automated systems to remove 'extremist content', but have not publically disclosed how their filters work (Menn and Volz, 2016[17]). Reddit has publically disclosed how their automated moderation system works (see Box 3.3).

This type of application can also present a threat to democracy; AI has already been blamed for creating online echo chambers based on a person's previous online behaviour, displaying only content a person would like to see based on previous personal interactions as well as those of similar users, instead of creating an environment for equally accessible and inclusive public debate. AI is also being used to spread misinformation, either through algorithms designed to push addictive content on users of social media or through the creation of fake content that appears legitimate. For example, AI can be used to create extremely realistic video, audio and images that are false or misleading, known as deepfakes. This can also present individual reputational harm, financial risks, and challenge free and fair decision making. In the aggregate this could lead to severe political and social polarisation.

3.2.5. Freedom of Association[8]

Freedom of association explicitly includes the right to form and join trade unions, and it is in particular here that certain trends in the use of AI can be identified that may provide reason for concern. The right to associate with others may come under pressure if AI is used to monitor, control and repress worker engagement. Data processing capabilities of AI used in combination with new productivity and movement tracking tools makes it possible to increase digital monitoring of workers and workplaces in ways that are unprecedented.

A glimpse of what is technically possible can be seen from the management of workplaces during the Covid-19 pandemic. In order to guarantee social distancing rules, new "biometric solutions for safer places" were introduced such as ultrasonic bracelets beeping every time workers came within virus-catching distance of a co-worker, or microchips allowing workers to enter the workplace in a contactless fashion (Aloisi and De Stefano, 2021[18]). Crucially, these tools permit private contact tracing. Increased telework during the pandemic was also accompanied by the use of new types of surveillance software measuring time spent online, the number of keystrokes, but also software reporting to managers when employees are distracted or when and for how long someone is away from their workstation. AI can be used to allow employers to turn extensive data sets of employee information into extensive behavioural profiles and patterns that can then be used to detect and predict the probability of workers organising themselves (Moore, 2020[19]).

In Autumn 2020, Amazon was reported to be looking to hire two intelligence analysts, to be charged with tracking "labour organizing threats" against the company (Palmer, 2020[20]). While these job vacancies were quickly withdrawn after widespread reactions in the public opinion, the Amazon-owned Whole Foods company is using technology and data to track and score stores it deems at risk of unionising. In Europe, Amazon's Intelligence Unit is reportedly also closely monitoring the labour and union-organising activity of their workers, as well as environmentalist and social justice groups on Facebook and Instagram. Intelligence analysts keep close tabs on how many warehouse workers attend union meetings; specific worker dissatisfactions with warehouse conditions, such as excessive workloads; updates on labour organizing activities at warehouses that include the exact date, time, location, the source who reported the action and the number of participants at an event (Gurley and Rose, 2020[21]).

By delivering enhanced information and knowledge tracking of worker activity and their possible engagement in organising themselves, AI can make it possible for businesses to discourage, interfere or even restrain efforts of workers to unionize, thus disrespecting a fundamental labour and human right.

3.3. RBC applied to AI supply chain actors

3.3.1. Six Step OECD Due Diligence Framework

Based on the recommendation in the Guidelines that companies conduct due diligence to identify and address adverse impacts in their own operations and their supply chains, the OECD has developed sector-specific guidance for carrying out supply chain due diligence in minerals, garment & footwear, agriculture, as well as for institutional investors. Most recently, and most relevant to the discussion on new technology, the OECD has developed a general OECD Due Diligence Guidance for Responsible Business Conduct (the Due Diligence Guidance) that draws from and builds on sector specific guidance, but can be applied to all sectors of the economy. The due diligence framework in the Due Diligence Guidance consists of six steps (see Figure 3.2). (OECD, 2018[22]).

Figure 3.2. The six steps of the OECD Due Diligence Guidance

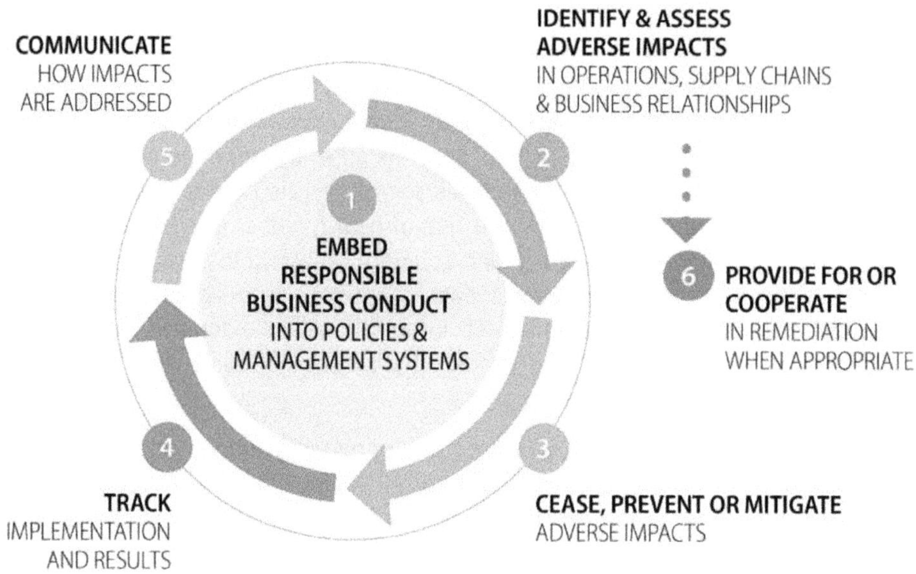

Source: (OECD, 2018[22]).

Due diligence is a tailored process, so when applied to the context of companies in the AI space, this could take a variety of forms depending on the size and location of the company, the type of product they are developing, its position in the value chain, the type of harm caused by its product, who its clients are, and a number of other factors.

Due diligence is also risk-based, meaning the measures that a company takes to conduct due diligence should be commensurate to the severity and likelihood of the adverse impact. When the severity and likelihood of the impact is high, as is presumably the case where the product developed has the capacity to be used in harmful ways, then due diligence must be more extensive.

Other key principles of due diligence to keep in mind when applying the due diligence framework are that it is flexible, progressive, consultative and transparent. The expectation on companies is that they initiate and continue the due diligence process; no one expects fully mapped out and impact-free operations and supply chains overnight. Businesses need to make difficult choices about the issues they prioritise and they need to show progressive improvement over time. This is a consultative and transparent approach whereby stakeholders expect to be consulted at each step of the due diligence process to ensure that efforts are effective. Companies are also expected to publically report on their efforts to conduct due diligence. Figure 3.2 demonstrates that these steps are not mutually exclusive and can all be undertaken simultaneously.

It is important for companies in business relationships with high risk end-users to keep in mind that the goal of due diligence is not to prevent them from doing business, but rather to promote increased responsible investment and trade, utilising the power of global business to leverage positive change. Global companies working with cutting edge technology have considerable leverage to address risks, for example by enforcing contractual terms, developing standards to ensure implementation of RBC across their value chains, and collaborating with other actors – such as international and regional organisations, national governments and civil society – to influence vendors and third parties.

The overall due diligence framework could be applied by all companies in the AI space. Companies should note that the Due Diligence Guidance goes into more detail on how exactly the steps can be implemented, however, a more detailed assessment of the technology and thorough consultation with all relevant stakeholders (including companies, government, and civil society) is necessary to develop guidance specific to AI. The examples on how RBC could be applied to AI in this chapter are drawn from the Due Diligence Guidance, engagement with experts and stakeholders and existing best practice.[9]

It is also important to note that application of the due diligence framework can assist companies in meeting expectations set out by the OECD Principles on AI[10], as each step of the Due Diligence Guidance tracks closely with the five principles.

Table 3.1. Linking the OECD AI Principles and the OECD Due Diligence Guidance

Values-based OECD AI Principles	OECD Due Diligence Guidance
1. Benefits to people and planet: AI should benefit people and the planet by driving inclusive growth, sustainable development and well-being.	Step 1 & 3: Companies should embed RBC into policies and management systems in order to ensure that commitments to benefit people and the planet are incorporated in the product's design, sale, and use. Companies can often most effectively prevent and manage risk of harm of its products by thinking of the opportunities to enhance positive impact / benefit.
2. Human-centred values and fairness: AI systems should be designed in a way that respects the rule of law, human rights, democratic values and diversity, and they should include appropriate safeguards – for example, enabling human intervention where necessary – to ensure a fair and just society.	Steps 2 & 3: Companies should identify adverse impacts and take steps to mitigate and prevent them, including through establishing safeguards like whistleblower mechanisms, kill switches, and allowing for human intervention, and also restricting sales/services to certain customers.
3. Transparency and explainability: There should be transparency and responsible disclosure around AI systems to ensure that people understand AI-based outcomes and can challenge them.	Step 5: Companies should publically report on due diligence efforts on a periodic basis, including tracking progress and efforts to expand the risk scope.
4. Robustness, security and safety: AI systems must function in a robust, secure and safe way throughout their life cycles and potential risks should be continually assessed and managed.	Steps 2 & 3: All companies in the AI lifecycle (and value chain more broadly) have a responsibility to ensure that negative impacts are addressed in its development, sale, and use. This not only includes technology companies, but non-technology companies that use AI, governments, and investors.
5. Accountability: Organisations and individuals developing, deploying or operating AI systems should be held accountable for the proper functioning of those systems throughout their lifecycle in line with the above principles.	Step 6: Companies should provide for or cooperate with remediation mechanisms if appropriate. Numerous judicial and non-judicial mechanisms exist to hold companies accountable and allow for impacts to be remediated.

Box 3.1. RBC in practice: Establishing a public company policy on human rights

(OECD Due Diligence Guidance Step 1)

Technology companies should implement and disseminate policies on the company's most significant adverse impacts to align their commitments to the Guidelines, including the commitment to refrain from causing harm and to conduct supply chain due diligence to address harms. As part of this step, companies should incorporate RBC expectations into their engagement with suppliers, customers and other business relationships. Companies should communicate clearly to suppliers and customers that certain uses or unintentional effects of their technology are unacceptable and may have consequences for the commercial relationship. Policies should also be updated on an ongoing basis, taking into account stakeholder views and learnings from the company's efforts to address risk.

In March 2018, Google announced a contract with the US Department of Defence to work on analysing military drone videos using AI, known as Project Maven. In response, over 4000 Google employees signed a letter calling on Google to cancel Project Maven and to draft, publicise and enforce a clear policy stating that neither Google nor its contractors will ever build warfare technology. A dozen employees also quit the company in protest. Following this opposition from employees, in early June 2018, Google announced that it will stop working on Project Maven when its current contract expires.

Since then, Google has published its AI Principles prominently on its website. The Principles are that AI should: "(1) Be socially beneficial, (2) Avoid creating or reinforcing unfair bias, (3) Be built and tested safely, (4) Be accountable to people, (5) Incorporate privacy design principles, (6) Uphold high standards of scientific excellence, (7) Be made available for uses that accord with these principles." And that Google will not pursue: "Technologies that cause or are likely to cause overall harm. (Subject to risk/benefit analysis.) Weapons or other technologies whose principal purpose or implementation is to cause or directly facilitate injury to people. Technologies that gather or use information for surveillance violating internationally accepted norms. Technologies whose purpose contravenes widely accepted principles of international law and human rights."

The Guidelines and related due diligence guidance aim to foster responsible business conduct in all sectors, even those which by nature are considered to be high-risk. The Guidelines do not necessarily suggest that companies disengage in high-risk activities, such as those in the defence sector. Instead, companies should seek to design strategies appropriate to their own risk appetite, with enhanced due diligence to identify and prevent or mitigate human right risks, prioritising actual or potential harms based on their severity. In this regard, RBC principles of transparency and stakeholder engagement are particularly important.

Notwithstanding Google's decision to disengage from this project, this anecdote serves as a strong example of a company applying the RBC approach with regards to stakeholder engagement and setting a public policy. Google responded to stakeholder feedback (in this case, the letter from the 4000 employees), made a decision to alter their approach to certain government contracts, and developed a clear public policy based on that stakeholder engagement, which will provide greater accountability to future undertakings.

Note: The Electronic Frontier Foundation (EFF), a watchdog on civil liberties issues relating to online platforms, publishes a helpful annual summary of public commitments to various human rights issues by the biggest online platforms: https://www.eff.org/wp/who-has-your-back-2019#transparent-about-legal-takedown-requests

Source: Coldewey, David (2018), "Google's new 'AI principles' forbid its use in weapons and human rights violations," TechCrunch, *https://techcrunch.com/2018/06/07/googles-new-ai-principles-forbid-its-use-in-weapons-and-human-rights-violations/?_guc_consent_skip=1615197403 ; Google's AI Principles, https://ai.google/responsibilities/.*

3.3.2. Roles/responsibilities of different supply chain actors

Different from a standard physical product, where the relationship between the manufacturers, retailers and consumer is linear, there is significant overlap and exchange in the AI landscape between developers, vendors and end-users. Indeed, the assigning of responsibility to the different AI actors who develop, sell, or deploy different technologies is still an open question. The OECD defines AI actors as "those who play an active role in the AI system lifecycle, including organisations and individuals that deploy or operate AI" (OECD, 2019[1]). Companies in this space should keep in mind that, given the broad definition of a 'business relationship' under the OECD Guidelines, these relationships commence prior to the execution of legally binding contracts (OECD, 2021, forthcoming[23]).

All supply chain actors are expected to carry out a broad scoping exercise to identify where RBC risks are most likely to be present and most significant. The scoping exercise should enable the company to carry out an initial prioritisation of the most significant risk areas for further assessment.

For AI, this exercise will consist of two primary elements: (1) a mapping of relevant business relationships and (see Figure 3.2); (2) a risk assessment of the product or service in question to determine the potential for misuse or negative side effects. As with all steps in the due diligence process, stakeholders such as civil society groups, representatives of potentially affected groups/communities, worker's unions and independent experts should be consulted in both of these elements in order to gain a more complete understanding of the risks.

Figure 3.3. A broad mapping of the AI supply chain

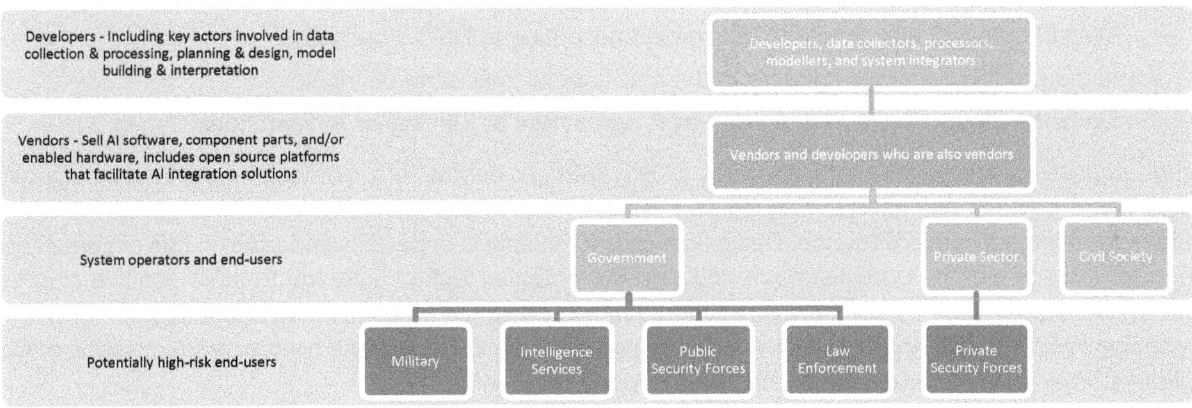

Note: This example landscape of different AI actors across an AI system value chain is provided as an illustration which does not necessarily include all actors in the value chain
Source: Based on the OECD Framework for the Classification of AI Systems for Policy makers (2021) https://oecd.ai/wonk/a-first-look-at-the-oecds-framework-for-the-classification-of-ai-systems-for-policy makers

Developers: Including key actors involved in data collection & processing, planning & design, model building & interpretation

AI products are created by developers, through the following process:[11]

- Ideation: Identifying a problem and priorities for the AI
- Data Gathering: Selecting the appropriate data set for the AI to learn from
- Method Selection: Selected the method for teaching the AI what to do with the data
- Performance Testing: Testing the AI's ability to perform the task it was taught

While due diligence should cover all stages of the product lifecycle, companies have the greatest opportunity to address risks during the product development of AI technologies. By applying a "human rights by design strategy," developers can prevent/mitigate potential risks of technologies at every step of development, so it is critical to map out the relevant actors and get them involved in the process early.

Developer due diligence could include asking questions such as:

- Who will likely use the product and for what purpose?
- Is the system robust, secure and safe? Is there the potential for misuse, poor handling or lack of enforcement of respective rules and standards?
- Is there a chance that vulnerable groups will be especially impacted by the use of the technology?
- Are appropriate safeguards in place to prevent negative impacts?
- Are processes and decisions made during the AI system lifecycle explainable and transparent?

Vendors

Once a product is developed, it is sold by vendors to end-users, who deploy and operate the technology. It is the responsibility of the vendor to conduct due diligence at the point of sale on the risks associated with the use of the product. Importantly, many AI developers also sell their own products. Other companies develop AI products that are distributed by its partners or third-party retailers. Developers may also be contracted directly to create specific products, and as such, take on extended responsibilities of due diligence. Vendors should review credible reports of the human rights records of the recipient or history of misuse of products.

Vendor due diligence could include asking questions such as:

- Was the product designed and assembled according to RBC standards?
- Is the product being sold directly to the end-user or to another distributor?
- Does the product come with an end-user agreement or training on AI limitations?

When end users are government agencies or government contractors, particularly militaries or private military and security companies, they present higher risks of the technology being used for harm and require more stringent due diligence. Due diligence prior to sale is especially important in this circumstance because the scale of the potential harm and also the potential lack of leverage to drive positive change. The United States State Department developed detailed guidance on conducting due diligence for selling technology with surveillance capabilities to foreign governments. Despite the narrow product scope of that guidance, many of recommendations can be extended to AI vendors.

Additional due diligence questions when selling to / contracting with a government include:

- Are there laws and oversight in the recipient country allowing for (or preventing) abuse of the technology (e.g. counter terrorism laws that unduly restrict freedom of expression or allow for arbitrary surveillance)?
- Are there data localisation requirements that may result in violation of privacy or other human rights in the country where the data is stored?
- Is the government involved in an on-going conflict where the technology can potentially be deployed?
- Is the government involved in on-going human rights abuses against protected groups?
- If the end-user is not the government, does the government have effective control over the end-user, opening the door for potential misuse of the technology or access to data?
- Can licenses be revoked or the product be disabled if misuse occurs?
- Does the product have a dual-use that is harmful?

End Users

End users can be anyone, ranging from a government, a government contractor, another company, or a civil society organisation. For many AI technologies that are licensed to end users, developers have the ability to monitor the product, creating opportunities for human rights due diligence directly between the developer and the end user. For example, developers and vendors can limit licensing renewals with end users.

End user due diligence could include asking questions such as:

- Was the product accompanied by guidance or training on its limitations?
- Has the product been altered in any way that may increase its potential RBC risks through resale channels?

Companies in the AI lifecycle should also assess whether the capabilities of its product or service may cause, contribute to or be directly linked to an adverse impact. This assessment should take into account the design, development, marketing, sale, licensing and deployment of its products and services. AI-based products and services could potentially linked to adverse impacts in a variety of ways.

Box 3.2. Investor due diligence and leverage to drive responsible AI development

In recent years, investors and financial institutions have become a major driving force for uptake of due diligence expectations in companies they lend to. The volume of "responsible" or "sustainable" financial products and strategies has grown exponentially in the past 10 years, driven largely by increased demand from beneficiaries and policy signals that the financial sector should be a driver in achieving global sustainability agendas.

Despite widespread funding and massive amounts of money raised for AI start-ups, the sector seems to be dominated by a relatively small number of venture capital funds. In 2019, the International Finance Corporation noted that AI start-ups in the United States raised $4.4 billion from 155 investments, while Chinese start-ups raised $4.9 billion from 19 investments (Xiaomin, 2019[24]). Together, US-based and Chinese start-ups represented over 80% of the monetary value of VC investments in AI start-ups in 2020. This compares to 72% of VC investments the two countries represented across all sectors (OECD, 2021, forthcoming[25]). If these funds were to incorporate human rights due diligence requirements as a condition for financing, it could have a significant impact on future AI development. To that end, the OECD developed a framework for financial institutions to identify, respond to and publicly communicate on environmental and social risks associated with their clients (OECD, 2019[26]).

There have already been high profile cases and backlash against large banks for their role in financing certain technology used in human rights abuses. For example, a Swiss bank is the subject of an NCP complaint due to alleged failure to observe the Guidelines regarding human rights due diligence with regards to its relationship with a Chinese surveillance technology firm (OECD, 2021[27]). Similarly, a large financial institution was reported to have sold its loan to an Israeli surveillance firm at a loss following reports of the firm's development and sale of technology allegedly used to spy on journalists and human rights defenders (Smith, 2019[28]).

3.3.3. Risk prevention/mitigation at different stages of the AI lifecycle

Based on the initial scoping and risk assessment companies should act to stop, prevent or mitigate the impact(s) identified. This involves developing and implementing plans that are fit-for-purpose. All impacts are expected to be addressed, with the most severe impacts taking priority. Stakeholders should be meaningfully involved in planning, enacting and monitoring impact prevention and mitigation efforts. Prevention/mitigation can take place at the design phase, as the product is being developed; at the procurement or sale phase; and after the produce has already been sold. With customers, companies can already mitigate potential impacts through contractual and procedural safeguards and strong grievance mechanisms.

At the design phase:

A growing community of researchers have called on developers to consider explainability (XAI), and fairness, accountability, and transparency (FATML) when developing products. Developers should strive to develop technology where the outcomes of decision making are readily interpretable (Council of Europe Expert Committee on human rights dimensions of automated data processing and different forms of artificial intelligence, 2019[29]). Similarly, techniques should be developed to identify and overcome problems of bias and discrimination arising from the use of data mining and other machine learning techniques (known as discrimination-aware' or 'fairness-aware' techniques for machine learning). This is also reflected in the OECD AI Principles which state that "AI actors should…provide meaningful information…to enable those adversely affected by an AI system to challenge its outcome based on plain and easy-to-understand information on the factors, and the logic that served as the basis for the prediction, recommendation or decision."[12]

Companies should also develop secure, accessible, and responsive communications channels and grievance mechanisms for both internal and external actors to report possible misuse of products or services.

At the contracting phase:

Contractual safeguards include, for example, end-use and end-user limitations, reserving the seller's right to terminate access to technology, and denying software updates, training, and other services.

After sale:

Technology companies tend to have a unique, on-going relationship with their customers that companies in other sectors lack (e.g. customer support, software updates, maintaining networks, etc). This provides them with very strong leverage should they identify misuse of their products or unintended side-effects that should be stopped or mitigated. Actions include:

- Tracking/Monitoring of product use
- Alerts of misuse
- Kill switches on certain features of the product (i.e. a way to rapidly shut down or disable those features or the entire product)
- Limiting customer support / updates

Currently, AI research and use of AI technology is currently under regulated and little is disclosed about internal whistleblowing mechanisms available to hold AI developers and users accountable, though this is increasingly changing (Katyal, 2018[30]). One of the central obstacles is the clash between human rights and the right of a business to not disclose proprietary information about an algorithm. This will increasingly become a problem as government agencies take data or AI service contracts from companies.

Again, the practical implications of RBC considerations in the context of the use of a technology product or service would be useful to explore and elaborate through multi-stakeholder processes. At a minimum, companies should explore all possible avenues to mitigate any new, unintended human rights risk and engage human rights experts and affected stakeholders when deliberating on dilemmas. Table 3.2 provides examples of specific mitigation actions depending on the type of harm.

Table 3.2. Risk mitigation based on the type of harm caused by AI

Type of harm	Examples	Illustrative risk mitigation options
Purposeful "harm by design"	Deepfake video designed to harm an individual's reputation and right to privacy.	Update company policies against developing this type of technology Investments in detection technology
Harm caused by inherent "side effects"	Biased police data leading to discrimination	Engagement with civil rights group during product development and roll out / transparent grievance mechanism / public oversight
	Social media algorithm promoting hate speech or false information	Policies that balance supporting freedom of expression with responsible content moderation. Transparent grievance mechanisms should be provided to inform users that content they uploaded has been filtered out or blocked, and to lodge complaints in case they do not agree with the assessment of the filtering system. Public reporting on the removal process and data in the aggregate
Harm caused by failure rates	Biased inputs leading to biased outcomes in hiring processes	Ensuring a balanced dataset, improving product validation and verification process, and engagement with civil rights groups during product development and roll out
Harm caused by intentional misuse	AI powered surveillance technology	Restrict sale and product support to certain governments Public oversight over how the technology is deployed

Source: Adapted from OECD (2019) briefing paper on RBC & AI, https://mneguidelines.oecd.org/RBC-and-artificial-intelligence.pdf.

Box 3.3. RBC in practice - transparency and accountability

(OECD Due Diligence Guidance Steps 4 & 5)

The Guidance recommends that companies publically report on the outcomes of their due diligence, and why the company is making certain decisions. Public reporting should include public policies, risk identification results, and a description of risk mitigation and tracking efforts. The flexible, transparent approach of this framework can help MNEs in particular overcome the lack of an internationally agreed view on many of the human rights concerns facing the technology sector (e.g. privacy, data ownership, and free speech).

In 2020, twelve of the biggest online platforms endorsed the Santa Clara Principles, which call for transparency by social media companies by publishing the numbers of removed posts, notifying users of content removal, and providing opportunities for meaningful and timely appeals. Only one site, Reddit fully implemented the principles into their platform, according to the Electronic Frontier Foundation. Reddit annually publishes data on content that was removed, accounts that were suspended, and legal requests received from third parties to remove content or disclose private user data. This includes information on which reports were removed by human users and which were filtered through AI-based "AutoMods" or automatic moderators. Reddit also publicly discloses how the AutoMods work and the reasoning behind its programming.

According to Reddit's Transparency Report, 99.76% of removals by AutoMods are spam. Of the remaining percentage, roughly one-quarter are posts containing minor sexualisation, hateful content, and harassment, 13.31% are violent content, 13% are involuntary pornography, and the rest include sale or promotion of prohibited goods and personally identifiable information.

Key to this process, and in line with expectations of the Guidance, is that Reddit also tracks progress made to reduce harmful content and updates made to its rules in order to improve. Data from their report shows a decrease in toxic comments per day from 11% to roughly 8% following the implementation of a ban wave.

Monitoring can be done by carrying out internal or third-party reviews or audits, as well as periodic assessments, to ensure that risk mitigation measures are being pursued or to assess the effectiveness of those measures. Many legislative proposals contain some general accountability requirements to ensure companies comply with their privacy programs, and some include self-audits or third-party audits. Paired with risk assessments and mitigation, auditing outcomes of algorithmic decision-making can help match foresight with hindsight. Auditing machine-learning routines remains a difficult and still developing field of research.

Source: Reddit Transparency Report 2020, https://www.redditinc.com/policies/transparency-report-2020-1.

3.4. National / International / Industry-led efforts to address AI risks

A wide range of tools are available to promote implementation of human rights due diligence by companies. Government policy to promote respect for human rights should involve a smart mix of voluntary, mandatory, national and international measures. Likewise, companies are encouraged to cooperate with each other, the government, and other stakeholders to jointly address sector-wide issues. This section provides a broad scoping of existing and future legislation, initiatives, and standards at the international / national / and industry-led level to address AI human rights risks.

3.4.1. Leveraging existing legislation

Although the Guidelines are directed primarily towards company behaviour, they acknowledge the role of governments as a key driver of RBC and there is widespread recognition that RBC cannot be achieved without governments taking part in these efforts. Experience from the minerals sector has shown that regulatory measures requiring human rights due diligence have had the largest impact in terms of driving business uptake of due diligence standards (OECD, 2016[31]). While voluntary standards have a role to play in promoting uptake, especially among the more progressive businesses, well-designed regulatory approaches have provided the strongest impetus for companies to change how they operate. Ultimately, a smart mix of market-based mechanisms driven by regulations will play an important role in scaling due diligence efforts and enforcement.

Dual-use export controls

Dual-use export controls can also play a significant role in addressing AI human rights risks, with many AI applications falling under the scope of these types of controls. Dual-use items are goods and technologies that may be used for both civilian and military purposes. Dual-use export controls not only manufacturers but also transport providers, academia and research institutions. In recent years there has been an increased focus on the role they can play in areas outside just military purposes, including preventing human rights abuses and controlling the trade in cyber-surveillance systems.

In March 2021, the European Parliament officially accepted the new EU regulation on its regime for export controls of dual use goods, amending previous rules set in 2009.[13] The new EU dual use goods regime will introduce new human rights-based catch-all controls over cyber-surveillance items. Specifically, it requires companies to produce due diligence findings about potential risks that the export of a non-listed cyber-surveillance item may be intended "for use in connection with internal repression and/or the commission of serious violations of international human rights and international humanitarian law."

In the United States, the International Traffic in Arms Regulations and the Export Administration Regulations (EAR) both govern the export and import of items and technology relevant to national security. On AI, the EAR has taken a very narrow approach. To date, the only restrictions have been on the export and re-export of AI software designed to analyse satellite images.[14] However, the US Department of State has released a due diligence guidance to assist US companies seeking to prevent their products or services with surveillance capabilities from being misused by foreign government end-users to commit human rights abuses, in line with the OECD Guidelines for Multinational Enterprises and the United Nations Guiding Principles on Business and Human Rights (United States Department of State, 2020[32]).

Data protection

Data is the key ingredient for AI applications, so data protection laws could have a significant impact on how AI technologies develop. In May 2018, the European General Data Protection Regulation (GDPR)[15] came into force. The regulation contains provisions and requirements related to the processing of personal data of individuals and applies to any company – regardless of its location and the data subjects' citizenship or residence – that is processing the personal information of data subjects inside the European Economic Area. This regulation has unified regulation within the EU, making compliance for companies within the EU easier. The GDPR also applies to the transfer of personal data outside the EU.

Key for this discussion is Article 22 of the GDPR which is a general restriction on automated decision making and profiling. It only applies when a decision is based solely on automated processing – including profiling – which produces legal effects or similarly significantly affects the data subject. Essentially, under the GDPR whenever companies use AI to make a significant decision about individuals, such as whether to offer a loan, the data subject has the right to have a human review that decision, including "meaningful information about the logic involved." However, it appears that explainability under the GDPR only extends to what data was collected to result in the decision, rather than the logic behind the decision, which in some cases is impossible for the developer to explain.

RBC legislation

RBC expectations are already integrated into a number of existing regulations in OECD countries. However, while the uptake of RBC expectations by companies within the scope of the regulations has increased, overall uptake remains low and enforcement efforts are lacking. Regulators should consider the human rights impacts of AI when prioritising regulatory oversight efforts.

Table 3.3 represents a brief accounting of existing RBC legislation that may be relevant to AI. Other less relevant legislation (e.g. UK Modern Slavery Act) is not included here, but may indeed have some sort of AI nexus not apparent to the author.

Broadly, due diligence legislation can be categorised as follows: those related to the mandatory disclosure and transparency of information and those relating to mandatory due diligence and other conduct requirements. The main distinction being that disclosure law does not include a requirement to take any affirmative steps in addressing RBC impacts.

Transparency and disclosure legislation requires companies to disclose risks they identify and whether they are taking or have taken any action to address those risks. To comply with this type of legislation, companies may have to follow certain standards and good practice when disclosing risks, but are not required to necessarily change their conduct, for example by addressing those risks. The idea behind this legislation is that it allows the market, including investors, consumers and civil society, to better assess companies. Examples of legislation focused on transparency and disclosure include the EU Non-financial disclosure directive, the Transparency Supply Chains Act in California, and the UK/Australian Modern Slavery Act.

Table 3.3. RBC Due Diligence Legislation in OECD Countries and the EU

FL / MS = Forced labour or Modern Slavery CL = Child labour

Country	Legislation or Legislative Proposals	Year	Enacted	Issue focus	Reporting expectation	Publication of reporting[i]	Due diligence expectation
Netherlands	Proposal for mandatory due diligence	Under discussion					
France	Duty of vigilance law	2017					
Denmark	Proposal for mandatory human rights due diligence	Under discussion					
Finland	Proposal for Corporate Responsibility Act	Under discussion					
Switzerland	Parliamentary initiative for MHRDD[ii]	Under discussion		FL/MS ; CL			
	Non-financial reporting directive[iii]	2014					
	Corporate Sustainability Reporting Directive	Under discussion					
European Union	Sustainable Finance Disclosure Regulation	2019					
	Proposal on directors duties under Sustainable Corporate Governance initiative	Under discussion					
	Proposal on mandatory due diligence under Sustainable Corporate Governance initiative	Under discussion					

Country	Legislation or Legislative Proposals	Year	Enacted	Issue focus	Reporting expectation	Publication of reporting[i]	Due diligence expectation
Austria	Proposal for Social Responsibility Act [viii]	Under discussion		FL/MS CL			
Germany	Due Diligence Act	2021					
Norway	Transparency Act	2021					

Notes: (i) Companies covered by the law are mandated to make their report publicly available; (ii) Counter proposal to Responsible Business Initiative; (iii) 2014/95/EU; (iv) 2018/0179(COD) - 24/05/2018 (v) Requires financial market participants to publish written policies on the integration of sustainability risks in investment decision making process; claiming products or services pursue sustainable investment objectives, obliging them to disclose information on the contribution of the investment decisions to the sustainable investment objectives. (vi) This regulation does not affect the garment sector but can represent a precedent as it is a successful conversion of voluntary self-certification into mandatory requirements stemming from the OECD Due Diligence Guidance for Responsible Supply Chains of Minerals from Conflict-affected and high risk areas. (vii) Update of the tariff act of 1930 (viii) Draft bill on social responsibility in the garment sector.

Mandatory due diligence legislation and other conduct requirements require companies to adhere to new forms of conduct and market practices, normally to prevent or mitigate RBC impacts and also to report on them. For example, the 2017 French Duty of Vigilance Law, which requires very large French companies and other companies with a substantial presence in France to publish and implement a "vigilance plan" and account for how they address human rights impacts in their global operations.

Most governments currently considering due diligence legislation have conducted independent studies confirming that voluntary standards do not lead to sufficient uptake (European Commission, 2020[33]; Netherlands Ministry of Foreign Affairs, 2020[34]; Norwegian Ethics Information Committee, 2019[35]; Business and Human Rights Resource Centre, 2020[36]; German Federal Ministry of Labour and Social Affairs (BMAS), 2020[37]). All the studies pointed out that smart mix of voluntary and mandatory rules is needed to increase uptake of due diligence implementation.

All proposed legislation currently under discussion plans to build on international standards (UN Guiding Principles on Business and Human Rights, the OECD Guidelines, and the OECD Due Diligence Guidance) in order to promote coherence and also to reduce legal uncertainty for multinational enterprises. The flexible, transparent approach of the Guidance framework can help MNEs in particular overcome the lack of an internationally agreed view on many of the human rights concerns facing the technology sector (e.g. privacy, data ownership, and free speech).

3.4.2. AI-specific initiatives

In November 2020, the OECD Centre for Responsible Business Conduct published a stocktaking of relevant national, international, and business-led initiatives, standards, and regulation on digitalisation and RBC, with a specific focus on social media platforms and artificial intelligence (OECD, 2020[38]).The paper found that governments are largely focused on developing AI strategies rather than regulation. Since 2015, governments increasingly include AI strategies in their national policies. This is particularly the case in OECD countries and key partners. Regulation on AI appears to remain minimal, with a clear concern from governments that they do not limit innovation with regulation that may place their country at a global disadvantage. More recently, the OECD Directorate for Science, Technology and Innovation developed a report on the state of implementation of the policy recommendations to governments contained in the OECD AI Principles (OECD, 2021[39]). This report presents a conceptual framework, provides findings, identifies good practices, and examines emerging trends in AI policy, particularly on how countries are implementing the five recommendations to policy makers contained in the OECD AI Principles.

Governments are increasingly developing strategies to advance their own efforts to create a conducive environment to innovation and digital transformation. Strategies commonly focus on the future of work, research, and incentivising innovation and leadership. Economic opportunities are driving state AI policies and research investments. Several states designate how AI will help specific sectors of their economies, often including agriculture, industry, healthcare and smart cities. Most national strategies or policies on AI address, in some form, the actual or potential impacts that artificial intelligence may have on people, planet and society.

The dominant focus areas in strategies dealing with AI in relation to RBC are competition issues, human rights, including privacy and discrimination in the workplace, labour market impacts, specifically on the future of work and consumer protection. About 40% of the strategies reviewed mention one or several of these elements. In addition, approximately 35% of the strategies reviewed also foresee some action on disclosure of AI systems by developers or users. The OECD AI Policy Observatory www.oecd.ai (OECD.AI), contains a database of national AI policies from OECD countries and partner economies and the EU. These resources help policy makers keep track of national initiatives to implement the recommendations to governments contained in the OECD AI Principles.

The OECD started work on AI in 2016. The resulting Recommendation of the Council on Artificial Intelligence, adopted in 2019, represents the first international, intergovernmental standard for AI and identifies AI Principles and a set of policy recommendations for responsible stewardship of trustworthy AI. Subsequently, the G20 Leaders have welcomed G20 AI Principles, drawn from the AI Principles contained in the OECD Recommendation. The AI principles focus on responsible stewardship of trustworthy AI, and include respect for human rights, fairness, transparency and explainability, robustness and safety, and accountability. The OECD AI Principles aim to complement existing OECD standards that are already relevant to AI. It refers to OECD standards in the field of privacy and data protection and digital security risk management, as well as to the Guidelines. There could be a role for the Guidelines also with respect to the implementation of the Recommendation.

In early 2020, the OECD launched OECD.AI, a platform to share and shape AI policies that provides data and multidisciplinary analysis on artificial intelligence. Also in early 2020, the OECD's Committee on Digital Economy Policy tasked the OECD.AI Network of Experts (ONE AI) with proposing practical guidance for implementing the OECD AI principles for trustworthy AI through the activities of three expert groups and one task force. The OECD.AI expert group on implementing trustworthy AI developed a report to on tools for trustworthy AI, to help AI actors and decision-makers implement effective, efficient and fair policies for trustworthy AI (OECD, 2021[27]). The OECD.AI expert group on the classification of AI systems is also developing a user-friendly framework to classify and help policy makers navigate AI systems and understand the different policy considerations associated with different types of AI systems.

In 2018, the EU presented a Strategy for AI. It includes the elaboration of recommendations on future-related policy development and on ethical, legal and societal issues related to AI, including socio-economic challenges. The Strategy has resulted, among other things, in the Policy and Investment Recommendations, which require accountability complements and the reporting about negative impacts; and the Ethics Guidelines for Trustworthy Artificial Intelligence (AI) (revised document of April 2019). These non-binding guidelines address, among other things, accountability and risk assessment, privacy, transparency, societal and environmental well-being. In February 2020, the European Commission issued a White Paper (European Commission, 2020[40]) and an accompanying report on the safety and liability framework, which set out policy objectives on how to achieve a regulatory and investment oriented approach that both promotes the uptake of AI and addresses the risks associated with certain uses of AI at the same time. In April 2021, the Commission published its AI package proposing new rules and actions aiming to turn Europe into the global hub for trustworthy AI (European Commission, 2021[6]).

In September 2019 the Ministers of the Council of Europe have set up an intergovernmental Ad hoc Committee on Artificial Intelligence (CAHAI), to examine the feasibility of a legal framework for the development, design and application of artificial intelligence. Important issues to be addressed include the need for a common definition of AI, the mapping of the risks and opportunities arising from AI, notably its impact on human rights, rule of law and democracy, as well as the opportunity to move towards a binding legal framework. It takes due account of a gender perspective, building cohesive societies and promoting and protecting rights of persons with disabilities in the performance of its tasks. The CAHAI adopted a Feasibility Study on a legal framework for AI in December 2020 (Council of Europe Ad Hoc Committee on Aritificial Intelligence, 2020[41]). The study examines the viability and potential elements of such a framework for the development and deployment of AI, based on the Council of Europe's standards on human rights, democracy and the rule of law.

In Latin America, Argentina, Mexico and Brazil have also developed national initiatives to support the development of AI aimed at addressing the Sustainable Development Goals. These initiatives involve financial support towards research on AI, grants for research & development of specific technologies, as well as support for development and awareness raising on AI ethics. In Mexico specifically, national strategy and research is focused on mitigating impacts of AI on the job market, in Argentina, the focus is on ethics, and in Brazil, the focus is on data protection and urban development.

The UN Human Rights Business and Human Rights in Technology (B-Tech) Project seeks to provide authoritative guidance and resources to enhance the quality of implementation of the United Nations' Guiding Principles on Business and Human rights with respect to a selected number of strategic focus areas in the technology space.[16] It aims to offer practical guidance and public policy recommendations to realise a rights-based approach to the development, application and governance of digital technologies. It uses an approach that includes attention for human rights risks, corporate responsibility and accountability by using the three pillars of the UNGPs: Protect, Respect, and Remedy. For example, it looks at the role of states and private actors in enhancing human rights in business models, human rights due diligence, and accountability and remedy. The project offers a framework for what responsible business conduct looks like in practice, regarding the development, application, sale and use of digital technologies and suggests a smart mix of regulation, incentives and public policy tools for policy makers that provide human rights safeguards and accountability, without hampering the potential of digital technologies to address social, ecological and other challenges.

Multi-stakeholder initiatives are also playing a critical role in helping clarify specific RBC issues in relation to digital technologies and support common action. For example, though not AI-specific, the Global Network Initiative provides a framework of principles and oversight for the ICT industry to respect, protect, and advance user rights to freedom of expression and privacy, in particular as it relates to requests for information by governments. The Partnership on AI primarily focuses on stakeholder engagement and dialogue seeking to maximise the potential benefits of AI for as many people as possible.

Civil society is actively involved in defining and promoting ethical principles for responsible development and use of digital technologies. While not consistently, many of the emerging principles reference some international RBC instruments (mostly from the United Nations). Leading efforts include the Santa Clara Principles. The Toronto Declaration is a human rights-based framework that delineates the responsibilities of states and private actors to prevent discrimination with AI advancements. Ranking Digital Rights is the first public tool to assess company performance on digital rights, seeking to trigger a 'race to the top'.

Companies have developed detailed policies dealing with a wide range of RBC issues. For AI, company policies tend to focus on transparency of AI systems, promotion of human values, human control of technology, fairness and non-discrimination, safety and security, accountability, and privacy. For online platforms, company policies tend to focus on mitigating violence and criminal behaviour, safety, mitigating objectionable content, integrity and authenticity, data collection, use, and security, sharing of data with third parties, user control, accountability, and promotion of social welfare. Broad commitments to human rights are included in most company policies reviewed. A brief analysis of company efforts shows that while many companies have publicly committed to human rights, their due diligence commitments largely focus on identifying and managing risk related to the above-mentioned policy issues, rather than tracking effectiveness, public reporting, or supporting remediation.

3.5. AI uses to support RBC

Going into detail on the specific applications of AI to support due diligence can standalone as its own report. AI's ability to analyse and interpret huge datasets quickly makes it an excellent tool to support supply chain due diligence. This section offers a brief look into AI applications for supply chain traceability and risk identification.

Physical supply chains (e.g. minerals/metals, garment, and agriculture) are extremely complex and fragmented. Many multinationals, particularly those involved in manufacturing, have thousands of suppliers and sometimes 10 – 15 tiers in their supply chains, with the exact relationship between those suppliers constantly changing. These supply chains include both informal and formal actors in developed and developing parts of the world, which makes it particularly difficult to track where the goods are coming from and who is handling the goods, which are both key sets of information for conducting supply chain due diligence.

Fraudulent misrepresentation of the origin of goods, money laundering, customs violations, bribery and tax evasion are common risks in physical supply chains, and are also often associated with or enablers of human rights abuses. Anomalous trade and production data can often by connected to these risks (e.g. an unusually high shipment of goods from a supplier, an unknown intermediary in a supply chain, or a shipment of raw material from a country known to not produce that material).

Currently, many of these anomalies are likely going unchecked given the overwhelming amount of data to sift through. AI can continuously analyse large amounts of rapidly changing data points along the supply chain (e.g. weather reports, shipping delays, payments made to customs agents, inventory, social media trends, financial and political news, etc.) to not only make supply chains more efficient, but quickly find hidden correlations between all these variables that potentially point towards illicit behaviour. A combination of AI-based analysis and human decision making could potentially allow for a less costly, more efficient due diligence process.

AI is also being used to evaluate company risk profiles for investors, linking information on RBC issues (human rights abuses, financial crime, and environmental degradation) with financial performance to support 'ESG investing'. One such use case is in sentiment analysis algorithms (Barrachin and Shoaraee, 2019[42]). These algorithms allow computers to analyse news and sustainability reporting by companies in order to determine how seriously a company takes an issue. For example, sentiment analysis programs might be trained to read the transcripts of a company's quarterly earnings calls to identify in which parts of the conversation the CEO talks about environmental degradation, and then infer from those words used how committed a company appears to be about mitigating risks. Once more data is gathered on the sustainability impacts of due diligence efforts (see for example (OECD, 2021[43]), AI systems could potentially be used to further link company rhetoric and efforts with change on the ground. However, this technology still certainly has its limits that human due diligence will be required to overcome. For example, companies aware of rating AI-based ESG rating systems may over represent ESG keywords in disclosures in an effort to game the system.

3.6. Looking forward

Given the wide-ranging RBC issues addressed in the stocktaking review described above, OECD RBC instruments continue to be relevant. They can provide cross-sectoral frameworks for looking at these issues holistically, and can help connect the dots between the different RBC issues. The broad scope of the Guidelines, covering all areas where business interacts with society, allows for addressing the manifold impacts of digitalisation on society and to enhance the use of new technologies for actually improving RBC and supply chain due diligence.

Specifically, the Guidelines and Due Diligence Guidance enable business to systematically address the impacts of their activities in all of their interactions with society. At the same time, it is clear from the review that policy-makers, industry, workers, trade unions and business/employers' organisations and other stakeholders could benefit from further work to integrate RBC standards and approaches into ongoing digitalisation efforts, and clarify the applicability of RBC instruments to specific digital issues. Companies can be supported through more specific research and targeted guidance on how to apply RBC standards to the development and applications of AI.

Technology companies should be aware that these *expectations* and *voluntary recommendations* may soon become *legal requirements*. Political and legislative efforts to make OECD recommended due diligence mandatory are multiplying across the globe, including in France, Germany, Finland, the US, the UK, Switzerland, as well as in the European Union, for which there is a legislative proposal to implement mandatory due diligence in 2021 (European Parliament, 2020[44]). Given the growing momentum, it is sensible for companies operating in this space to stay ahead of the curve. Not only will early implementation and active engagement with stakeholders help reduce future legal and reputational risks, it could also give companies a seat at the table in helping frame the rule making to make future rules on this topic as practically implementable as possible.

References

Aloisi, A. and V. De Stefano (2021), "Essential jobs, remote work and digital surveillance: addressing the COVID-19 pandemic panopticon", *International Labour Review*, https://doi.org/10.1111/ilr.12219. [18]

Baraniuk, C. (2019), "The new weapon in the fight against crime", *BBC*, https://www.bbc.com/future/article/20190228-how-ai-is-helping-to-fight-crime. [11]

Barrachin, M. and S. Shoaraee (2019), "Sentiment Analysis: Is It All The Same?", *S&P Global Market Intelligence*, https://www.spglobal.com/marketintelligence/en/news-insights/research/sentiment-analysis-is-it-all-the-same. [42]

Bedoya, A. (2016), *The Perpetual Line-Up: Unregulated Police Face Recognition in America*,, Georgetown Law Center on Privacy and Technology, https://www.perpetuallineup.org/. [3]

Business and Human Rights Resource Centre (2020), *Germany: Cabinet passes mandatory due diligence proposal; Parliament now to consider & strengthen*, https://www.business-humanrights.org/en/latest-news/german-due-diligence-law/ [36]

Chouhan, K. (2019), "Role of an AI in Legal Aid and Access to Criminal Justice", *International Journal of Legal Research*, Vol. 6/2 (1), https://ssrn.com/abstract=3536194. [13]

Council of Europe Ad Hoc Committee on Aritificial Intelligence (2020), *Feasibility study on AI legal framework*, https://rm.coe.int/cahai-2020-23-final-eng-feasibility-study-/1680a0c6da. [41]

Council of Europe Expert Committee on human rights dimensions of automated data processing and different forms of artificial intelligence (2019), *Responsibility and AI*, Council of Europe, https://rm.coe.int/responsability-and-ai-en/168097d9c5. [29]

Council of Europe Committee of Experts on Internet Intermediaries (2018), *Algorithms and human rights - Study on the human rights dimensions of automated data processing techniques and possible regulatory implications*, Council of Europe, https://edoc.coe.int/en/internet/7589-algorithms-and-human-rights-study-on-the-human-rights-dimensions-of-automated-data-processing-techniques-and-possible-regulatory-implications.html. [9]

Destin, J. (2018), "Amazon scraps secret AI recruiting tool that showed bias against women", *Reuters*, https://www.reuters.com/article/us-amazon-com-jobs-automation-insight-idUSKCN1MK08G. [8]

European Commission (2021), *Artificial intelligence: threats and opportunities*, https://www.europarl.europa.eu/news/en/headlines/society/20200918STO87404/artificial-intelligence-threats-and-opportunities. [7]

European Commission (2021), *Europe fit for the Digital Age: Commission proposes new rules and actions for excellence and trust in Artificial Intelligence*, https://ec.europa.eu/commission/presscorner/detail/en/ip_21_1682. [6]

European Commission (2020), *Study on due diligence requirements through the supply chain*, https://op.europa.eu/en/publication-detail/-/publication/8ba0a8fd-4c83-11ea-b8b7-01aa75ed71a1/language-en. [33]

European Commission (2020), *White Paper on Artificial Intelligence - A European approach to excellence and trust*, https://ec.europa.eu/info/publications/white-paper-artificial-intelligence-european-approach-excellence-and-trust_en. [40]

European Parliament (2020), *Towards a Mandatory EU system of due diligence for supply chains*, EPRS | European Parliamentary Research Service, https://www.europarl.europa.eu/thinktank/en/document.html?reference=EPRS_BRI(2020)659299. [44]

Floridi, L., B. Mittelstadt and S. Watcher (2017), "Why a Right to Explanation of Automated Decision-Making Does Not Exist in the General Data Protection Regulation", *International Data Privacy Law*, Vol. 7/2, https://academic.oup.com/idpl/article/7/2/76/3860948. [15]

Gasparri, G. (2019), "Risks and Opportunities of RegTech and SupTech Developments", *Frontiers in Artificial Intelligence*, https://doi.org/10.3389/frai.2019.00014. [16]

German Federal Ministry of Labour and Social Affairs (BMAS) (2020), *Respect for human rights along global value chains - risks and opportunities for sectors of the German economy*, https://www.bmas.de/DE/Service/Publikationen/Forschungsberichte/fb-543-achtung-von-menschenrechten-entlang-globaler-wertschoepfungsketten.html. [37]

Gurley, L. and J. Rose (2020), *Amazon Employee Warns Internal Groups They're Being Monitored For Labor Organizing*, Vice News, https://www.vice.com/en/article/m7jz7b/amazon-employee-warns-internal-groups-theyre-being-monitored-for-labor-organizing. [21]

Katyal, S. (2018), "Private Accountability in the Age of Artificial Intelligence", *UCLA Law Review*, https://papers.ssrn.com/sol3/papers.cfm?abstract_id=3309397. [30]

Kerry, C. (2020), *Protecting privacy in an AI-driven world*, Brookings Institution, https://www.brookings.edu/research/protecting-privacy-in-an-ai-driven-world/. [2]

Menn, J. and D. Volz (2016), "Google, Facebook quietly move torward automatic blocking of extremist videos", *Reuters*, https://www.reuters.com/article/us-internet-extremism-video-exclusive-idUSKCN0ZB00M. [17]

Moore, P. (2020), *Data subjects, digital surveillance, AI and the future of work*, Panel for the Future of Science and Technology for the Directorate-General for Parliamentary Research Services of the Secretariat of the European Parliament, https://www.europarl.europa.eu/thinktank/en/document.html?reference=EPRS_STU(2020)656305. [19]

Mozur, P. (2019), "One Month, 500,000 Face Scans: How China Is Using A.I. to Profile a Minority", *The New York Times*, https://www.nytimes.com/2019/04/14/technology/china-surveillance-artificial-intelligence-racial-profiling.html. [5]

Netherlands Ministry of Foreign Affairs (2020), *Evaluation and revision of policy on Responsible Business Conduct (RBC)*, https://www.government.nl/topics/responsible-business-conduct-rbc/evaluation-and-renewal-of-rbc-policy. [34]

Niiler, E. (2018), "Can AI Be a Fair Judge in Court? Estonia Thinks So", *WIRED*, https://www.wired.com/story/can-ai-be-fair-judge-court-estonia-thinks-so/. [12]

Norwegian Ethics Information Committee (2019), *Report on Supply Chain Transparency - Proposal for an Act regulating Enterprises' transparency about supply chains, duty to know and due diligence*, https://www.regjeringen.no/contentassets/6b4a42400f3341958e0b62d40f484371/ethics-information-committee---part-i.pdf. [35]

OECD (2021), *Monitoring and Evaluation Framework: OECD Due Diligence Guidance for Responsible Supply Chains of Minerals from Conflict-Affected and High-Risk Areas*, OECD, https://mneguidelines.oecd.org/monitoring-and-evaluation-framework.pdf. [43]

OECD (2021), "State of implementation of the OECD AI Principles: Insights from national AI policies", *OECD Digital Economy Papers*, No. 311, OECD Publishing, Paris, https://dx.doi.org/10.1787/1cd40c44-en. [39]

OECD (2021), "Tools for trustworthy AI: A framework to compare implementation tools for trustworthy AI systems", *OECD Digital Economy Papers*, No. 312, OECD Publishing, Paris, https://dx.doi.org/10.1787/008232ec-en. [27]

OECD (2020), *Digitalisation and Responsible Business Conduct Stocktaking of Policies and Initiatives*, https://mneguidelines.oecd.org/Digitalisation-and-responsible-business-conduct.pdf. [38]

OECD (2019), *Artificial Intelligence in Society*, OECD Publishing, Paris, https://dx.doi.org/10.1787/eedfee77-en. [1]

OECD (2019), *Due Diligence for Responsible Corporate Lending and Securities Underwriting*, OECD Publishing, https://mneguidelines.oecd.org/due-diligence-for-responsible-corporate-lending-and-securities-underwriting.htm. [26]

OECD (2019), "Scoping the OECD AI principles: Deliberations of the Expert Group on Artificial Intelligence at the OECD (AIGO)", *OECD Digital Economy Papers*, https://doi.org/10.1787/d62f618a-en. [47]

OECD (2018), *Due Diligence Guidance for Responsible Business Conduct*, OECD Publishing, http://mneguidelines.oecd.org/due-diligence-guidance-for-responsible-business-conduct.htm. [22]

OECD (2016), *Report on the Implementation of the Recommendation on Due Diligence Guidance for Responsible Supply Chains of Minerals from Conflict-Affected and High-Risk Areas*, https://one.oecd.org/official-document/COM/DAF/INV/DCD/DAC(2015)3/FINAL/en. [31]

OECD (2011), *OECD Guidelines for Multinational Enterprises, 2011 Edition*, OECD Publishing, Paris, https://dx.doi.org/10.1787/9789264115415-en. [48]

OECD (2021, forthcoming), *Considering the purposes of the Guidelines and the notion of the "multinational enterprise" in the context of initial assessments.* [23]

OECD (2021, forthcoming), *Venture Capital Investments in Artificial Intelligence.* [25]

OECD Watch (2020), *Society for Threatened Peoples Switzerland vs UBS Group*, https://www.oecdwatch.org/complaint/society-for-threatened-peoples-switzerland-vs-ubs-group/. [45]

Palmer, A. (2020), *How Amazon keeps a close eye on employee activism to head off unions*, CNBC, https://www.cnbc.com/2020/10/24/how-amazon-prevents-unions-by-surveilling-employee-activism.html. [20]

Russell, S. (2019), *Human-compatible*, Penguin Books, http://ISBN 9780525558637. [46]

Smith, R. (2019), "Jefferies and Credit Suisse set to lose on Israeli cyber security deal", https://www.ft.com/content/e390685a-5a10-11e9-939a-341f5ada9d40. [28]

Sweeny, L. (2013), "Discrimination in Online Ad Delivery: Google ads, black names and white names, racial discrimination, and click advertising", *ACM Queue*, Vol. 11/3, https://dl.acm.org/doi/10.1145/2460276.2460278. [10]

United States Department of State (2020), *Guidance on Implementing the UN Guiding Principles for Transactions Linked to Foreign Government End-Users for Products or Services with Surveillance Capabilities*, https://www.state.gov/key-topics-bureau-of-democracy-human-rights-and-labor/due-diligence-guidance/. [32]

Vincent, J. (2020), "NYPD used facial recognition to track down Black Lives Matter activist", *The Verge*, https://www.theverge.com/2020/8/18/21373316/nypd-facial-recognition-black-lives-matter-activist-derrick-ingram. [4]

Walter, J. (2019), *AI Could Give Millions Online Legal Help. But What Will the Law Allow?*, https://www.discovermagazine.com/technology/ai-could-give-millions-online-legal-help-but-what-will-the-law-allow. [14]

Xiaomin, M. (2019), "Artificial Intelligence: Investment Trends and Selected Industry Uses", *EM Compass* Note 71, https://www.ifc.org/wps/wcm/connect/7898d957-69b5-4727-9226-277e8ae28711/EMCompass-Note-71-AI-Investment-Trends.pdf?MOD=AJPERES&CVID=mR5Jv. [24]

Notes

[1] The Guidelines were adopted as part of the broader 1976 OECD Declaration on International Investment and Multinational Enterprises. The Guidelines are regularly reviewed and revised and have been updated five times since 1976, most recently in 2011 (OECD, 2011[48])).

[2] See Chapter IX, "Science and Technology," (OECD, 2011[48]).

[3] Universal Declaration of Human Rights, Article 12.

[4] Article 9, Regulation (EU) 2016/679 of the European Parliament and of the Council on the protection of natural persons with regard to the processing of personal data and on the free movement of such data, and repealing Directive 95/46/EC (General Data Protection Regulation), https://eur-lex.europa.eu/legal-content/EN/TXT/HTML/?uri=CELEX:32016R0679&rid=3#d1e2051-1-1.

[5] Universal Declaration of Human Rights, Article 7.

[6] Universal Declaration of Human Rights, Articles 10 & 11.

[7] Universal Declaration of Human Rights, Article 19.

[8] Universal Declaration of Human Rights, Article 20.

[9] See for example, United States Department of State (2020), *Guidance on Implementing the "UN Guiding Principles" for Transactions Linked to Foreign Government End-Users for Products or Services with Surveillance Capabilities*, https://www.state.gov/key-topics-bureau-of-democracy-human-rights-and-labor/due-diligence-guidance/; Danish Institute for Human Rights (2020), *Human rights impact assessment of digital activities*, https://www.humanrights.dk/publications/human-rights-impact-assessment-digital-activities; United Nations Office of the High Commissioner on Human Rights B-Tech Project, Foundational Papers, https://www.ohchr.org/EN/Issues/Business/Pages/B-TechProject.aspx.

[10] OECD (2019), Recommendation of the Council on Artificial Intelligence, https://legalinstruments.oecd.org/en/instruments/OECD-LEGAL-0449.

[11] Adapted from Data Robot (2019), "Machine Learning Life Cycle," https://datarobot.com/wiki/machine-learning-life-cycle/; Brook, Adrien (2019), "10 Steps to Create Your Very Own Corporate AI Project," Towards Data Science, https://towardsdatascience.com/10-steps-to-your-very-own-corporate-a-i-project-ced3949faf7f.

[12] OECD (2019), Recommendation of the Council on Artificial Intelligence, https://legalinstruments.oecd.org/en/instruments/OECD-LEGAL-0449.

[13] European Parliament legislative resolution of 25 March 2021 on the proposal for a regulation of the European Parliament and of the Council setting up a Union regime for the control of exports, transfer, brokering, technical assistance and transit of dual-use items (recast) (COM(2016)0616 – C8-0393/2016 – 2016/0295(COD)), https://www.europarl.europa.eu/doceo/document/TA-9-2021-0101_EN.pdf.

[14] United States Federal Register, Addition of Software Specially Designed To Automate the Analysis of Geospatial Imagery to the Export Control Classification Number 0Y521 Series,

https://www.federalregister.gov/documents/2020/01/06/2019-27649/addition-of-software-specially-designed-to-automate-the-analysis-of-geospatial-imagery-to-the-export.
https://www.govinfo.gov/content/pkg/FR-2020-01-06/pdf/2019-27649.pdf

[15] EU Regulation 2016/679 (2016), on the protection of natural persons with regard to the processing of personal data and on the free movement of such data, and repealing Directive 95/46/EC (General Data Protection Regulation), https://eur-lex.europa.eu/eli/reg/2016/679/2016-05-04.

[16] See OHCHR webpage on the B-Tech Project for full list of materials, https://www.ohchr.org/EN/Issues/Business/Pages/B-TechProject.aspx.

4 Competition and AI

This Chapter explores some of the potential competition risks stemming from the use of AI, namely collusion and abuses of dominance, and highlights the challenges they pose for competition policy. It is still too early to tell whether many of these risks will materialise, and their overall impact on markets. However, it is clear that competition policy will have a role to play in ensuring that AI reaches its procompetitive potential.

Beyond the need for sufficient technical capacity to assess AI technologies and their effects in markets, competition authorities may find that certain market outcomes caused by AI may be difficult to address under current enforcement frameworks. Nonetheless, competition authorities still have tools at their disposal to address at least some concerns regarding AI. These tools include merger control, market studies, competition advocacy and co-operation with other regulators. Further, some jurisdictions are considering additional legislative measures that may help.

4.1. Introduction

AI has the potential to fundamentally reshape how firms make decisions, in particular by generating predictive analytics, automating decision-making, and optimising business process (OECD, 2017[1]). This transformation is a natural extension of trends that are already well underway, for example two-thirds of EU e-commerce retailers use software to automatically adjust their prices to competitors (European Commission, 2017, p. 5[2]). This means competitive dynamics could be changing in ways that are difficult to predict. The speed and nature of decision-making with respect to prices, product design (including customisation to individual consumers), targeting marketing efforts, and managing costs and investments may all evolve.

The benefits to consumers (including business consumers) from this transformation are significant and wide reaching. Consumers have access to an ever-growing range of digital products and services, for example online platforms that rely on searching or matching functionality. Established markets are being transformed by new entrants harnessing digital technologies, for example in the financial sector, where competition is being spurred by new and cheaper services (explored in Chapter 2). Further, even in traditional markets, significant supply-side efficiencies may be passed on in the form of lower prices or better responsiveness to consumer preferences, for example when supermarkets are able to better adjust their selection in response to trends in consumer demand. More broadly, one estimate suggests that AI technologies will increase labour productivity in developed economies by up to 40% by 2035 (Accenture, 2017[3]).

AI applications may also enable a faster detection and response to changes in consumer preferences, making markets responsive to the evolution of demand. They may also be used to detect unsafe products and fix them remotely through software updates. More broadly, the rapid development of AI technology has triggered rivalry on an important dimension of competition: innovation.

At the same time, AI can also provide new tools for consumers to make decisions. AI applications may use the ever-increasing amount of data available about products and consumers in order to develop personalised products and transactions that better fit individuals' and businesses' needs. AI can also help guide consumers in markets with complex or uncertain prices and conditions, in order to select the best offer based on their needs and preferences. They may also give rise to "algorithmic consumers" whose decision-making is at least partially automated through the application of algorithms (Gal and Elkin-Koren, 2017[4]).

These examples demonstrate the significant procompetitive potential of AI applications in markets, both on the supply and the demand side. However, as AI begins to play a greater role in decision-making, particularly with respect to pricing, it may also dampen competition in some markets. Predictability, transparency and frequent interactions between competitors' algorithms can undermine competitive dynamics. For instance, while price transparency may facilitate consumer decision-making, it may also lead firms to compete less aggressively by facilitating co-ordination. Competition authorities may find that addressing these concerns will require new technical capacities to assess AI technologies and their effects in markets. Further, certain market outcomes caused by AI will be difficult to address with current enforcement tools. This chapter explores some of the potential competition risks stemming from the use of AI, namely collusion and abuses of dominance, and highlights the challenges this poses for competition policy. It also notes that research is still developing on the likelihood of these risks, as well as the potential for AI to play a destabilising role in collusive agreements.

Concerns about AI-related competition problems fit within a broader discussion about competition in digital-intensive markets. Data-intensive digital technologies can involve high fixed costs and low variable costs, economies of scale and scope, significant first-mover advantages, strong network effects,[1] and switching costs or other consumer behaviours that lead to lock-in. These characteristics may contribute to market power that is (1) durable and (2) brought to bear in multiple markets. AI technologies can exemplify these market dynamics, particularly given the importance of data access and processing involved (OECD, 2016[5]).

Indicators of potentially durable market power, which suggest that markets are less contestable for new innovations and less open to competitive pressure, have been observed across OECD economies, and particularly in digital-intensive sectors. For example, the mark-ups firms charge over marginal costs are on the rise (Calligaris, Criscuolo and Marcolin, 2018[6]; Bajgar, Criscuolo and Timmis, 2021[7]), and the rate of new firm entry in digital-intensive sectors has declined (Calvino and Criscuolo, 2019[8]).

Digital markets may feature a significant degree of vertical integration (e.g. when the operator of an e-commerce platform offers its own products for sale on the platform) or conglomerate business models (when digital firms are active in multiple related markets featuring overlapping consumers). AI technologies can directly lead toward these types of business models, given that they can either be an important input in some markets, or be repurposed across multiple markets. One recent paper finds empirical support for this idea: specifically that AI investments in one market are associated with greater investment activity in other related markets (Babina et al., 2020[9]). These business models offer significant benefits to consumers in the form of economies of scope and convenience, but may also give rise to competition problems, including higher collusion risk due to multi-market contact of conglomerate firms (since multi-market contact can facilitate communication and enhance incentives for collusion) and the potential for abusive conduct by dominant firms (OECD, 2020[10]; Fletcher, 2020[11]).

In sum, AI, like many digital technologies, has the potential to produce wide-reaching benefits for consumers, but it may also contribute to durable market power in digitalised markets, and give rise to new forms of competition concerns. It can facilitate the implementation of collusive agreements and abusive conduct by dominant firms. It can also lead to new market dynamics that depress competitive pressures without clear anticompetitive conduct, creating challenges for the existing competition policy toolbox. These challenges are explored further below.

4.2. Competition problems associated with AI

The use of AI to support and automate business decisions may usher in a new age for competitive dynamics in markets. With this new age may come competition harms stemming from collusion, abusive conduct on the part of dominant firms, or mergers, as described further below.

4.2.1. AI and collusion

For competition policy purposes, the term collusion refers to "any form of co-ordination or agreement among competing firms with the objective of raising profits to a higher level than the non-cooperative equilibrium" (OECD, 2017, p. 19[11]). Collusion is not limited to agreements on prices; rather, it can include the allocation of different segments of a market among competitors, agreements regarding product quality or total output, and even harmonising the terms and conditions to be offered to consumers.

The widespread use of AI in a market can be associated with a higher risk of collusion, specifically market dynamics that make collusive outcomes more stable or rewarding. First, AI applications rely on consumer data, the offer of competitors, and transactions in a market. When there is a high degree of market transparency due to the availability of data on competitor pricing or transactions, for example in online marketplaces, collusion is more likely. This is because it is easier for firms to communicate through pricing signals, detect any deviations from a collusive agreement, or implement algorithms to implement collusion (OECD, 2017, pp. 21-22[11]). Secondly, AI may be deployed in markets in which frequent interactions with competitors are feasible (through rapid price adjustments), which can make the implementation and monitoring of collusive agreements easier. Third, as noted above, since there are indications that AI applications are likely to be associated with conglomerate business models, firms active in AI technologies may be more likely to compete in multiple markets. Research suggests that, when competitors are in contact with one another across multiple markets, it makes collusion more likely by increasing the gains of collusion (OECD, 2015[12]). Nonetheless, the UK Competition and Markets Authority has indicated that AI-facilitated collusion will be most likely in markets already susceptible to collusion (for example due to homogeneity of products and firms) (Competition and Markets Authority, 2018, p. 31[13]).

Beyond its deployment in markets whose conditions make collusion more likely, stable and profitable, AI may also directly lead to collusive outcomes, whether by design or not. Collusion can take two different forms, both of which can be implemented through AI (OECD, 2017, p. 19[1]):

> ***Explicit collusion*** *refers to anti-competitive conduct that is maintained with explicit agreements, whether they are written or oral. The most direct way for firms to achieve an explicit collusive outcome is to interact directly and agree on the optimal level of price or output.*
>
> ***Tacit collusion****, on the contrary, refers to forms of anti-competitive co-ordination which can be achieved without any need for an explicit agreement, but which competitors are able to maintain by recognising their mutual interdependence. In a tacitly collusive context, the non-competitive outcome is achieved by each participant deciding its own profit-maximising strategy independently of its competitors. This typically occurs in transparent markets with few market players, where firms can benefit from their collective market power without entering in any explicit communication.*

AI and explicit collusion

Explicit collusion (or forming a cartel) is considered one of the most serious breaches of competition law. Reflecting this seriousness, cartel formation is generally a *by object* or *per se* infringement – meaning that a cartel agreement is illegal regardless of its effectiveness. AI can be used as a tool for implementing and maintaining collusive agreements.

Collusive agreements can be difficult to maintain for a variety reasons. First, communication between the parties will be limited, since they will want to avoid detection and proof of their agreement. Thus, the agreement's stability may be undermined if the parties interpret its terms differently, for instance if costs or demand change. Second, there can be incentives for firms to deviate from an anticompetitive agreement, for example by slightly undercutting the agreed-upon price to earn more revenue. While a cartel can seek to punish deviators through targeted, aggressive competition, it can sometimes be difficult to detect deviations, and to co-ordinate a punishment response. Third, collusive agreements can be difficult to maintain as the number of participants increases, differences between participants or their products emerge, or innovations reshape the market.

AI can be a tool to overcome the challenges that threaten the stability of cartels. In particular, an algorithm can avoid misinterpretations or errors in implementing cartel agreements by implementing pricing or other decisions according to pre-established parameters – particularly when a common flow of data is available to all parties. In addition, more sophisticated AI applications can be used to monitor implementation, uncover deviations from collusive agreements, and even implement punishment strategies. Finally, AI can help market participants respond to more fundamental changes in markets as well, for example if all participants use the same technology to make decisions in response to change in markets.

First, monitoring algorithms can take advantage of available data in order to monitor conditions in a market and determine whether any cartel participants have deviated from the agreement. When paired with technologies such as screen scraping, which allows data available to users (including prices or outcomes of search results) to be automatically gathered, these algorithms could make it easy to identify any deviations, and thus discourage such deviations. These algorithms can also prevent the misinterpretation of firm behaviour, which could lead cartel members to inaccurately believing deviations have taken place, thus undermining the stability of the agreement even if all members comply (Competition and Markets Authority, 2018, p. 24[13]).

Monitoring algorithms have been used to implement collusive agreement between poster sellers in the UK and US. The sellers agreed not to undercut each other's prices, and used automated pricing software (the same software in the US case) to implement this agreement when setting prices on Amazon (US Department of Justice, 2015[14]; Competition and Markets Authority, 2016[15]). While the algorithm used here was relatively simple, it demonstrates the potential for AI as an instrument for facilitating collusive agreements.

Box 4.1. The European Commission Eturas case

On 21 January 2016, the Court of Justice of the European Union (CJEU) handed down a preliminary ruling on questions from the Supreme Administrative Court of Lithuania.

The case concerned the use by travel agents of a uniform online travel booking system for package tours (E-TURAS), on their respective websites. The Competition Council of Lithuania (Competition Council) had found that the users of the platform (travel agencies) and the platform administrator (Eturas) had breached Article 101 TFEU by colluding in relation to the applicable discounts applied to transactions on E-TURAS.

Users of the online platform had access to an internal message system. Eturas sent a message to at least two concerned travel agencies about a proposal to limit the discount rate applied to transactions on the platform. Platform users then received a system notification of the reduction and technical modifications that were made to apply this cap to the platform. In order for travel agencies to apply a different discount, they were required to carry out additional technical steps.

The Competition Council argued that the E-TURAS system was used by agencies to coordinate prices by fixing a maximum discount. Travel agencies knew that other agencies were using this common booking system and that the same conditions would apply to all users. It claimed the tacit agreement of platform users could be characterised as collusion (specifically, a "concerted practice") and that users that had not expressed any objection would be liable, along with Eturas, as the facilitator.

The CJEU referral related to certain specific legal issues (regarding the burden of proof and questions regarding evidence), but provides some insights into collusion involving platforms. In particular, the CJEU found that travel agencies receiving the messages via the platform and aware of the collusive practice can be presumed to be participating in the practice, unless they publicly distance themselves from the conduct or report it to authorities.

Source: Case C-74/14 https://eur-lex.europa.eu/legal-content/EN/TXT/HTML/?uri=CELEX:62014CJ0074&from=EN>

Collusive outcomes can sometimes be facilitated by parties other than firms competing with one another, such as industry associations, upstream suppliers, or downstream sellers. Thus, artificial intelligence need not be employed by the competing firms to facilitate collusion – a central "hub" can be used to transmit information, execute collusive agreements, and monitor compliance (Competition and Markets Authority, 2021[16]). This could occur, for example, when all parties use a common provider for selling to consumers which limits price competition, as illustrated in the case in Box 4.1. This scenario is not new in competition enforcement, as traditional cartels have in the past used third parties to set terms, and monitor as well as enforce collusive agreements. However, AI may be able to do so more effectively and discreetly than ever before.

Competition authorities in several jurisdictions have determined that imposition of fixed or minimum resale prices by manufacturers (also called "resale price maintenance"), could be a means of implementing a collusive agreement (OECD, 2019, p. 28[17]). This conduct may also be facilitated with algorithms. For example, the European Commission recently imposed fines totalling EUR 111 million on a manufacturer of consumer electronics for imposing resale price maintenance on retailers, and using monitoring algorithms to verify compliance (see Box 4.2).

Box 4.2. The European Commission ASUS case

On 24 July 2018, the Commission fined Asus Computer GmbH and Asus France SARL (Asus) €63.5 million for resale price maintenance (RPM). This case was initiated following information obtained in the EU e-commerce sector inquiry. Denon & Marantz, Phillips and Pioneer, three other consumer electronics manufacturers were also fined in separate decisions, with the total fine in all four cases amounting to over €111 million.

The Commission found that Asus restricted the ability of retailers to independently determine their resale prices in Germany and France for certain electronic products. It engaged in a strategy to keep resale prices at the level of recommended resale prices, thus limiting resale price competition. The Commission found conduct of Asus amounted to RPM, an infringement of Article 101 of the Treaty on the Functioning of the European Union (TFEU).

Asus monitored retail prices of its products through price comparison websites and through internal software monitoring tools and identified retailers that were selling its products below their recommended retail prices. Non-compliant retailers were threatened or sanctioned and asked to adjust their prices or to remove their products from price comparison websites. In Germany, for example, Asus introduced a premium partner program where it set out price lists for networking equipment and a similar program for display products, which additionally provided for a conditional bonus for compliance with recommended retail price lists. The programs were implemented through internal monitoring lists, which provided an overview of the resale prices of all retailers and indicated non-compliant retailers, who were then contacted by Asus employees. For certain products, Asus used other tools such as an "online map" which "gave employees on a daily basis an overview of regional as well as online pricing in Germany" [para 47]. Again, identified non-compliant retailers were contacted by Asus employees and asked to adjust their prices.

Retailers were aware of the business policy and complained when other retailers failed to adhere to it. The Commission decision explains that retailers also used price comparison websites to monitor the prices of their competitors, but also pricing robots, that were used to crawl competitor's websites and match prices [para 58].

Source: Decision of the European Commission of 24 July 2018, Case AT.40465 – ASUS, available at https://ec.europa.eu/competition/antitrust/cases/dec_docs/40465/40465_337_3.pdf.

Firms seeking to form a cartel or implement a cartel agreement may attempt to communicate with one another in indirect ways, known as "signalling". Algorithms can help firms identify signals (for example, in relation to price or quantity), act on them according to pre-established decision rules, and even determine whether fellow cartel members have accepted a signalled proposal. This type of co-ordination can be difficult for competition authorities to tackle as explicit collusion. Among other challenges, it can sometimes be difficult to distinguish from procompetitive behaviour, such as certain types of information disclosure or algorithmic exploration (Autorité de la concurrence and Bundeskartellamt, 2019, pp. 53-55[18]). However, in a past case described in Box 4.3, the US Department of Justice argued that signalling through online airline reservation platforms constituted a per se infringement.

While the body of research in this area is growing, more needs to be done to understand whether AI can in fact play a role in *undermining* collusive outcomes, namely by allowing cartel participants to more effectively deviate from an agreement (Petit, 2017[19]). Greater research in this area would enable a more informed assessment of the underlying risks.

Box 4.3. The US Department of Justice airline reservation case

During the early 1990's, the US Department of Justice (DoJ) investigated tariff fixing activities in the airline industry, where the cartel members were able to implicitly coordinate tariffs using a third party centre and sophisticated signalling mechanisms.

In the US airline industry, airline companies send fare information on a daily basis to the Airline Tariff Publishing Company (ATPCO), a central clearinghouse that compiles all the data received and shares it in real time with travel agents, computer reservations systems, consumers and even the airline companies themselves. The database published by ATPCO includes, among other things, information about prices, travel dates, origin and destination airports, ticket restrictions, as well as first and last ticket dates, which indicate the time range when the tickets at a particular fare are for sale.

According to the case presented by the DoJ, airline companies were using first ticket dates to announce tariff raises many weeks in advance. If the announcements were matched by the rivals, when the first ticket date arrived all companies would simultaneously raise the tariff. Some of the coordination strategies were more complex, involving the use of fare code numbers and ticket date footnotes to send signals or negotiate multimarket coordination.

According to the DoJ's case it was the existence of a fast data exchange mechanism to monitor tariffs and react rapidly to price changes that enabled companies to collude without explicitly communicating. The DoJ reached a settlement agreement with the airline companies, under which the latter agreed to stop announcing most price increases in advance, with the exception of a few circumstances where early announcements could enhance consumer welfare. All of the airline defendants' fares had to be concurrently available for sale to consumers.

Source: Excerpted from OECD (2016, p. 23[5]).

AI and tacit collusion

The role of AI in implementing explicit collusive agreements is relatively straightforward. However, many of the concerns about AI and collusion involve situations without an explicit agreement among competitors. While this type of collusion can still harm consumers, it is generally not covered under competition law, making the distinction particularly important.

AI may lead to tacit collusion outcomes, in which firms make decisions that jointly maximise profits, without the need for any co-ordination or collective decision-making on the part of those firms. First, the use of AI in business decisions may create the conditions for tacit collusion to emerge. As firms invest in AI solutions to make pricing and other business decisions, the overall level of transparency and data availability can be expected to increase. In particular, competitive pressures may drive firms to collect and observe data in the market once at least one firm begins to do so (OECD, 2017, p. 22[1]). Thus, even in markets where tacit collusion may have been difficult in the past due to a lack of awareness of competitor decisions, AI and its associated technologies could make tacit collusion viable by making firms more predictable (Ezrachi and Stucke, 2017, pp. 1789-1790[20]).

Second, AI can affect the incentives of firms to tacitly collude. A firm will be less likely to undertake aggressive competitive decisions, such as a price cut, if it knows that competitors' algorithm will be able to rapidly and without delay respond, for example with a price cut of its own. This could render any such decisions unprofitable, and disincentivise aggressive price competition (Ezrachi and Stucke, 2017, pp. 1791-92[20]).

Third, AI, and particularly machine learning algorithms tasked with making business decisions independently, may arrive at a tacitly collusive outcome on its own. Take the example of a machine learning algorithm tasked with maximising profits by setting pricing decisions using available data on demand and competitor prices. Without AI, the best profit-maximising strategy could be to compete and potentially out-innovate rivals, since a tacitly collusive outcome would be too difficult to achieve (for example due to analytical complexity, the propensity for human error or the lack of transparency), even if it would deliver greater profits. Machine learning algorithms, on the other hand, may reach a tacitly collusive outcome which does in fact maximise profits. This outcome could be the result of the repeated interactions of each firm's pricing algorithms which, after a period of trial and error, avoid aggressive competition to protect profits (Ezrachi and Stucke, 2017, p. 1795[20]). The risk could be particularly pronounced if competing firms purchase the same algorithm or data stream from a third-party provider, resulting in a form of "hub and spoke" collusion (Competition and Markets Authority, 2018, p. 31[13]).

Empirical research on the subject of tacit collusion engendered by AI is still developing. Findings remain mixed, and recent experiments suggest that the current state of AI technology may not lead to tacit collusion without a facilitating factor, such as common algorithm design (Deng, 2018[21]). However, one recent paper provides an example in which it appears to have occurred. Specifically, the authors investigated the adoption of algorithmic pricing software by German gasoline stations (Assad et al., 2020[22]). They found that the adoption of the software increased the margins of gasoline stations facing competition by on average 9%, but had no impact on the margins of stations that were monopolies in their area. Further, in markets with only two gas stations, the authors found that margins would only increase if both stations adopted the software, and that the nature of this margin change was consistent with the software gradually reaching a tacitly collusive outcome.

Tacit collusion, which generally arises in more concentrated markets with homogeneous products (for example commodity markets where firms compete primarily on price), is generally characterised by a lack of dynamism, stable prices, steady profit margins and few significant variations in market shares. When these outcomes are observed and firms in the market use algorithms to make pricing and other decisions, the precise cause may nonetheless be unclear. Machine learning algorithms can constitute a "black box", since the process behind a given pricing decision, for example, may not be observable. Thus, it may not be possible to know whether competing algorithms have reached a joint profit maximisation outcome, for example by signalling and monitoring each other's responses, or whether the cause of a lack of market dynamism is simply a high degree of transparency and simplistic algorithmic pricing rules. This opacity can compound challenges for competition policy makers, as explored further below.

In sum, AI, in the presence of transparent prices and other market data, can dampen competition by making collusion more durable, more feasible, or even the unintentional result of profit maximisation algorithms (especially when firms purchase the same algorithm from a single provider). However, there is only limited research available on the competitive impact of machine learning and other AI applications in firm decision-making. The precise effect of AI in a given market may well vary significantly based on the conditions of the market, the design of the algorithm, and data availability, among other characteristics. For example, it is not clear how the risk of algorithmic collusion will be affected by the market characteristics that normally make collusion more difficult, such as differentiated products, significant dynamism due to innovation, and substantial differences in competing firms (such as large discrepancies in firm size). On one hand, AI applications that rely on predictability and clear market patterns may be unable to reach a collusive outcome in rapidly changing and differentiated markets. On the other hand, sophisticated AI could be effective in implementing collusive strategies in complicated markets with highly differentiated products – collusion that would break down if implemented by humans due to the risk of error or limited capacity.

4.2.2. AI and abuses of dominance

AI could also lead to more aggressive competition in some markets, in contrast to the concerns about collusion outlined above. AI could, for instance, become a major differentiator among firms in terms of how quickly they are able to respond to changes in markets, how accurately they are able to forecast and interpret data, and how they are able to harness AI to develop better, cheaper products. Aggressive profit-maximisation algorithms could even disrupt tacitly collusive outcomes in markets, depending on their design. This scenario of aggressive competition being spurred by AI suggests that, rather than dampening competition, AI could encourage competition. This may depend on the characteristics of specific markets – concentrated markets with homogeneous products and firms may be more prone to tacit algorithmic collusion, whereas in dynamic, markets characterised by firm heterogeneity, AI could intensify competition. However, there are also risks associated with the latter scenario.

In digital markets exhibiting features that create a tendency toward concentration and market power, such as strong network effects, large discrepancies in access to data, and switching costs for consumers, the aggressive competitive strategies employed by AI may in fact cross into the category of abusive conduct.

Competition laws generally either prohibit certain types of abusive conduct by firms deemed to be "dominant" (i.e. hold significant market power), or attempts to obtain or retain a monopoly position (for further discussion, see OECD (2020[23])). Enforcement of these prohibitions generally involves an assessment of the effects of the conduct in question, in contrast to *by object* or *per se* collusion cases which do not require such an assessment. This reflects the economic theory associated with the conduct: certain strategies that are harmless or even procompetitive when employed by small firms could in fact be anticompetitive and harmful to consumers when employed by dominant firms. This logic would apply to any potentially abusive conduct associated with the use of AI.

Markets in which AI plays a significant role in competitive decision-making and product design may, like many digital markets, exhibit certain features that make dominant positions more common. AI investments involve significant economies of scale and scope, given the data and technical capacity required. When AI is a part of the product offered to consumers, it is also likely to exhibit network effects, since greater user numbers can improve the quality of the algorithms involved. Thus, AI applications as well as the data flows and intangible assets used to operate them can be a source of competitive advantage, and barriers to entry, enabling the emergence of market power and potentially dominance. Recent OECD work suggests that these effects have led to higher barriers to technology diffusion and declining business dynamism (Berlingieri et al., 2020[24]; Calvino, Criscuolo and Verlhac, 2020[25]).

AI developing or implementing anticompetitive strategies

When AI drives the competitive decision-making of a dominant firm on prices or other important dimensions of quality, it could choose anticompetitive strategies. For example, machine-learning algorithms with a sufficiently long-term perspective could choose to use predatory pricing[2] or margin squeeze[3] strategies without specific instructions to do so. These strategies can both lead to consumer harm, by excluding competitors from a market or hampering their access to either inputs or downstream distribution.

In fact, these strategies may be more effective when implemented by AI. This is because planning a predatory pricing strategy aimed at driving a competitor out of the market, for example, requires information on the competitor's cost structure, available resources and capacity to withstand certain price increases. AI could be used to more effectively analyse available data to determine these characteristics, or infer them from observable characteristics such as the competitor's response to changes in the market (Dolmans, 2017, p. 8[26]).

Anticompetitive design of consumer-facing AI

When AI is part of a product provided to consumers (e.g. when a platform provides search results based on a search algorithm), rather than a mechanism for making business decisions, different competition concerns may arise. In particular, dominant firms may seek to leverage their position to exclude competitors in downstream or related markets. As noted above, AI applications can exhibit significant economies of scope, in that they can be used for multiple different products and generate useful insights across product markets. Thus, to the extent AI leads to more conglomerate business models, there may be a risk of leveraging through, for example, bundling and tying of products together (OECD, 2020[10]).

The most prominent concern, however, may stem from vertical relationships, for example when AI can be used in online platforms that connect firms with final consumers. In particular, as a result of the market characteristics described above, the operators of online platforms which incorporate algorithms may become "gatekeepers" in certain markets (Crémer, de Montjoye and Schweitzer, 2019[27]). For instance, a dominant online marketplace platform can serve as an important gatekeeper between a seller and its consumers. The design of AI used to display products to consumers that enter a search query would, in this case, have a significant impact on the prospects of the seller. Thus, it may be used to exclude firms from the market or provide advantages to firms that make commercial arrangements with the gatekeeper, affecting the experience of users without their awareness. In other cases, online platform firms may also compete downstream, for example offering products for sale on the platform they operate. This could lead to anticompetitive conduct in order to leverage platform market power into downstream markets using that platform.

One example was highlighted in allegations set out in a Majority Staff Report from the US House of Representatives Subcommittee on Antitrust. The Report described how an online marketplace could use its gatekeeper status and preferential access to third-party seller data to identify popular products, copy their features and introduce its own version (Majority Staff, Subcommittee on Antitrust, Commercial and Administrative Law, 2020, pp. 273-274[28]). While this conduct may be a procompetitive strategy in some instances, it may constitute abusive conduct in others. Indeed, the European Commission has opened an investigation into Amazon for these practices (European Commission, 2019[29]). AI technologies may be used to implement these strategies by assessing market data and identifying opportunities for product launches, for instance.

Another example of competition concerns when a product involves the use of algorithms is "self-preferencing" – when a firm provides advantages to its own products in search results, for example, which could constitute a an abuse of dominance (OECD, 2020, p. 54[23]). This was the theory of harm underlying the European Commission's case involving Google Shopping, as described in Box 4.4.

More generally, there is growing interest in the role that changes to algorithm design and behavioural "nudges" can play in shaping consumer behaviour. For example, an online platform may take advantage of the tendency of consumers to consult only the first few results on a search query, or use prominent display features to try to encourage a given choice – all while consumers assume that they are obtaining neutral or unbiased results (see, for example, Costa and Halpern (2019[30])). More broadly, AI can be used to analyse consumer decision-making patterns and alter the "choice architecture" available to consumers in order to take advantage of consumer behavioural biases without the knowledge of consumers (Competition and Markets Authority, 2021[16]). The implications of such strategies go beyond competition policy, and have particular relevance for consumer protection authorities.

In some jurisdictions, abuse of dominance prohibitions extend beyond conduct aimed at harming competition by excluding competitors or narrowing their margins. Specifically, some jurisdictions prohibit dominant firms from imposing terms on consumers or suppliers that are deemed to be unfair or discriminatory (referred to as exploitative abuses of dominance) (OECD, 2020, p. 50[23]). These cases involve numerous conceptual as well as legal challenges, and they represent only a small proportion of abuse of dominance cases brought by competition authorities (OECD, 2018, p. 27[31]). However, a recent case by the German competition authority against Facebook regarding exploitative abuse of dominance (Bundeskartellamt, 2019[32]) suggests that this tool may be considered in some jurisdictions to address competition concerns in digital markets. Whether authorities opt to pursue concerns associated with AI strategies using provisions regarding exploitative abuses of dominance (for example when platforms impose on manufacturers the type of practices enabling product copying described above) remains to be seen, however.

Box 4.4. The European Commission Google Shopping case

In June 2017, the European Commission fined Google €2.42 billion for abusing its dominant position in the general search market by favouring its own vertical comparison shopping service in its search results page. The theory of harm considered in this case was novel.

The Commission found that Google provided an "illegal advantage" to its own comparison shopping service by demoting rivals and presenting its own service in a more favourable position in its search results. In particular, Google was found to have leveraged its position in the market for general search results to benefit its offering in comparison shopping services (found by the Commission to constitute a separate market from general search). The Commission identified specific evidence of drops in traffic to rival comparison-shopping services because of Google's practices. The Commission argued that Google's self-preferencing conduct foreclosed competing comparison shopping sites from the market, which reduced consumer choice.

It is interesting to note that the US FTC conducted an investigation into Google's search practices but ultimately closed its investigation into allegations of Google's "search bias". The FTC found that changes in how Google displayed its content (through algorithm and design changes) could be viewed as quality improvement for the product (search results) and did not find the practices were anticompetitive. The Turkish Competition Authority also discontinued a similar investigation.

Source: European Commission Decision in Case AT.39740. 27 June 2017, https://ec.europa.eu/competition/antitrust/cases/dec_docs/39740/39740_14996_3.pdf. Box excerpted from OECD (2020, p. 36[23]).

Personalised pricing

Of particular relevance to AI is the question of whether personalised pricing, or price discrimination across consumers, could constitute an exploitative abuse of dominance. In contrast to the concerns about stable prices, uniformity, dampened competition and tacit collusion described above, AI may lead to highly dynamic and specialised markets (Dolmans, 2017, p. 8[26]).

Price discrimination occurs when consumers are charged different prices based on their characteristics or consumption patterns. For example, rather than offering a uniform service, many airlines offer different cabin types and services according to a consumer's willingness to pay. This can be an effort to capture additional revenues from certain groups of consumers, for example those travelling for business versus leisure.

With AI, firms can process a growing amount of data on consumers and their characteristics. This allows firms to set prices not just based on broad categories of consumers, but in some cases individually tailored prices based on estimates of the consumer's willingness to pay, as ascertained using multiple data points – also called personalised pricing (OECD, 2018, p. 8[31]). In particular, AI applications may be able to generate inferred data (such as consumption preferences, brand loyalty, and purchasing behaviours) based on data provided by and observed about consumers in a way that was not possible beforehand

(OECD, 2018, p. 11[31]). While data can make some degree of personalisation possible in many digital markets, AI decision-making can enable more extensive, more accurate and more granular personalisation. However, it may not be able to overcome all challenges associated with implementing personalised pricing, such as potential consumer arbitrage behaviour which would help some consumers avoid higher prices.

Beyond personalised pricing, AI can be used to personalise the functionality and information provided to consumers. In fact, personalisation may become significantly more widespread thanks to AI applications. For example, it can play a role in the ranking of products in a search query, or in the timing and content of notifications directed to consumers (Competition and Markets Authority, 2021[16]). Further, this personalisation may occur without a consumer's knowledge.

Personalisation, including personalised pricing, is not automatically cause for competition concerns – in many cases it can improve overall efficiency in markets, and could even improve the accessibility of products. For example, personalised pricing could result in lower prices for some consumers who would not purchase a product if there were only a single, market-wide price. In particular, those with a lower willingness to pay could be offered a price below the previous market-wide price, potentially offset by higher prices for consumers with a higher willingness to pay (OECD, 2018[31]). It may also allow greater customisation to meet a consumer's needs, and provide a strategy for new firms to develop a foothold in a market (Competition and Markets Authority, 2021[16]). However, significant concerns may arise in some cases. The line between human decision-making and outcomes can be blurred in these situations, particularly when the decision-making process of "black box" algorithms tasked with a broad objective cannot be observed.

Some of these concerns can fall squarely within the realm of competition law. For example, a dominant firm may use algorithms to identify users of rival products and implement "selective pricing" or use behavioural nudges in order to lure them away (OECD, 2018, p. 28[31]). Such strategies could constitute an exclusionary abuse of dominance, depending on the circumstances.

Other concerns associated with personalised pricing may be raised in the context of the more rare exploitative abuse of dominance cases described above. For example, in some jurisdictions, complaints may arise about a dominant firm exploiting its market power by using an algorithm to impose excessive prices on some consumers. However, caution may be needed in these circumstances, particularly if intervention could threaten access to consumers who may have access to a product thanks to cross-subsidisation and personalised pricing.

Finally, personalised pricing may give rise to broader societal concerns that are better addressed outside of competition law, even if it is being implemented by firms with market power. Consumer protection concerns may arise out of the opacity of personalisation algorithms, which can put consumers at an informational disadvantage and make shopping around more difficult. Broader concerns could also arise out of the potential for AI to set personalised prices that result in discrimination, including on the basis of an individual's age, gender, location, or race (Competition and Markets Authority, 2021[16]). Concerns about this type of discrimination are more fully explored in Chapter 3333.

4.2.3. AI and mergers

Competition authorities may also need to assess the risks of market power stemming from AI when reviewing mergers. Many of these risks apply across a broad range of digital markets, and overlap with concerns stemming from data access as well as network effects. For example, a merger that alleviates the competitive pressure on a firm may also reduce its incentives to innovate, thus limiting the positive potential of AI technologies for consumers (OECD, 2018[33]). However, the dynamics associated with AI may also lead to unique concerns. For example, a merger that combines two firms' datasets or AI capacity could result in market power that can be hard to contest given the substantial economies of scale and scope associated with data and AI applications (OECD, 2016[5]).

While these harms will be most straightforward with respect to mergers between two product market competitors, there has been growing interest in vertical mergers (i.e. mergers between firms and their suppliers or downstream distributors) in the digital sector (OECD, 2019[34]). Competition harms may result from vertical mergers if the post-merger firm can cut its competitors off from the supply of an essential input (such as data or AI technology), although the analysis in these cases can be complex.

Finally, conglomerate mergers (i.e. mergers between firms that are neither competitors nor in a supply relationship), may also give rise to harm in particular circumstances. These circumstances may be particularly common in digital markets, including those featuring AI technology. In particular, a digital firm with market power in one market may use a merger to enter another market with an overlapping user base. It may then leverage its market power in the original market to foreclose competition in the new market, for example by bundling products together in some situations (OECD, 2020[10]).

Merger control is a preventative measure that can also help address the risks of anticompetitive conduct before it occurs. Thus, in markets in which AI is used for competitive decision-making, or as a component of a product offered to consumers, the risks of the merger facilitating algorithmic collusion or abuses of dominance could be considered by authorities. For example, authorities could consider whether one of the merging parties used a different pricing strategy or algorithm from other firms in a market – meaning the merger could be depriving the market of a "maverick" that encourages competition. Further, if a merger risks significantly increasing transparency in a market (due, for example, to one of the parties' tendency to disclose significant detail on its prices and products beyond what is needed for consumers), it may also lead to collusive outcomes.

4.3. Challenges for competition policy in addressing AI-related competition problems

The discussion above identifies a range of potential competition problems associated with AI, either as a decision-maker, implementer of firm strategies, or component of a product offered to consumers. Further, while limited, there have been some cases by competition authorities to address anticompetitive conduct associated with algorithms, as well as one initial empirical indication that algorithms could dampen competition. The question remains, however, whether competition policy and in particular enforcement frameworks are equipped to address the potentially significant impact of AI on competitive dynamics in markets. The OECD Competition Committee held an initial discussion on this subject in 2017, which served to identify some of the key challenges facing competition authorities as well as some proposed solutions. This section explores these challenges and the developments that have occurred since the discussion.

4.3.1. Legal challenges

For the purposes of competition law, harms associated with AI can be divided into three categories: (1) the use of AI to implement anticompetitive agreements or strategies developed by humans; (2) the implementation of identifiable anticompetitive strategies by AI without explicit instructions by humans; and (3) AI coinciding with a reduction in competitive intensity without explicit evidence of anticompetitive strategies or agreements.

The first category involves the most straightforward application of competition law. Explicit cartel agreements among competitors are infringements of competition law regardless of whether they are executed through phone calls, meetings, or pricing algorithms designed to mirror one another's behaviour. The collusion cases involving poster sellers in the US and UK described above illustrate this point.

Similarly, the use of algorithms to implement abuses of dominance (including the self-preferencing issues described above) would be subject to the same legal standards as the implementation of these strategies through other means. Recent reform proposals by the European Commission and UK Government have included additional rules and oversight regarding gatekeeper platforms, however.[4] These reforms reflect concerns about the ability of existing competition laws to address concerns regarding self-preferencing, for example in terms of speed or coverage of the law.

The second category may apply in cases where an abuse of dominance has occurred as a result of the decisions made by an algorithm. Unlike hard-core collusive arrangements, which are assumed to be anticompetitive given past experience, abuses of dominance are assessed in terms of their effect, and rooted in economic theories of harm. Thus, even if an algorithm is not explicitly programmed to exclude competitors, for example, firms using "black box" algorithms that execute anticompetitive behaviour on their own are likely to be liable for the effects of this conduct. For example, when investigating a potential exploitative abuse of dominance case involving the possibility of excessive airfares, the President of the Bundeskartellamt stated (Bundeskartellamt, 2018[35]):

> *The use of an algorithm for pricing naturally does not relieve a company of its responsibility. The investigations in this case have also shown that the airlines specify the framework data and set the parameters for dynamic price adjustment separately for each flight. The airlines also actively manage changes to these framework data and enter unanticipated events manually, which are not automatically accounted for by the system.*

The third category remains the most prominent legal challenge to enforcing competition laws in the presence of AI. In particular, competition law does not apply to tacit collusion outcomes reached without any co-ordination among the firms involved. This is because tacit collusion may in fact be the most rational response to conditions in certain markets, even if it is not ideal from an economic perspective, and thus it could be difficult to fashion an effective remedy that would improve market outcomes (OECD, 2017, p. 18[1]).

Collusion cases are generally prosecuted according to whether an *agreement* has taken place among firms. The precise definition of an agreement varies across jurisdictions, but proof is generally required that an allegedly collusive outcome was the result of direct or indirect communication rather than purely independent decision-making by the firms involved. Some jurisdictions supplement this by also considering other forms of collusion. *Concerted practices* are "a form of coordination between undertakings by which, without it having reached the stage where an actual agreement has been concluded, practical cooperation between them substitutes the risks of competition" (European Commission, 2019, p. 4[36]). *Facilitating practices*, which are "positive, avoidable actions, engaged in by market players, which allow firms to easier and more effectively achieve coordination, by overcoming the impediments to coordination" (Gal, 2017, p. 18[37]).

The challenge posed by tacit collusion enabled by algorithms is thus similar to that posed by tacit collusion more broadly, particularly in oligopolistic markets (OECD, 2017, pp. 35-36[1]): in the presence of strong entry barriers and homogeneous products, there may be strong incentives for firms to avoid aggressive competition. Some have suggested that algorithmic collusion in these situations could be addressed as part of a broader competition policy debate about attempting to tackle tacit collusion through competition law (Gal, 2017, p. 21[37]). In particular, the reliance on an explicit agreement to prove an infringement may need to be revised.

In the absence of such a significant and controversial change, some alternative approaches tailored to algorithms could be considered. One such approach is to consider algorithms facilitating practices, particularly if they enable tacitly collusive outcomes to be reached more efficiently, according to the analysis set out in Figure 4.1 (Gal, 2017, p. 18[37]). For example, the use of similar pricing algorithms could be considered a harmful facilitator of collusion. An equivalent practice in more traditional sectors would be a decision to publicise detailed price and product information, in a manner beyond what would be useful to consumers, to clearly signal competitors and enable collusion. However, there may be a significant evidentiary burden for proving that an algorithm constitutes such a practice in some jurisdictions (Ezrachi and Stucke, 2017, pp. 20-21[38]).

Alternatively, there may be a case in some situations for considering that an agreement between firms may have been reached through a "meeting of algorithms" (OECD, 2017, p. 38[1]). In particular, if a collusive outcome has been reached through rapid algorithmic pricing decisions, it could be interpreted as a case of explicit collusion. In particular, the algorithms could be deemed to have reached an indirect agreement by signalling to each-other in order to reach a mutually-acceptable price. However, competition authorities are still grappling with whether this interpretation may fit within current competition law, particularly given that this sort of algorithmic communication may still be limited in today's markets (Autorité de la concurrence and Bundeskartellamt, 2019, p. 53[18]).

Figure 4.1. Method developed by Gal for assessing whether decision-making algorithms constitute a facilitating practice

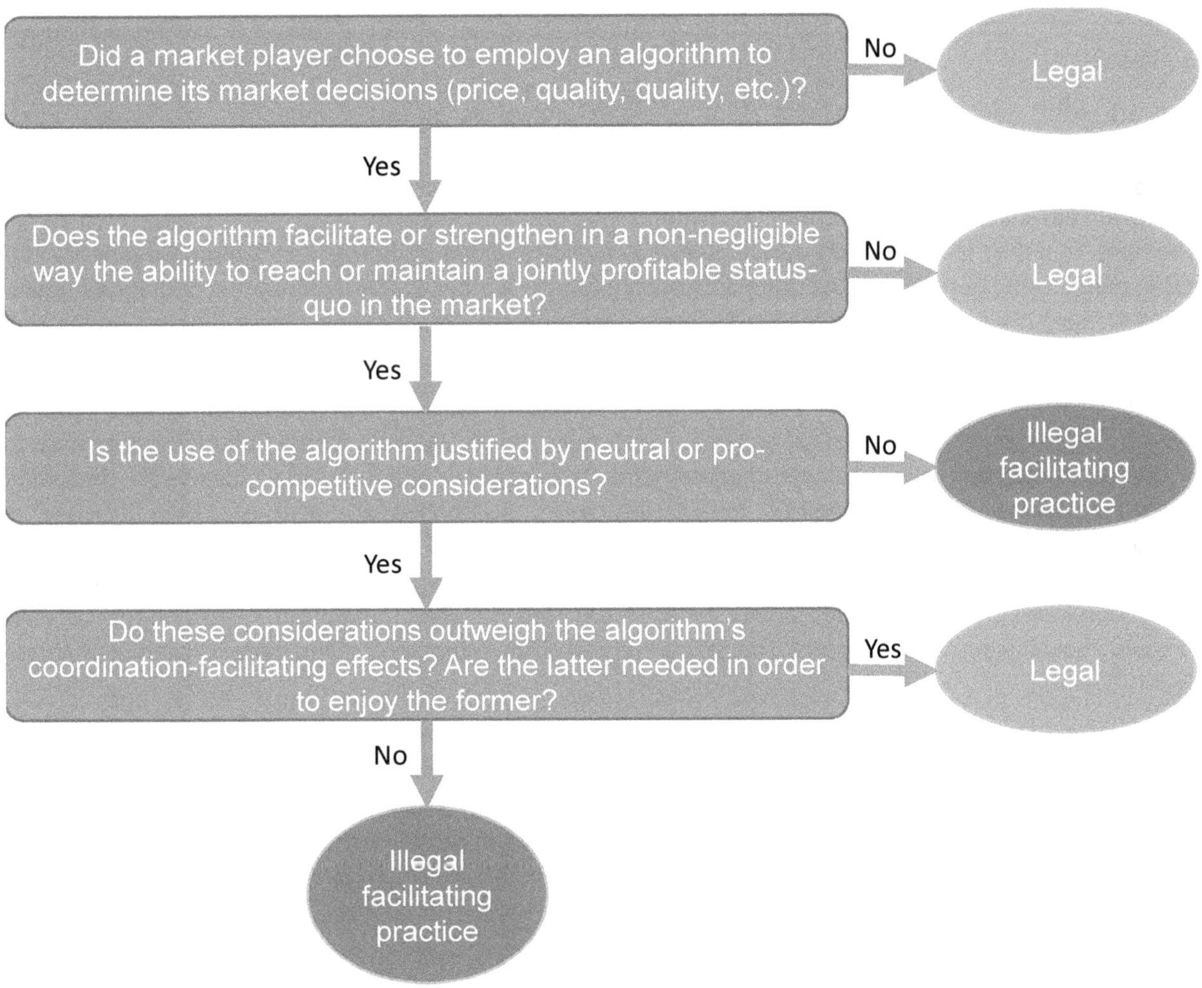

Source: Excerpted from Gal (2017, p. 23[37])

These theories have yet to be tested extensively in competition authority proceedings. Doing so will require addressing important questions, including liability. For example, if a firm procures a black box machine-learning algorithm from a third party developer, and the latter does not explicitly include collusion objectives in programming the algorithm, who should bear liability for any collusive outcomes that result? Some authorities have suggested a duty on the part of firms to avoid collusive outcomes, in the same way that a firm would not escape liability if an employee engaged in collusion without knowledge of the firm's owners (Autorité de la concurrence and Bundeskartellamt, 2019, p. 58[18]; Vestager, 2017[39]).

In the event the legal challenges to tackling tacit algorithmic collusion prove insurmountable, authorities may need to make use of the alternative measures described in Section 4.3.3 below.

4.3.2. Investigative challenges

Investigations into collusion and abusive conduct each involve their own unique challenges – challenges that may be exacerbated when algorithms are involved.

In the case of collusion investigations, which are a priority in many jurisdictions, detection is a particular challenge.[5] Firms that collude generally seek to maintain the secrecy of their agreement, for instance by minimising communication, or using indirect or informal communication that does not leave behind evidence. In this sense, explicit cartels using AI tools involve the same detection challenges as many other cartels. However, AI may be an effective means of further limiting communication between cartel participants, for example by using signalling techniques to help co-ordinate a cartel's response to changes in a market.

There are some techniques available to competition authorities to tackle detection challenges. First, competition authorities have developed leniency programs that allow a cartel member to come forward with information about the cartel in exchange for a lesser penalty (OECD, 2001[40]). A leniency application may be an attractive option for cartel participants that are not satisfied with the outcome of a cartel agreement, or if they fear detection and prosecution by competition authorities (including the potential for another cartel member revealing the cartel and applying for leniency). While leniency is a primary detection method in many markets, its efficiency will depend on the existence of a credible threat of detection through other means. Thus, authorities are continuing to explore alternative detection methods.

One such method of cartel detection is the use of screening tools by competition authorities (OECD, 2013[41]). These can include structural screens, which may identify markets where authorities may wish to pay particular attention given certain characteristics that might make collusion more likely (including product homogeneity and oligopolistic market structure). Authorities are also exploring the use of behavioural screens, which use available data on firm behaviour to flag potential collusion.[6] This could include looking for patterns of unusual or unexplained behaviour (such as uniform price rises across a market not related to changes in demand or input prices), and identifying "structural breaks" in market data that could show the implementation of a cartel agreement or the adaptation of the cartel to market changes (OECD, 2013[41]).

Screens are generally only helpful in providing indications of potential cartel activity – that is, in order for prosecution to occur, further investigation will be required. However, they can create disincentives for cartel formation, and encourage leniency applications, to the extent they create the threat of detection. Further, screens involve a range of technical and analytical challenges in their implementation, but AI may in fact help competition authorities in surmounting these challenges, as described in the following Chapter.

Beyond detection, competition authorities also face the challenge of investigating potential collusion facilitated by AI that straddles the line between explicit and tacit. Gal (2017, pp. 24-25[37]) proposes that authorities prioritise certain situations where competition harm may be more clear-cut; including: when firms consciously use similar algorithms, when they use similar data and make it easier for rivals to observe this data, or when firms reveal the content or design of their algorithms, making it easier for rivals to copy them.

Finally, competition authorities face a significant technical challenge in analysing AI-related competition concerns, whether they pertain to collusion or abusive conduct. While competition authority staff always face the need to become acquainted with an industry, its players and its dynamics when undertaking investigations, the assessment of AI can pose a particular challenge. This is due not only to the technical aspects of AI design and functioning, but also the opaque nature of AI, particularly when machine learning functionality is involved.

The UK Competition and Markets Authority (2021[16]) has recently published a report that identifies a range of investigative techniques allowing competition authorities to better assess AI. Specifically:

- When authorities do not have direct access to an algorithm or the data it uses, they may nonetheless monitor the behaviour of market participants through, for example: "mystery shopping" (in which authority staff mimics a consumer), scraping techniques (which extract data from websites or applications), or access to application programming interfaces (APIs, which can facilitate access to data on an online platform).
- When authorities have access to the data used by the AI, or data regarding its outputs, they may be able to undertake analysis on the nature and effects of the AI decision-making. For example, in its investigation regarding Google's practice of promoting its own comparison shopping service, the European Commission used data on 1.7 billion search queries in order to estimate the effect of search result ranking on consumer decisions (European Commission, 2017[42]).
- When authorities have access to the code underlying AI, they may attempt a review of the code (to determine, for example, whether there are explicit anticompetitive instructions included), although this may involve substantial technical and practical difficulty. Alternatively, authorities may engage in testing the algorithm in order to better understand its functioning and outputs.

Each of these approaches are likely to require that competition authorities have access to sufficient technical expertise. Several authorities are investing in this capacity, including being able to not only assess algorithms but also deploy them for their own purposes, as outlined in the following Chapter. At the same time, more traditional evidence gathering can help in some situations. For example, the collection of internal firm documents that help explain the business strategy associated with AI techniques can be valuable for investigations (Deng, 2018, p. 91[21]).

4.3.3. Competition policy approaches to addressing competition issues raised by AI

As the discussion above highlights, there are a range of competition and other policy concerns that may not be easily addressed through current competition enforcement tools. These range from tacit collusion, to the modification of consumer-facing algorithms in ways that may not qualify as an abuse under current standards, to wide-ranging consumer protection and even human rights concerns. There are several opportunities for competition policy makers to help address these concerns.

Market studies and advocacy

AI may affect competitive dynamics in a market without leading to explicit collusion or abuses of dominance. As noted above, tacit collusion facilitated by AI may depress market dynamics and make competitor decisions more predictable. AI may also be designed in a way that takes advantage of consumers' behavioural biases or makes switching to other providers more difficult.

Many OECD competition authorities have the ability to conduct market studies, in cases where competition is not functioning well but an antitrust investigation is not warranted.[7] A limited number of jurisdictions also have the power to order the implementation of remedies in response to any issues identified (generally through a complementary instrument called a market investigation).

Market studies may be of particular value in identifying the conditions that are leading to dampened competition in markets featuring AI decision-making, or in assessing the supply- and demand-side factors enabling other uncompetitive outcomes. One such example is the European Commission's sector inquiry on e-commerce, which observed issues regarding price transparency and automated price adjustments, as summarised in Box 4.5. The findings of market studies can be used to support recommendations for regulatory change, measures to inform consumers, or follow-on investigations by competition or other regulators. For example, they can discuss the balance between promoting data access for procompetitive reasons and the risks of collusion. Market studies can also highlight risks associated with market concentration among AI service providers (which could lead to symmetry in pricing behaviour, for example).

Box 4.5. The European Commission E-Commerce Sector Inquiry

On 10 May 2017, the EU Commission adopted the final report in its e-commerce sector inquiry, where it discussed key market trends and competition issues in e-commerce in relation to the online sale of consumer goods and the online distribution of digital content.

The final report highlighted the increase in online price transparency and the use of price monitoring software in the e-commerce sector, noting the significant implications for consumers, retailers and manufacturers.

The report noted that such enhanced transparency may increase price competition but could also affect other diameters of competition, for example, innovation and quality. The report found that both retailers and manufactures track prices using price monitoring software or "spiders", which provide a large amount of price related information in a timely manner, often with real time updates and alerts. Further, the majority of retailers that use such software adapt their prices to their competitors, adjusting prices manually and/or automatically through pricing software.

The report identified two ways in which increased transparency and the use of price monitoring software could impact the competitive process, facilitating and strengthening the implementation of:

- **Pricing restrictions and recommendations of manufacturers**. The inquiry noted an increase in vertical restraints as one of the key market trends, and that pricing restrictions or recommendations were the most prevalent vertical restraint imposed on online retailers. In the e-commerce sector, manufactures are better able to monitor the pricing behaviour of retailers. They are able to detect when retailers do not implement recommended prices and thus may be more likely to take action against non-compliant retailers. This also reduces the incentive of retailers to set their prices independently.
- **Tacit and implicit collusion.** Enhanced transparency and monitoring techniques can facilitate cartel conduct and strengthen existing arrangements, as market players are able to easily monitor the pricing behaviour of their competitors. Specifically, they are able to identify and react immediately to a deviation from an agreement. This reduces the incentive to deviate from any anticompetitive agreement by limiting the potential gains.

Source: Final report on the E-commerce Sector Inquiry, https://ec.europa.eu/competition/antitrust/sector_inquiry_final_report_en.pdf; Commission Staff Working Document, https://ec.europa.eu/competition/antitrust/sector_inquiry_swd_en.pdf

In addition, market studies and other competition authority advocacy efforts can be used to identify ways to better-equip consumers to face AI-related conduct generating competition concerns. Competition authorities are beginning to explore the greater use of measures focusing on the consumer side of the market, in recognition of the fact that competition problems may be enabled through certain demand side characteristics (see, for example, the background note prepared by the UK Competition and Markets Authority to support an OECD discussion on this topic (2018[43])). Some potential measures of relevance here including leveraging AI to enable comparison tools and services acting as an intermediary between consumers and online platforms, transparency requirements, and data portability as well as interoperability (see, for example, Costa and Halpern (2019[30])). The OECD is exploring the application of these measures, for example with a discussion earlier this year on data portability, interoperability and competition in the Competition Committee.[8]

Co-operation with other regulators and stakeholders

Beyond the importance of international co-operation among competition authorities given the borderless nature of many digital markets, addressing concerns regarding AI will require close and ongoing co-ordination with other regulators, including consumer protection and data protection authorities as well as sector regulators. The use of AI to take advantage of consumer behavioural biases, for example, may not be easily addressed using competition enforcement tools even if it does shape market dynamics, in which case competition authorities may wish to support further consumer protection or data protection interventions. In addition, data protection frameworks can have a significant impact on the competitive dynamics associated with AI in markets; for instance, poorly-designed data protection regulations may enhance the advantage of incumbents and reduce market contestability (see, for example, (OECD, 2020[44])). Further, as a greater range of regulators begins to respond to AI issues within their own mandates, competition authorities can also play a role in ensuring that these responses do not unduly harm competition and lead to unintended consequences for consumer welfare. For instance, authorities may need to highlight situations in which competition enforcement can more effectively address certain concerns than regulation – particularly when rapid innovation could render regulation obsolete, or when the concern can be addressed by leveraging the forces of competition.

In addition, the competition concerns outlined above present a range of novel conceptual and practical challenges for competition authorities. Authorities can benefit from co-operation with researchers when seeking to assess how AI is currently affecting competitive dynamics, and the ensuing effects on consumers. Further, this co-operation can help explore how widespread certain anticompetitive practices are, and develop tools for detecting and analysing them.

Policy makers may also need to consider the role of trade policy when seeking to promote the evolution of AI in a procompetitive manner. For instance, discussions at the World Trade Organization regarding e-commerce have covered potential competition distortions in trade policy that could affect AI applications. This includes requirements that firms transfer their software source code when seeking to operate in a given jurisdiction.[9] In addition, data localisation policies could affect the evolution of AI applications, either by limiting the combination of datasets or creating competition distortions, and will thus need to be considered carefully.

4.3.4. Considering reforms to current enforcement frameworks and new regulatory measures

Concerns about the role of algorithms in facilitating or reaching collusive outcomes have been on the radar of competition authorities for several years (as demonstrated by the OECD's 2017 roundtable on the topic). Since that time, interest and analysis regarding competition issues in digital markets more broadly has grown significantly. Governments have commissioned expert reports,[10] competition authorities have undertaken market studies,[11] and elected officials have held hearings.[12]

These studies emphasise the importance of protecting and promoting competition in digital markets, given their growing role in the economy and their importance for future growth. They also point to changes needed to address growing concerns about competitive dynamics in the wake of digitalisation. In some cases, these changes relate to strengthening competition enforcement frameworks, such as enhancing merger control or enabling faster competition authority intervention in the case of abuses.

Further, a growing set of jurisdictions are also developing new legislation and new regulatory frameworks to address competition concerns that may not be easily addressed within existing competition frameworks, including proposals made by the European Commission[13] and UK Government,[14] among others. This reflects the view that current competition enforcement procedures may be too slow, too reactive instead of proactive, or may not capture all competition concerns that arise in digital markets.

The scope of these regulatory proposals extend well beyond addressing concerns regarding AI, including competition risks stemming from bundling of digital products together, self-preferencing by vertically-integrated firms, and concerns about the bargaining relationship between large online platforms and businesses using them. While the full extent of these proposals is beyond the focus of this Chapter, the OECD Competition Committee will be holding a roundtable on the topic of ex ante regulation in digital markets in December 2021.

Of particular relevance to the assessment of AI-related competition issues, both the EU and UK proposals referenced above seek to impose specific rules on online platforms acting as gatekeepers. These measures rectify perceived gaps in competition enforcement frameworks, namely their ability and speed in addressing concerns about self-preferencing and other issues of relevance to AI applications. The precise application of these measures is still being developed, but they suggest the need to consider asymmetric measures for particular dominant firms, including with respect to the design and operation of their algorithms.

Other policy measures are being developed to specifically address AI-related competition concerns. For instance, the European Commission has set out guidelines under the EU Platform-to-Business (P2B) regulation regarding the ranking of choices presented to consumers on platforms. While not legally binding, these guidelines can demonstrate how platforms can comply with their obligations under the P2B regulation. They include transparency with respect to the main parameters of algorithmic ranking, improving the information available to businesses that use platforms and encouraging fairness in the application of ranking algorithms (European Commission, 2020[45]).

4.4. Conclusion

This chapter highlights how AI may lead to competition problems, particularly collusion and abusive conduct. Further, the nature of these outcomes may not be easily addressed using existing competition enforcement tools. This is particularly the case with tacit collusion, which one commentator likened to a "crack" in enforcement frameworks that could be widened into a "chasm" due to AI (Mehra, 2016, p. 1340[46]).

The competition policy community's understanding of exactly how AI will affect competitive dynamics is still developing, and rooted in theory. By enabling more efficient decision-making, new products and services, AI holds substantive procompetitive potential, and may even serve to undermine the stability of some collusive outcomes. At the same time, competition risks could emerge if AI dampens competition by making markets predictable, transparent and stagnant, or if it leads to the implementation of aggressive strategies that exclude competitors from markets. More broadly, AI gives rise to a range of concerns that cannot be neatly confined within a competition law context, and will require the attention of consumer protection regulators as well as policy makers to address more fundamental questions about discrimination.

Despite concerns about the significant potential legal and investigative challenges that may arise due to these AI-related competition problems, it is clear that competition authorities' toolboxes are not empty. They can capture a wide range of conduct using existing tools, as demonstrated by some of the cases summarised above. They can manage risks of anticompetitive conduct through careful merger control, conduct market studies to identify procompetitive measures (including those aimed at supporting consumer information and decision-making), and engage in advocacy and co-operation with other regulators. However, additional legislative tools may be required to capture the full range of competition concerns, and competition authorities will need access to the technical capacity and knowledge needed to understand how AI works in markets. In fact, there are numerous opportunities for authorities to harness AI to improve their work, as will be explored in the following chapter.

In sum, it is still too early to say whether AI will deliver on its potential for significant procompetitive consumer benefits, or whether it will lead to widespread competition harm. However, it is clear that competition policy will have an important role to play in managing the potential dark sides of AI technology for consumers, businesses that may be harmed by AI-enabled anticompetitive conduct, and the economy more broadly. This will involve ensuring regulatory frameworks support innovation and procompetitive AI applications without unnecessary burdens or competition barriers, ensuring enforcers have the right tools to enforce competition laws, and co-ordinating across regulatory and policy disciplines.

References

Accenture (2017), *How AI Boosts Industry Profits and Innovation*, https://www.accenture.com/fr-fr/_acnmedia/36dc7f76eab444cab6a7f44017cc3997.pdf. [3]

Assad, S. et al. (2020), "Algorithmic Pricing and Competition: Empirical Evidence from the German Retail Gasoline Market", *CESifo Working Paper* No. 8521, https://www.econstor.eu/bitstream/10419/223593/1/cesifo1_wp8521.pdf. [22]

Australian Competition & Consumer Commission (2019), *Digital Platforms Inquiry: Final Report*, https://www.accc.gov.au/publications/digital-platforms-inquiry-final-report. [51]

Autorité de la concurrence and Bundeskartellamt (2019), *Algorithms and Competition*, https://www.autoritedelaconcurrence.fr/sites/default/files/algorithms-and-competition.pdf. [18]

Autorité de la concurrence and Bundeskartellamt (2016), *Competition Law and Data*, https://www.bundeskartellamt.de/SharedDocs/Publikation/DE/Berichte/Big%20Data%20Papier.pdf?__blob=publicationFile&v=2. [49]

Babina, T. et al. (2020), *Artificial Intelligence, Firm Growth, and Industry Concentration*, https://papers.ssrn.com/sol3/papers.cfm?abstract_id=3651052. [9]

Bajgar, M., C. Criscuolo and J. Timmis (2021), *Intangibles and Industry Concentration: Supersize Me*, OECD, https://one.oecd.org/document/DSTI/CIIE(2019)13/REV1/en/pdf. [7]

Berlingieri, G. et al. (2020), *Last but not least: laggard firms, technology diffusion and its structural and policy determinants*, OECD, https://www.oecd-ilibrary.org/science-and-technology/laggard-firms-technology-diffusion-and-its-structural-and-policy-determinants_281bd7a9-en. [24]

Bundeskartellamt (2019), *Case Summary: Facebook, Exploitative business terms pursuant to Section 19(1) GWB for inadequate data processing*, https://www.bundeskartellamt.de/SharedDocs/Entscheidung/EN/Fallberichte/Missbrauchsaufsicht/2019/B6-22-16.pdf?__blob=publicationFile&v=4. [32]

Bundeskartellamt (2018), *Press Release: Lufthansa tickets 25-30 per cent more expensive after Air Berlin insolvency – "Price increase does not justify initiation of abuse proceeding"*, https://www.bundeskartellamt.de/SharedDocs/Meldung/EN/Pressemitteilungen/2018/29_05_2018_Lufthansa.html. [35]

Calligaris, S., C. Criscuolo and L. Marcolin (2018), "Mark-ups in the digital era", *OECD Science, Technology and Industry Working Papers*, No. 2018/10, https://www.oecd-ilibrary.org/industry-and-services/mark-ups-in-the-digital-era_4efe2d25-en. [6]

Calvino, F. and C. Criscuolo (2019), "Business dynamics and digitalisation", *OECD Science, Technology and Industry Policy Papers*, No. 62, OECD Publishing, Paris, https://dx.doi.org/10.1787/6e0b011a-en. [8]

Calvino, F., C. Criscuolo and R. Verlhac (2020), *Declining business dynamism: structural and policy determinants*, OECD, https://www.oecd-ilibrary.org/science-and-technology/declining-business-dynamism_77b92072-en. [25]

Competition and Markets Authority (2021), *Algorithms: How they can reduce competition and harm consumers*, https://www.gov.uk/government/publications/algorithms-how-they-can-reduce-competition-and-harm-consumers/algorithms-how-they-can-reduce-competition-and-harm-consumers#theories-of-harm. [16]

Competition and Markets Authority (2020), *Online platforms and digital advertising: Market study final report*, https://assets.publishing.service.gov.uk/media/5efc57ed3a6f4023d242ed56/Final_report_1_July_2020_.pdf. [50]

Competition and Markets Authority (2018), *Designing and Testing Effective Consumer-facing Remedies: Background Note for OECD Competition Committee Working Party No. 3*, OECD, https://one.oecd.org/document/DAF/COMP/WP3(2018)2/en/pdf. [43]

Competition and Markets Authority (2018), *Pricing algorithms: Economic working paper on the use of algorithms to facilitate collusion and personalised pricing*, https://assets.publishing.service.gov.uk/government/uploads/system/uploads/attachment_data/file/746353/Algorithms_econ_report.pdf. [13]

Competition and Markets Authority (2016), *Decision of the Competition and Markets Authority: Online Sales of Posters and Frames - Case 50223*, https://assets.publishing.service.gov.uk/media/57ee7c2740f0b606dc000018/case-50223-final-non-confidential-infringement-decision.pdf. [15]

Costa, E. and D. Halpern (2019), *The behavioural science of online harm and manipulation, and what to do about it*, The Behavioural Insights Team, https://www.bi.team/wp-content/uploads/2019/04/BIT_The-behavioural-science-of-online-harm-and-manipulation-and-what-to-do-about-it_Single.pdf. [30]

Crémer, J., Y. de Montjoye and H. Schweitzer (2019), *Competition policy for the digital era*, https://ec.europa.eu/competition/publications/reports/kd0419345enn.pdf. [27]

Deng, A. (2018), "What Do We Know About Algorithmic Tacit Collusion?", *Antitrust*, Vol. 33/1, https://awards.concurrences.com/IMG/pdf/fall18-denga-published.pdf?46593/5e118cee876a9c4a37e32bc8c9451a34c54e18d9. [21]

Digital Competition Expert Panel (2019), *Unlocking digital competition: Report of the Digital Competition Expert Panel*, https://assets.publishing.service.gov.uk/government/uploads/system/uploads/attachment_data/file/785547/unlocking_digital_competition_furman_review_web.pdf. [48]

Dolmans, M. (2017), *Artificial Intelligence and the future of competition law – further thoughts*, Cleary Gottlieb Steen & Hamilton LLP, https://www.coleurope.eu/sites/default/files/uploads/event/dolmans.pdf. [26]

European Commission (2020), *Press Release: European Commission publishes ranking guidelines under the P2B Regulation to increase transparency of online search results*, https://ec.europa.eu/digital-single-market/en/news/european-commission-publishes-ranking-guidelines-under-p2b-regulation-increase-transparency. [45]

European Commission (2019), *Hub-and-spoke arrangements – Note by the European Union for the OECD Competition Committee Roundtable Discussion*, https://one.oecd.org/document/DAF/COMP/WD(2019)89/en/pdf. [36]

European Commission (2019), *Press Release: Antitrust: Commission opens investigation into possible anti-competitive conduct of Amazon*, https://ec.europa.eu/commission/presscorner/detail/en/ip_19_4291. [29]

European Commission (2017), *Final report on the E-commerce Sector Inquiry*, https://ec.europa.eu/competition/antitrust/sector_inquiry_final_report_en.pdf. [2]

European Commission (2017), *Press Release: Antitrust: Commission fines Google €2.42 billion for abusing dominance as search engine by giving illegal advantage to own comparison shopping service*, https://ec.europa.eu/commission/presscorner/detail/en/IP_17_1784. [42]

Ezrachi, A. and M. Stucke (2017), *Algorithmic Collusion: Problems and Counter-Measures: Note for the Competition Committee Roundtable on Algorithms and Collusion*, OECD, https://one.oecd.org/document/DAF/COMP/WD(2017)25/en/pdf. [38]

Ezrachi, A. and M. Stucke (2017), "Artificial Intelligence & Collusion: When Computers Inhibit Competition", *University of Illinois Law Review*, https://papers.ssrn.com/sol3/papers.cfm?abstract_id=2591874. [20]

Fletcher, A. (2020), *Digital competition policy: Are ecosystems different?*, https://one.oecd.org/document/DAF/COMP/WD(2020)96/en/pdf. [11]

Gal, M. (2017), *Algorithmic-facilitated Coordination: Note for OECD Competition Committee Roundtable on Algorithms and Collusion*, OECD, https://one.oecd.org/document/DAF/COMP/WD(2017)26/en/pdf. [37]

Gal, M. and N. Elkin-Koren (2017), "Algorithmic Consumers", *Harvard Journal of Law & Technology*, Vol. 30, https://jolt.law.harvard.edu/assets/articlePDFs/v30/30HarvJLTech309.pdf. [4]

Majority Staff, Subcommittee on Antitrust, Commercial and Administrative Law (2020), *Investigation of Competition in Digital Markets: Majority Staff Report and Recommendations*, https://judiciary.house.gov/uploadedfiles/competition_in_digital_markets.pdf?utm_campaign=4493-519. [28]

Mehra, S. (2016), "Antitrust and the Robo-Seller: Competition in the Time of Algorithms", *Minnesota Law Review*, Vol. 100, https://papers.ssrn.com/sol3/papers.cfm?abstract_id=2576341. [46]

OECD (2020), *Abuse of dominance in digital markets: Background note by the Secretariat*, http://www.oecd.org/daf/competition/abuse-of-dominance-in-digital-markets-2020.pdf. [23]

OECD (2020), *Consumer Data Rights and Competition: Background note by the Secretariat*, https://one.oecd.org/document/DAF/COMP(2020)1/en/pdf. [44]

OECD (2020), *Roundtable on Conglomerate Effects of Mergers - Background note by the Secretariat*, https://one.oecd.org/document/DAF/COMP(2020)2/en/pdf. [10]

OECD (2019), *Practical approaches to assessing digital platform markets for competition law enforcement: Background note by the Secretariat for the Latin American and Caribbean Competition Forum*, https://one.oecd.org/document/DAF/COMP/LACF(2019)4/en/pdf. [47]

OECD (2019), *Roundtable on Hub-and-Spoke Arrangements: Background Note by the Secretariat*, https://one.oecd.org/document/DAF/COMP(2019)14/en/pdf. [17]

OECD (2019), "Vertical Mergers in the Technology, Media and Telecom Sector", https://one.oecd.org/document/DAF/COMP(2019)5/en/pdf. [34]

OECD (2018), *Considering non-price effects in merger control: Background note by the Secretariat*, https://one.oecd.org/document/DAF/COMP(2018)2/en/pdf. [33]

OECD (2018), *Personalised Pricing in the Digital Era: Background note by the Secretariat*, https://one.oecd.org/document/DAF/COMP(2018)13/en/pdf. [31]

OECD (2017), *Algorithms and Collusion: Competition Policy in the Digital Age*, https://www.oecd.org/competition/algorithms-collusion-competition-policy-in-the-digital-age.htm. [1]

OECD (2016), *Big data: Bringing competition policy to the digital era: Background paper by the Secretariat*, https://one.oecd.org/document/DAF/COMP(2016)14/en/pdf. [5]

OECD (2015), *Serial offenders: Why some industries seem prone to endemic collusion - Background Paper by the Secretariat*, https://one.oecd.org/document/DAF/COMP/GF(2015)4/en/pdf. [12]

OECD (2013), *Roundtable on Ex Officio Cartel Investigations and the Use of Screens to Detect Cartels: Background note by the Secretariat*, https://one.oecd.org/document/DAF/COMP(2013)14/en/pdf. [41]

OECD (2001), *Policy Brief: Using Leniency to Fight Hard Core Cartels*, http://www.oecd.org/daf/competition/1890449.pdf. [40]

Petit, N. (2017), *Antitrust and Artificial Intelligence: A Research Agenda*, https://orbi.uliege.be/bitstream/2268/235346/1/Artificial%20Intelligence%20Juin%202017.pdf. [19]

US Department of Justice (2015), *Press Release: Former E-Commerce Executive Charged with Price Fixing in the Antitrust Division's First Online Marketplace Prosecution*, http://www.justice.gov/atr/public/press_releases/2015/313011.docx. [14]

Vestager, M. (2017), *Speech at Bundeskartellamt 18th Conference on Competition - Algorithms and competition*, https://wayback.archive-it.org/12090/20191130155750/https://ec.europa.eu/commission/commissioners/2014-2019/vestager/announcements/bundeskartellamt-18th-conference-competition-berlin-16-march-2017_en. [39]

Notes

[1] Gains enjoyed by consumers of a product when more consumers use that product (OECD, 2019, p. 6[47]).

[2] Predatory pricing refers to a strategy by a firm to cut prices in order to push competitors out of the market and then, with the market power obtained thanks to barriers to entry that protect the firm's position after the exit of competitors, raise prices afterward.

[3] Margin squeeze strategies arise when a firm reduces its rival's margins, specifically when it has market power either upstream (i.e. over an input) and competes with rivals downstream, or when it has market power downstream (e.g. over retail distribution) and competes with rivals upstream.

[4] The proposed EU Digital Markets Act package imposes specific rules on digital gatekeepers: https://ec.europa.eu/info/strategy/priorities-2019-2024/europe-fit-digital-age/digital-markets-act-ensuring-fair-and-open-digital-markets_en. In the UK, a Digital Markets Unit will enforce a code of conduct applicable to dominant digital firms: https://www.gov.uk/government/news/new-competition-regime-for-tech-giants-to-give-consumers-more-choice-and-control-over-their-data-and-ensure-businesses-are-fairly-treated.

[5] This is less of an issue with respect to abuses of dominance where competitor and consumer complaints help with detection.

[6] See, for instance, the OECD Workshop on cartel screening in the digital era, https://www.oecd.org/competition/workshop-on-cartel-screening-in-the-digital-era.htm.

[7] Find additional resources at: https://www.oecd.org/daf/competition/market-studies-and-competition.htm

[8] Find additional resources at: http://www.oecd.org/daf/competition/data-portability-interoperability-and-competition.htm.

[9] See, for instance, proposals by the European Union) and Singapore regarding WTO Disciplines and Commitments Relating to Electronic Commerce (https://docs.wto.org/dol2fe/Pages/FE_Search/FE_S_S009-DP.aspx?language=E&CatalogueIdList=253794,253801,253802,253751,253696,253697,253698,253699,253560,252791&CurrentCatalogueIdIndex=6&FullTextHash=&HasEnglishRecord=True&HasFrenchRecord=True&HasSpanishRecord=True and https://docs.wto.org/dol2fe/Pages/FE_Search/FE_S_S009-DP.aspx?language=E&CatalogueIdList=253794, respectively).

[10] See, for instance, reports commissioned by the European Commission (Crémer, de Montjoye and Schweitzer, 2019[27]) and UK Government (Digital Competition Expert Panel, 2019[48]).

[11] See, for instance, studies undertaken by the Australian (Australian Competition & Consumer Commission, 2019[51]), French and German (Autorité de la concurrence and Bundeskartellamt, 2016[49]), and UK (Competition and Markets Authority, 2020[50]) competition authorities.

[12] (Majority Staff, Subcommittee on Antitrust, Commercial and Administrative Law, 2020[28])

[13] The Digital Markets Act package, which imposes specific rules on digital gatekeepers: https://ec.europa.eu/info/strategy/priorities-2019-2024/europe-fit-digital-age/digital-markets-act-ensuring-fair-and-open-digital-markets_en

[14] Including the establishment of a Digital Markets Unit to enforce a code of conduct applicable to dominant digital firms: https://www.gov.uk/government/news/new-competition-regime-for-tech-giants-to-give-consumers-more-choice-and-control-over-their-data-and-ensure-businesses-are-fairly-treated.

5 The use of SupTech to enhance market supervision and integrity

Digital technologies and data – including Artificial Intelligence (AI) -- hold the potential to automate and thus improve the efficiency and effectiveness of regulatory, supervisory and enforcement activities. These functions have become increasingly complex, given the substantial increase of data of regulatory relevance to be processed in recent years, along with the growth of digital market forces posing new challenges. Market regulators and public enforcement authorities have turned to supervisory technology (SupTech) tools and solutions as a means to improve their surveillance, analytical and enforcement capabilities, which can in turn have important benefits for financial stability, market integrity and consumer welfare. This chapter takes stock of the most common uses of SupTech by regulatory, supervisory and enforcement authorities to date, identifies its associated benefits, risks and challenges, and outlines considerations for devising adequate SupTech strategies.

5.1. Introduction

Digital technologies and data are transforming the ways in which people, firms, and governments live, interact, work and produce at an accelerating rate (OECD, 2019[1]). This chapter considers the implications of this transformation for the supervisory and enforcement practices of market regulators and public enforcement authorities, which can be rendered more efficient through the use of supervisory technology (SupTech), including a growing potential for the use of AI.

SupTech usually refers to the use of digital tools and solutions – including hardware and software – by public sector regulators and supervisors to carry out their responsibilities (FSB, 2017[2]; BCBS, 2018[3]). While some variations exist[1] as to what falls under the umbrella of SupTech, the term has mainly been used to refer to supervisory practices involving financial institutions and securities markets (World Bank, 2018[4]; di Castri et al., 2019[5]). However, recognising the potential of digital technologies and data to automate and thus improve the efficiency and effectiveness of supervisory and enforcement processes, this chapter considers the relevance of SupTech applications and concepts for a wider range of institutions with regulatory and enforcement responsibilities for private sector conduct – including not only securities and financial regulators, but also competition authorities and anti-corruption authorities – whose functions entail protecting investors and consumers, ensuring that markets are fair, efficient and transparent, and reducing systemic risk. By improving surveillance, analytical and enforcement capabilities of authorities, SupTech can have important benefits for financial stability, market integrity and consumer welfare (FSB, 2020[6]).

Beyond enhancing the overall capacity and efficiency of supervisory oversight at a general level, SupTech applications may be particularly relevant to better detect insider trading, market manipulation and misconduct, as well as to better determine compliance with and enforce regulatory requirements that are principle-based or comprise judgment-based rules, such as corporate disclosure requirements. In particular, the increased availability of data on the outcomes arising from different policy interventions that were previously imperfectly observable – or only observable at significant costs – enables improved monitoring and supervision, and more effective enforcement of policies (OECD, 2019[7]).

By extension, SupTech solutions also have the potential to alleviate the regulatory burden on regulated entities, which have themselves turned to regulatory technology (RegTech) tools to improve compliance outcomes against regulatory requirements and enhance risk management capabilities. Such solutions hold the potential to reduce costs related to regulatory reporting, data collection and risk management (ESMA, 2019[8]).

According to IBM estimates (2018[9]), poor data quality costs the United States economy around USD 3.1 trillion a year, and one in three US business leaders do not trust the information they use to make decisions. Research also suggests that while financial authorities have access to a growing wealth of data to guide their decisions and actions, they tend to lack the infrastructure or skills to make use of this data, with increasing amounts of data often simply translating into more manual data processing and leading to "analysis paralysis" down the line (R^2A, 2019[10]). As data continues to increase in volume, velocity, variety and complexity, it is essential that both regulators and market participants develop systems to appropriately process, monitor and analyse datasets of regulatory relevance.

This chapter takes stock of the most common uses of SupTech by supervisory and enforcement authorities to date, identifies the main benefits, risks and challenges associated with its adoption, and outlines considerations for devising adequate SupTech strategies. It draws upon insights from reports prepared by international bodies[2] and other surveys, reviews of cases and research[3] which appear to reflect an emerging consensus around some of the benefits and challenges related to the application of Suptech for market supervision. As part of the broader SupTech framework, the use of AI and its further potential is also addressed, illustrating both SupTech and AI use for market oversight, with a particular focus on the review of cases related to the enforcement of securities, competition and anti-bribery and corruption laws and regulations.

5.2. Drivers and typology of SupTech developments

Demand and supply drivers have simultaneously spurred the development and application of SupTech tools and methods by supervisory and enforcement authorities across policy areas (ESMA, 2019[8]; FSB, 2020[6]). While supply drivers permeate all three policy areas considered in this chapter, and include the availability of new analytical methods and tools at lower costs that allow large datasets to be collected, stored and analysed more efficiently, demand drivers are specific to each policy area and context. However, all converge on the need for authorities to adopt tools to process the increasing volume and availability of data being produced with respect to both traditional and digital markets.

In particular, financial and securities regulators have turned to digital tools to enhance their supervisory capability and efficiency in the aftermath of the 2008 global financial crisis, which led to an increasing complexity and volume of regulations, in turn leading to a substantial increase in regulatory data to process (FSB, 2020[6]). Competition agencies face similar challenges, with firms using digital technologies to engage in anticompetitive conduct (as discussed in Chapter 4), requiring consideration of a growing volume and complexity of data on market conduct. Recognising that the right infrastructure and expertise are needed to enforce competition laws in digital markets– especially when faced with well-resourced merging parties and defendants, competition authorities have recognised the importance of building up their capabilities.

Public enforcement authorities involved in the fight against corruption and foreign bribery have similar but also specific drivers to adopt SupTech tools. For instance, as non-trial resolutions in foreign bribery cases involving companies are becoming increasingly available in several jurisdictions with many more considering their introduction, self-reporting and cooperation with authorities is encouraged[4] (OECD, 2019[11]). As these types of multi-jurisdictional cases involve large-scale investigations, companies are increasingly deploying AI tools in their cooperation efforts with authorities[5]. Therefore, authorities need to be able to understand how AI tools operate, how the information that is being provided to them through this process is selected and, most importantly, be able to analyse this amount of data in order to effectively exercise their enforcement functions.

Overall, as the volume and frequency of both structured and unstructured data being produced increases substantially, so does the need for architectures or systems that are able to collect, store, analyse and visualise these new forms of data[6]. For instance, in addition to regulatory returns from regulated entities, authorities leverage open source information (e.g. social media posts) to enhance their insights. According to a recent survey undertaken by the FSB (2020[6]), while regulatory, statistical, and market structured data make up the majority of data types collected from reporting institutions (respectively 45%, 22% and 12%), unstructured data amount to around one-fifth of the data collected by authorities (14% of regulatory unstructured data, 4% of statistical unstructured data, and 3% of market unstructured data). While unstructured data may offer useful insights, it is often collected in a format that makes it difficult to process and analyse.

The greater availability of "big data" itself stems from the increasing volume, frequency and granularity of reporting requirements, combined with the growth of the digital economy. Characterised by the "4 Vs" (volume, variety, velocity, validity), big data can pose data governance challenges for authorities, which have turned to technologies enabling sophisticated data processing techniques and generating advanced analytics. Despite the wide range of supervisory technologies available, their distinct features make their respective applications most relevant in specific areas of the data lifecycle. For instance, machine learning (ML) and natural language processing (NLP) are mostly applied by authorities for data analysis, processing and validation, while cloud computing is most often used for data storage, and blockchain is considered to offer potential for data collection (FSB, 2020[6]).

SupTech applications evolve along with technological innovations. To date, SupTech initiatives may – allowing for a certain degree of simplification – be classified as belonging to four successive technological layers or "generations", which respectively generate descriptive, diagnostic, predictive and prescriptive analytics (

Figure 5.1) (di Castri et al., 2019[5]). While the first generation covers primarily manual data management workflows, the second involves the digitisation[7] of certain paper-based processes in the data pipeline. These early generations of data architecture support mostly *descriptive* and *diagnostic* analytics (i.e. describing what happened and diagnosing why it happened). In a continuum, the third generation covers big data architecture, and the fourth involves AI as its main attribute – both enabling *predictive* and *prescriptive* analytics, in addition to enhanced descriptive and diagnostic analytics (i.e. predicting what will happen and prescribing anticipatory action).

As authorities' use of predictive and prescriptive analytics have emerged only recently, they are still at the experimental or development stages, but are gaining momentum. By fully automating data processing and optimising data storage and computation through the use of big data architectures involving tools such as application programming interfaces (APIs) and robotic process automation (RPA), big data architectures[8] can process larger datasets with greater computing power – in turn generating advanced insights such as predictive analytics. As AI-enabled solutions require large volumes of data and significant computing power in order to generate valid and actionable results, they are usually built upon pre-existing big data architectures. This fourth generation is characterised by machine-driven data management and analysis – which may involve natural language processing and machine learning to collect unstructured and disparate data, as well as recommendation engines suggesting courses of action. Chatbots may also be leveraged to perform tasks such as responding to and resolving complaints (di Castri et al., 2019[5]).

Figure 5.1. The four generations of SupTech

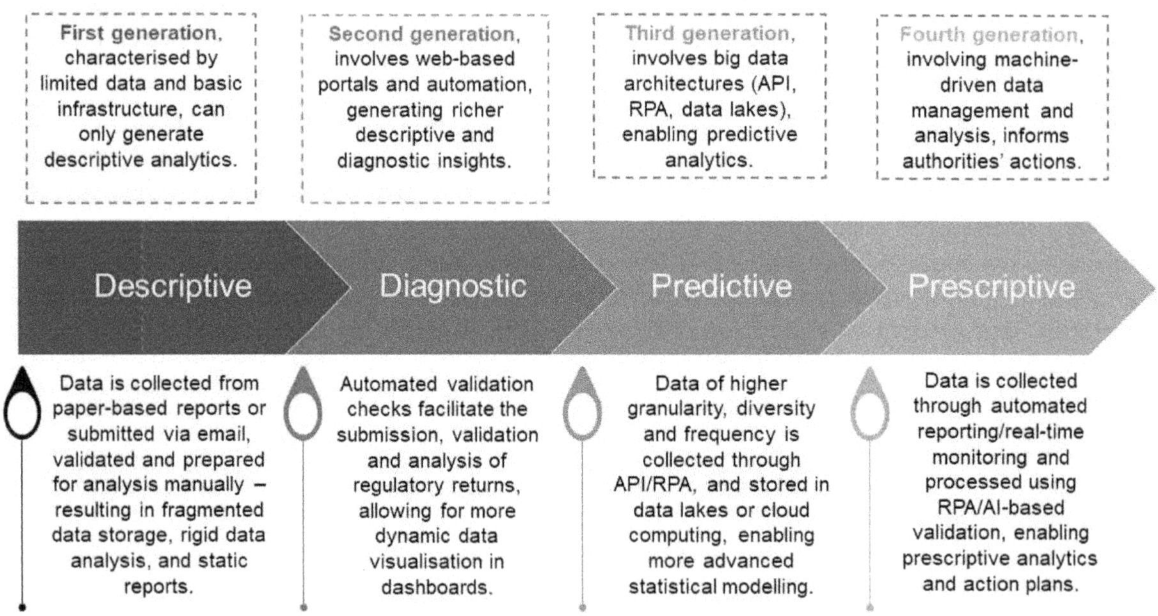

Source: Authors, adapted from (di Castri et al., 2019[5]).

According to a recent survey from the Financial Stability Board (FSB) undertaken among FSB members (2020[6]), the first and second generations of SupTech initiatives encompass the majority of technologies used by supervisory authorities, with 49% of surveyed authorities using data analysis functions for descriptive outputs and 32% for diagnostic outputs. Only a minority of respondents report using technologies comprised in the third predictive category (11%), and the fourth prescriptive category (8%). Echoing these findings, a recent report from FinCoNet (2020[12]) based on survey responses from 21 market conduct and financial consumer protection authorities similarly demonstrates that while some SupTech tools currently deployed in this arena are used to make predictions, the majority are designed to collect or analyse data or automate workflows.

While third-generation data collection solutions and fourth-generation data analytics potentially yield the most value for authorities by enabling forward-looking supervision[9] and greater storage and mobility capacity, technologies comprised within earlier SupTech generations can still generate sufficient information and substantial efficiency gains to be beneficial as well – especially with regards to enforcement processes[10] (di Castri et al., 2019[5]; Dias and Staschen, 2017[13]).

5.3. The benefits of SupTech

As regulatory, supervisory and enforcement authorities all rely on data, internal procedures and working tools, as well as human and other resources, they all face common challenges – albeit to varying degrees – related to low data quality and time-consuming manual procedures (Dias and Staschen, 2017[13]). SupTech applications can help authorities address these challenges by enhancing their capability, efficiency and effectiveness in terms of data collection and analysis – in particular by enabling the automation of routine tasks, the development of new analytical techniques, and the provision of better insights. By using tools to analyse increasing volumes of both structured and unstructured data of supervisory and enforcement relevance, authorities can shift their focus away from labour-intensive tasks to activities requiring human judgement and expertise, allowing them to better allocate human resources and reduce costs over time. SupTech applications can be developed in-house, by external vendors, or a combination of both.

Overall, SupTech tools in the areas of corporate governance, competition and anti-corruption are most commonly applied by supervisory and enforcement authorities to i) enhance their detection capabilities, and ii) increase the efficiency of enforcement actions. While these two purposes are not mutually exclusive and should be envisaged as intertwined, the *first* focuses on adoption of tools by authorities that enable the detection of new forms of market manipulation and anti-competitive conduct that analog tools cannot detect, while the *second* focuses on efficiency gains enabled by digital technologies in pre-existing enforcement processes. SupTech tools can also help authorities improve their data collection and management capabilities, which can in turn improve data quality – itself a pre-requisite for enhanced data analysis.

5.3.1. Improving detection capabilities

Evidence suggests that securities regulators, competition authorities and law enforcement agencies involved in combatting corruption are increasingly using SupTech tools to respectively better detect i) insider trading and other types of misconduct (such as money laundering, terrorist financing, mis-selling and fraud), ii) anti-competitive behaviour, and iii) foreign bribery and corruption allegations. SupTech applications – including AI tools – are particularly relevant for these purposes, as conduct supervision relies on the analysis of large amounts of granular, time-sensitive and unstructured data from disparate sources. In addition, as digital technologies enable new forms of money laundering, terrorist financing, mis-selling, fraud and anti-competitive behaviour to arise, new tools are required to detect and tackle them.

Use cases by financial and securities regulators: better detecting market manipulation and insider trading

According to a recent FSB survey (2020[6]), SupTech applications have gained most momentum in recent years for misconduct analysis, with the largest increase in the number of reported use cases by authorities since 2016. Evidence suggests that authorities use advanced analytics such as machine learning, natural language processing, text mining and network analysis to enhance their capacities – especially with regards to detecting networks of related transactions, identifying anomalies and unusual behaviours, and drawing insights from extensive amounts of structured and unstructured data (Coelho, De Simoni and Prenio, 2019[14]).

For example, Mexico's National Banking and Securities Commission (CNBV) has developed a prototype for an NLP application to detect what a suspicious Anti-Money Laundering/Combatting the Finance of Terrorism network is 'talking about', thus facilitating the detection of unusual transactions, relationships, and networks events to identify potential money laundering issues that cannot be identified by people. The rationale for developing such a prototype is the rise of digital financial products and services posing new challenges for Mexico's financial authorities, which entails that traditional methods and models of capturing and analysing regulatory data are ill-suited to cope with the surfeit of data being generated by new platforms, products, and customers (CNBV/R2A, 2018[15]).

Central Bank of Brazil (BCB) also launched a SupTech - Natural Language Processing Applications for Supervision project (SupTech-NLP) in 2020, with the aim to incorporate into supervision processes AI applications for document processing based on NLP techniques. Within the Suptech-NLP, BCB's conduct supervision department developed a prototype for a robot that downloads data from financial consumer complaints' websites and categorizes them through machine learning. Access to official consumer complaints' databases is currently being discussed with consumer protection authorities from the Ministry of Justice.

Authorities can also leverage big data architectures to perform real-time market surveillance. Securities regulators have started to leverage these technologies to transform large datasets into usable patterns for detecting potential insider trading and market manipulation. However, designing and implementing tools focused on certain aspects of market surveillance can be complex due to the large volume and variety of data required (i.e. regulatory and market data and intelligence). As new technologies become available, they may facilitate their development and deployment (FSB, 2020[6]). Nevertheless, some authorities have already successfully deployed these solutions.

For instance, the Australian Securities and Investments Commission (ASIC) developed a Market Analysis and Intelligence (MAI) platform, which collects real-time data feeds from all Australian primary (ASX) and secondary (Chi-X) capital markets for equity and equity derivatives products and transactions (Box 5.1). Likewise, in the European Union (EU), the German Federal Financial Supervisory Authority (BaFin) is setting up an integrated automated alarm and market monitoring system (ALMA) for analysing potential market abuse cases, including insider trading and market manipulation (BaFin, 2017[16]). In North America, the Canadian Securities Administrators (CSA) is developing its Market Analysis Platform (MAP) to collect post-trade data from exchanges, alternative trading systems (ATSs) and dealers/brokers in order to facilitate enforcement investigation of potential insider trading and market abuse cases (CSA, 2018[17]).

Box 5.1. Market Analysis and Intelligence (MAI) platform by the Australian Securities and Investments Commission (ASIC)

The Australian Securities and Investments Commission (ASIC) has developed a Market Analysis and Intelligence (MAI) platform, which collects real-time data feeds from all Australian primary (ASX) and secondary (Chi-X) capital markets for equity and equity derivatives products and transactions. In particular, the MAI platform has a real-time alert monitor that detects and identifies abnormalities in order and trade messaged in traded securities. It also contains standard reports to allow analysts to drill down and analyse market data to identify trading accounts of interest that may be undertaking market misconduct such as insider trading and market manipulation. Overall, the standard dashboards within MAI include Real-Time Alert Monitor, Market Summary, Market Manipulation and Insider Trading Reports and the Market Replay, which allow for real-time or historical review of the market for a particular security. The MAI platform was preceded by the SMARTS market intelligence system.

ASIC has recently upgraded MAI from a non-cloud, Flex system to a cloud-based, HTML5 system, and has the latest version of its current vendor's platform which includes enhanced functionality to ingest, analyse and visualise data. ASIC intends to leverage the enhanced functionality of the upgraded SMARTS market intelligence system to increase its surveillance capabilities of the Fixed Income Clearing Corporation markets and further utilise information received from the Australian Tax Office. This work is being undertaken in-house and is experimental/in-development. This capability was developed on the upgraded MAI system's sandbox environment called Kx Analyst. Datasets that have beeningested include OTC Trade Repository Data, Bond Clearing information from Austraclear and Global Legal Entity Identifier data.

The Kx Analyst environment uses proprietary KDB+ technology and interfaces with various open source languages such as python and R, providing ASIC analysts with a single data science environment. ASIC currently receives trading account information and their related relationship information, including spousal and residential and business address information from the Australian Tax Office. From this information, ASIC has created a data set of an anonymised map of linked trading accounts. This data set will be ingested into Kx Analyst and will be linked to MAI trading data to create different analytics to improve ASIC's market surveillance capability of identifying market misconduct.

Source: ASIC.

Use cases by agencies involved in combatting corruption: better detecting criminal allegations and fraud

Law enforcement agencies become aware of corruption and foreign bribery allegations through many different sources – including through media articles, embassies, international cooperation, self-reporting, financial intelligence units (FIUs), tax authorities, and whistleblowers (OECD, 2017[18]). Some of these sources depend on the processing of large amounts of diverse sets of data to detect suspicious transactions or patterns that could lead to an investigation. Against this backdrop, survey results suggest that the use of AI tools by law enforcement agencies can stand as a catalyst to better identify such transactions and patterns, in turn leading to greater detection rates.

In particular, the use of AI tools appears to be most relevant for financial intelligence units (FIUs) to better detect criminal allegations. This is because anti-money laundering regulations generally require multiple reporting obligations from financial institutions and Designated Non-Financial Businesses and Professions (DNFBPs), and FIUs also usually use information from other sources to prepare financial intelligence reports. As such, many countries appear to have already adopted – or are aiming to adopt – AI tools to sort, connect, and prioritise data in suspicious transactions reports. For instance, the German FIU reports that one of the main benefits of using AI tools would be to facilitate the identification of potentially relevant suspicious transactions reports connected to serious crime without the need to exhaustively describe all characteristic attributes of various typologies in the form of mathematical rules. Instead, these rules would be automatically derived from labeled training data.

Governmental auditing authorities also appear to be using AI tools to detect irregularities in public procurement and to screen corruption reports. For instance, Brazil's Comptroller General reported the use of AI tools to sort and triage corruption reports from ombudsman platforms and to decide which cases merit further investigation (FARO System). Brazil and another member of the OECD Working Group on Bribery (WGB) also reported using AI tools to help raise red flags that allow authorities to intervene in tainted public procurement procedures before the awarding of the contract.

Use cases by competition authorities: better detecting cartels and other types of anti-competitive practices

While reactive methods of detecting anti-competitive conduct, such as leniency regimes and complaints, continue to be effective methods of detection, proactive detection tools are particularly important in the digital world, where business practices evolve quickly and firms use new technologies to implement anticompetitive conduct. Increasing data availability regarding traditional markets can also facilitate the use of these tools. Overall, predictive SupTech tools can be used by competition authorities to better detect atypical signs or suspicious behaviours in the market, and in turn help determine enforcement priorities and initiate in-depth investigations. Difficulties may arise, however, in ensuring that predictive models are applicable when working across different sectors and markets where the data and the related challenges are distinct.

Cartel screening

Market screens are economic tools that can assist competition authorities in their investigations. As described in Chapter 4, these can include structural screens, which may identify markets where authorities may wish to pay particular attention given certain characteristics that might make collusion more likely (including product homogeneity and oligopolistic market structures). Authorities are also exploring the use of behavioural screens by looking for patterns of unusual or unexplained behaviour, and identifying "structural breaks" in market data that could show the implementation of a cartel agreement or the adaptation of the cartel to market changes. The use of such screens is supported by the OECD 2019 Recommendation of the Council concerning Effective Action against Hard Core Cartels, which recommends the use of "pro-active cartel detection tools such as analysis of public procurement data, to trigger and support cartel investigations" in implementing an effective cartel detection system (OECD, 2019[19]). In the fight against collusion, digital cartel screening tools are becoming increasingly important, especially for behavioural screens, which tend to be data and resource intensive. Such screens have been most notably used to detect bid-rigging cartels, which represent a significant share of cartel enforcement in many jurisdictions.[11]

Screening methods can include statistical and econometric techniques, network analysis and machine learning methods – and as such can particularly benefit from advanced data analysis solutions.[12] Some of these techniques can be carried out supervised or unsupervised (OECD, 2020, p. 3[20]). For instance, the Spanish competition authority makes use of data mining techniques "such as applying statistical, econometric and machine learning to try to detect patterns of behaviour that evidence the existence of anticompetitive agreements". Where data are limited, techniques such as web scraping or text mining can locate data (OECD, 2020, pp. 2-3[20]).

Recognising the potential of digital screens in their enforcement activities, several competition agencies have invested significant resources in the development of market screening tools based on algorithms that help to identify possible signs of collusion, such as suspicious patterns or pricing. Some jurisdictions have developed specific screening programmes that use data from electronic government procurement databases to monitor bids and bidding patterns to identify collusive bidding. For example, the Brazilian competition agency has a data analytics and screening project (Project Cérebro), and the Korean Fair Trade Commission's (KFTC) has developed a Bid Rigging Indicator Analysis System (BRIAS), which provides for the automatic review of procurement data (Box 5.2).[13] Other jurisdictions such as Spain and Canada are currently developing similar screening tools (OECD, 2020, p. 6[21]).

Box 5.2. Examples of Digital Cartel Screens

Brazil's Cérebro (Brain) Project

Brazil's competition authority, the Administrative Council for Economic Defense (CADE) has developed a screening project called Cérebro (the "Brain"). Cérebro is a platform that allows the integration of large public procurement databases by applying data mining tools and economic filters capable of identifying and measuring the probability of cartels occurring in public bids.

Cerebro's data mining tools allow for the automation of the analyses formerly conducted by investigators and case handlers. The objective is both the identification of evidence of cartels in public bids, such as suspicious, implausible facts or behavioural patterns, and the provision of relevant information for the investigation of the cases. The economic filters in the platform are based on specialist literature and econometrics. They seek to provide generalised evidence of the existence of cartels based on data related to prices, costs, profit margins, market share, etc. Through the identification of firms' behaviour as described in academic articles, CADE derived mathematical models as statistical tests for general use in a kind of reverse engineering process.

Since 2014, CADE has initiated some investigations thanks to the Cérebro tool. The tool continues to evolve. The project team is exploring possibilities of using machine-learning algorithms to preselect digital evidence more likely to contain information relevant for the investigation (OECD, 2019[22]). Currently, CADE has three ongoing investigations based on findings obtained using the Cérebro platform, and is about to start formal proceedings supported by findings from its first investigation's use of screening techniques.

Korea's Bid Rigging Indicator Analysis System (BRIAS)

In 2006, the Korean Fair Trade Commission (KFTC) developed the Bid Rigging Indicator Analysis System ("BRIAS") to help detect bid rigging. BRIAS is an automatic quantitative analysis IT system that analyses large amounts of online public procurement data and, based on indicators incorporated in it, quantifies the likelihood of bid rigging.

BRIAS collects online public procurement data concerning large-scale contracts awarded by central and local administrations within 30 days of the contract award. Then, the system analyses the data and generates scores on the likelihood of bid rigging by assessing factors like tender method, number of bidders, number of successful bids, number of failed bids, bid prices above the estimated price, and price of winning bidder. Each of these factors is assigned a weighted value and all values are then added up. For instance, higher rates of successful bids and lower number of participating companies are indicative of a possibility of collusion. All bids are also screened according to search criteria like the name of the winner candidate, or bids with similar score.

Source: (OECD, 2020, p. 21[23])

Colombia's Sherlock Project

Colombia's competition authority, the Superintendence of Industry and Commerce (SIC), has launched a screening project (Project Sherlock) that seeks to support the SIC's investigators in the identification of signs or patterns that suggest potential anticompetitive behaviors in the data available from public procurement processes.

The first stage of the project consisted of developing a tool that could facilitate the access of investigators to public procurement data available online. The tool collects and organises public procurement data and provides simple descriptive analysis to the investigators in a user-friendly manner. In this first stage of the project, the investigators are still tasked with identifying suspicious, implausible facts or behavioural patterns based on the data presented by the tool. The second stage of the project involves the automation of the above-mentioned tasks in which the tools would automatically identify red flags in the procurement process, in addition to simple descriptive analysis of the data.

Source: SIC

Adapting techniques to investigate harm facilitated by algorithms

Some competition authorities have also adapted their techniques to investigate harm facilitated by algorithms. In a recent paper, the UK CMA outlines inter alia techniques that could be used without access to firms' data and those that could be used once an investigation has been launched or from available information disclosed as part of remedies[14]. Without access to firms' data and algorithms, the analysis authorities can conduct will depend on the level of transparency. Where an algorithm's outputs are transparent, such as when an algorithm sets the price offered to consumers on a website, techniques such as mystery shopping can be used to better understand the operation of the algorithm. Crawling and scraping can help increase transparency by extracting data and reverse engineering methods, including the use of APIs can help locate outputs in more complex cases. It is not always necessary to have access to the code to identify the harm. An authority could conduct an analysis where the input data used by the algorithm is available, or as mentioned above, where the algorithm's outputs are transparent. When competition authorities "have access to the code", the UK CMA describes three possible methods: dynamic analysis, static analysis and a manual code review. The first method involves "automated testing through execution of the code" and is considered to be the most effective (OECD, 2019, p. 40[22]).

Price monitoring tools

Digital tools can also be used to monitor firms' pricing strategies and to detect anticompetitive practices such as resale price maintenance (RPM). While algorithms can facilitate anticompetitive conduct, they can also be a powerful detection tool for competition authorities. For example, the UK CMA's DaTA unit has developed an in-house price-monitoring tool, which was used to make it easier for the case teams to detect resale price maintenance in the musical instruments sector (OECD, 2014[24]). These types of price monitoring tools can also be useful for investigation teams in determining whether the anticompetitive conduct is more widespread than the targets of the investigation. There are challenges however in using such tools to identify RPM from other normal market behaviour, as signals identified by price monitoring software are not necessarily linked to a RPM strategy (see Chapter 4). Colombia's SIC has also developed a price-monitoring tool under its project "Sabueso" that collects data on products sold on-line in order to help its investigators discover suspicious pricing behaviour in e-commerce. The tool relies on machine learning to identify the same product in different on-line stores sold under different names and descriptions (OECD, 2020[25]).

5.3.2. Improving efficiency in enforcement actions

AI tools can significantly increase efficiency in enforcement actions, as investigations and prosecutions demand extensive time and resources. In particular, authorities are often required to devote extensive human resources to cope with increasingly complex cases, often in an environment of scarce resources. As the average duration of a foreign bribery case is 7.3 years, the OECD Working Group on Bribery (OECD WGB) has recommended in 10 out of its 15 Phase 4 evaluation reports published so far[15] that its member countries increase the resources allocated to law enforcement agencies fighting foreign bribery (OECD, 2014[24]). Competition authorities face similar challenges, as their budgets have decreased in real terms by approximately 5% on average between 2015 and 2018 (OECD, 2019[22]). Likewise, securities regulators also have resource limitations that constrain their ability to supervise and enforce corporate governance standards, as many securities regulators are less well funded than banking regulators (OECD, 2014[24]).

Against this background, AI tools can be useful to review large-scale evidence by ensuring that submissions comply with format and structure requirements, and analysing evidence using machine learning techniques such as NLP. Overall, AI tools are particularly well suited to standardise procedures and repetitive tasks involving large amounts of data. In the case of competition authorities and given the tight timelines for investigations, it can however be difficult to design sophisticated applications that are tailored to individual cases.

Use cases by securities regulators: better determining compliance with disclosure requirements and guiding enforcement actions

As many authorities continue to rely on heavily manual processes, challenges remain as to how to make effective use of unstructured or qualitative data, such as information comprised within disclosure materials or annual reports. SupTech tools can be leveraged by authorities that must undertake complex, qualitative analyses to determine compliance with legislation or regulation that is often principle-based or comprises judgment-based rules (World Bank, 2018[4]). AI tools – including machine learning and natural language processing – are particularly relevant in that respect.

For instance, the Malaysian Securities Commission (SC Malaysia) uses artificial intelligence (AI) to monitor the adoption of corporate governance best practices and quality of disclosures by listed companies on the Malaysia Stock Exchange (Bursa Malaysia). Since 2017, listed companies are required to report on their adoption of the Malaysian Code on Corporate Governance using a prescribed template for corporate governance reports. This template is designed to facilitate data extraction, evaluation and analysis by the AI system, which considers *inter alia* the type of information disclosed, depth of explanation, and in relation to departures, the strength of alternative practices. The use of AI has enabled SC Malaysia to annually report data and observations in relation to the adoption of the Malaysian Code on Corporate Governance and the quality of disclosures, including year-on-year progress, in SC Malaysia's Corporate Governance Monitor report. The data also supports evidence-based regulatory measures to improve corporate governance practices or address areas of concern – including practices with low score for disclosure (SC Malaysia, 2020[26]).

AI tools can also be used to guide authorities' enforcement actions related to suspicious trading activities that may constitute market manipulation. For instance, the Monetary Authority of Singapore (MAS) has deployed an augmented intelligence system called "Apollo" that automates the computation of key metrics used in the analysis of suspicious trading activities, and assesses the likelihood that certain types of market manipulation have occurred. As a "Robo-Expert", it seeks to predict the likelihood of positive prosecution outcomes for new cases by understanding how experts analyse market misconduct cases. MAS built and trained Apollo using expert reports and the trading data from cases that they had successfully prosecuted in the past. Several benefits have resulted from its implementation. Automated trade analysis reduces the need for manual computation, helps to identify fraudulent transactions with higher market impact and provides greater insight into market trading behaviours. In particular, it allows for the testing of various case scenarios to fine-tune investigation strategies for individual cases, thus also helping with case prioritisation and guiding decisions on the appropriate courses of enforcement actions (MAS, 2019[27]).

Use cases by agencies involved in combatting corruption and foreign bribery: better resolving cases

The majority of the respondents to the OECD WGB survey mentioned efficiency as part of the benefits of using AI tools. Corruption and foreign bribery investigations often require the analysis of data from several sources, including companies' books and records, third-party sources and government authorities including tax and corporate registry information and financial intelligence, among others. AI tools can allow investigators of ongoing cases to timely and effectively detect patterns and extract better evidence from different sets of data, in turn increasing the efficiency of enforcement actions.

In particular, as the language in foreign bribery tends to be very obscure – including code words and colloquialisms to hide the discussions around the transactions – machine learning tools can be used to find more material that is relevant to investigations with those words, faster than traditional keywords. Image-based classification models can also allow authorities to derive pictures of documents and hand-written notes faster from seized devices. In addition, information retrieval and e-discovery algorithms such as email threading, near duplication and graphing technologies can also be used by authorities to better review and understand the evidence collected.

In practice, many law enforcement agencies appear to already be using advanced analytical tools – including AI tools – to solve corruption and foreign bribery cases. For instance, the Australian Federal Police reported the use of text-based AI tools to analyse data seized during an investigation and identify language potentially indicating bribery transactions (Box 5.3). In Lithuania, the Special Investigation Service has not yet adopted AI, but reports that it has used big data analytics to aggregate data from different public registries and information systems in order to reveal inconsistencies in public procurement relevant to an ongoing investigation. In Costa Rica, the Judicial Investigation Body reports that the use of AI tools to date has reduced the time of investigations and increased trustworthiness of the evidence obtained from data analysis.

The UK Serious Fraud Office was the first to use AI in a criminal case in the United Kingdom to assist the removal of legally professional privileged documents. In particular, scanning as many as 600,000 documents a day, AI reduced the pool of legally professional privileged material needing to be reviewed by independent counsel by 80%,. Beyond saving resources by reducing the timeline of the review process from two years to a few months, the use of AI also resulted in a more accurate and consistent review of the evidence.[16]

Box 5.3. Australian Federal Police's Use of AI tools to increase the efficiency in enforcement actions

Operation T

In 2012, Operation T was initially conducted using a traditional investigative methodology and was later benchmarked using an AI classifier. The data received was approximately 10 TB and the use of keywords originally found 900 000 documents which would have taken approximately 687 working days for one reviewer to analyse, while also potentially missing a significant amount of the key language being used. It took investigators several years to understand the terminology being used for the key persons of interest, the bribe and how it transpired, as obscure terminology was used. After using an interactive review process with AI – including seven rounds of document review equalling approximately 5600 documents over the span of two weeks – investigators started to see patterns in both the language and the communications of material found that have allowed investigators to piece together the transaction much faster.

Source: Australian Federal Police.

Use cases by competition authorities: facilitating evidence review in cartel investigations and enhancing the monitoring of remedies

As competition authorities have access to a greater volume of data in digital form – which is also harder to destroy – investigations that use digital search are more likely to discover relevant evidence (OECD,

2018[28]). While competition authorities are increasingly using advanced digital tools and techniques in collecting, preserving and analysing digital evidence, the use of digital forensics in cartel investigations in particular allows competition authorities to collect and analyse data in a more efficient way.

Given the large amounts of data that can result from digital searches, the use of forensic search software enables better search strategies through sophisticated search methods. In particular, forensic search software such as *EnCase* and *Nuix* can enable more sophisticated keyword searching, for example, by identifying misspelled versions of keywords and producing results based on self-learning algorithms. In addition to basic keyword searches, these types of software also allow "concept" searching, which can make it easier for the authorities to find relevant evidence (OECD, 2020, p. 9[23]). Spain has noted some of the advantages of software platforms, such as Nuix, explaining that it "enables analysis of multiple databases and offers a high-speed indexing engine. This software allows the use of various clustering algorithms and other machine learning techniques. Additionally, it offers the option of social network analysis, which can improve information filtering" (OECD, 2020, p. 3[21]).

In addition to the collection of files and documents, forensic examination of how the device in question has been used is also important (OECD, 2018[28]). For example, agencies in the United States have noted that metadata can reveal "when files have been accessed and modified, internet search history, attachment of USB storage devices, and other traces of information that indicate how an individual used the device" (OECD, 2020, p. 7[21]).Such forensic information "be useful to show knowledge or intent, to corroborate witness statements, and to counteract defendants' claims that they had no knowledge or control over particular documents or shared network spaces" (OECD, 2020, p. 7[21]). Additionally, authorities can obtain necessary information to carry out additional tasks, for example to decrypt encrypted data.

Alongside cartel investigations, competition authorities must undertake large-scale evidence review in other areas. The UK CMA has built its own data science platform, which it uses in its various functions, to sort and analyse large amounts of data. The tool applies natural language processing techniques, and has been used in both merger review[17], and market studies (OECD, 2019[22]).[18] For example, the tool was used by the UK CMA to analyse 3-4 billion search events seen by Google and Bing (over a one-week sample period) for the purposes of its market study on *Online platforms and digital advertising* (OECD, 2019, p. 93[22]).

Overall, competition authorities have noted the efficiency of these new digitised procedures. They allow authorities to search through high volumes of data in a swift manner and with a high degree of accuracy. The Portuguese Competition Authority (Autoridade da Concorrência), for example, compared its old (analog) and new (digitised) models in cartel investigations, noting that in 2013, under the old model, it seized 5 million documents and used 2 000 documents to prove infringements, while in 2017, under the new model, it seized 40 000 relevant documents and recorded a low percentage of irrelevant data. Under the old model, the authority noted a "long and very difficult data review process" while under the new model, thanks to a preliminary onsite assessment, the data review was much quicker (4 000 documents per week thanks to the use of forensic software). Consequently, in 2017, the statement of objections was issued within 12 months, while in 2013, it took around three years (Autoridade da Concorrência, 2018[20]).

AI also offers potential to automate competition authorities' monitoring of remedies, although these efforts are nascent. For instance, following the UK CMA's market investigation into the payday lending market, the UK CMA published an order to address the identified market features that may prevent, restrict or distort competition (UK CMA, 2015[30]). The order set out publication requirements on those supplying payday loans (i.e. information to be supplied, timeframe for publication, duty to display a hyperlink to a UK FCA-authorised payday loan price comparison website) (UK CMA, 2015, pp. 7-11[30]). The UK CMA has been able to automate some of its monitoring, using its in-house tool to monitor parties' websites and determine compliance with some remedies, such as presentation of information requirements.

5.3.3. Improving data collection

Use cases by financial and securities regulators: improving regulatory reporting

SupTech tools are mainly used by financial and securities regutors to improve regulatory reporting. As regulatory reporting has become increasingly complex, authorities face challenges related to collecting delayed and poor quality reporting data – which can in turn impact their ability to supervise (FCA, 2020[31]; European Commission, 2020[32]; European Commission, 2018[33]). Some reports suggest that regulatory reporting has also become increasingly time-consuming and expensive for regulated entities. In a 2018 report, the European Commission estimated most firms' regulatory reporting costs at around 1% of total operating costs.[19] However, industry feedback suggests that the total burden on regulated entities is likely even higher, as the cost of building or amending reports tends to be higher than ongoing running costs (European Commission, 2018[33]).

In the aim of improving data collection, some financial authorities have piloted the adoption of both "push" and "pull" technologies in recent years. While the former refers to pre-defined data being delivered from the regulated entity to the regulator, the latter enables the authority to draw data from the regulated entity as required. Some authorities have also developed APIs to allow regulated entities to submit data – thus lowering reporting costs and enabling better communication between both parties (FSB, 2020[6]).

Taking these efforts one step further, some authorities have begun exploring how to translate rules into a machine-readable format, in order to automate regulatory reporting and further facilitate compliance (World Bank, 2018[4]; Dias and Staschen, 2017[13]; European Commission, 2020[32]). This entails digitising reporting instructions and converting them into code to make them machine executable[20] (FCA, 2020[31]; Mohun and Roberts, 2020[34]; European Commission, 2020[32]). However, it is worth noting that while digitising regulatory reporting rules might entail additional benefits such as regulatory simplification, it is currently being hindered by the absence of common standards (FSB, 2020[6]; European Commission, 2020[32]). [21] To address this challenge, the European Commission will develop a strategy on supervisory data in 2021, to help ensure that "(i) supervisory reporting requirements (including definitions, formats, and processes) are unambiguous, aligned, harmonised and suitable for automated reporting, (ii) full use is made of available international standards and identifiers including the Legal Entity Identifier, and (iii) supervisory data is reported in machine-readable electronic formats and is easy to combine and process" (European Commission, 2020[32]).

Use cases by competition and anti-corruption authorities: improving the collection of evidence during unannounced inspections

Law enforcement authorities usually have powers to conduct unannounced inspections or "dawn raids" at business and private premises in order to access and obtain documents and information necessary, for example with respect to proving cartel conduct or in relation to corruption or foreign bribery investigations (OECD, 2019[19]). During dawn raids, digital evidence is collected either through the physical seizure of data carriers (i.e. computers, smartphones, USBs) or by searching the data carriers and servers on site. During an onsite inspection, a competition authority may copy or make forensic images of the digital data. The techniques used depends on the availability and form of data. Forensic IT tools may be used to collect digital evidence, and some competition authorities use live forensics to capture data, which cannot be obtained once the device is turned off (OECD, 2020, p. 6[23]). The ability to analyse data offsite has become more important during the COVID-19 pandemic.

5.3.4. Improving data management

The three main tasks within data management include validation, consolidation and visualisation – each referring to specific target points in the data management cycle. Validation refers to the quality control checks of completeness, correctness and consistency of data against reporting rules, whereas consolidation relates to the aggregation of data from multiple sources and in varying formats, and visualisation involves the presentation of information in a legible manner (di Castri et al., 2019[5]). A wide range of SupTech tools can be leveraged to improve data management – and in particular cloud computing, which allows for greater and more flexible storage, mobility capacity and computing power (Broeders and Prenio, 2018[35]).

For instance, Mexico's CNBV is currently implementing the second phase of a project involving cloud computing to process large amounts of anti-money laundering (AML) compliance data, thus allowing for a greater and more flexible storage, mobility capacity and computing power to support AML supervision of all supervised financial institutions. The platform will also enable the development of both basic and advanced, prospective analytics to strengthen monitoring activities and better identify atypical patterns.

5.4. Challenges and risks of SupTech

Adopting SupTech solutions also comes with challenges and risks, including those that commonly arise upon large technology platform and software transitions, as well as risks that are transversal in nature due to the digital environment itself. The main issues and constraints principally revolve around data quality, resourcing, and skills. Other practical and legal challenges can also arise upon the integration of SupTech tools into legacy systems. Case studies reviewed for this chapter also identified insufficient communication across all stakeholders involved as a potential hindrance to the effective implementation of SupTech solutions. Technical issues and risks stemming from the digital nature of SupTech solutions also need to be accounted for, including risks related to: cyber and data security; third party dependencies; data localisation (potentially resulting in cross-border issues), as well as poor-quality algorithms or data, and opacity in the design and outputs of SupTech tools (i.e. a "black box issue" potentially entailing reputational risks).

While most of these challenges and risks arise across the three policy areas considered, some are also specific to certain authorities, their particular functions and remit.

5.4.1. Data quality, standardisation and completeness

SupTech applications rely on machine-readable data – i.e. in a format that can be processed by computer programmes. As such, quality, standardisation and completeness of data are key requirements and can pose major challenges, especially upon leveraging unstructured data collected from non-traditional sources of information (e.g. open source or social media). For instance, SC Malaysia mentions that getting the buy-in from listed companies to disclose the information and data in a structured manner was a key enabler to using AI, which required effort by listed companies to change their reporting format.

Providing sufficient amounts of quality data to build machine learning applications can also be an issue. For instance, in relation to its Project Apollo, Singapore's MAS reported the scarcity of training data – particularly expert reports associated with prosecution outcomes – as a main challenge. Having a sufficient volume of such data is a key requirement to continually improve the accuracy and robustness of the algorithms, and to validate Apollo's models and methodologies in order for its results to be admissible for use in a court of law.

Likewise, several law enforcement agencies involved in combatting corruption also identify data quality and standardisation as primary challenges for the effective use of AI, in particular for the detection and enforcement of corruption and foreign bribery offences. As such, it is important to ensure that information provided by companies to law enforcement authorities (either voluntarily through self-reporting and cooperation or under some form of compulsion) is in a format that authorities' systems can read. Standardisation is often obtained through protocols or guidance from the authorities themselves or by using industry standard protocols.

5.4.2. Legal and procedural challenges

The use of SupTech tools and AI have raised a range of legal and procedural challenges for supervisory and law enforcement authorities, which in some cases may require amendments to existing legal frameworks to facilitate their more effective use for enforcement purposes. For example, Switzerland noted that their legal framework does not currently allow for the use of AI technology in a generalised manner. However, they are undertaking pilot projects using anonymised data to assess the added value of this technology and are at a preliminary stage of reviewing the legal basis for its use.

Another challenge could be the acceptance by the courts of the use of AI technology, particularly in criminal cases. In civil cases, the use of AI (predictive coding) has already been accepted by courts in various countries as a legitimate means for document discovery in court proceedings but the position is less clear for contested criminal cases, where defendants may wish to challenge the use of the technology, its accuracy and reliability.

Due process rights of companies as a legal challenge

The use of digital technologies for enforcement purposes has led to the identification of several legal challenges across jurisdictions, including the respect of due process rights of the companies that are subject to the authorities' investigations (OECD, 2019[22]). While digital technologies allow authorities to collect a large amount of data from businesses during dawn raids – including any information that is stored in digital forms – the respect of due process rights of the investigated companies requires that such broad powers of investigation aided by digital technologies be exercised within the limit of proportionality. As such, the scope of data collected from businesses needs to be proportionate to the purposes of the authorities' investigations. For example, while digital technologies allow seizing entire hard-drives or servers for examination of the documents contained therein, there is a legal risk that this goes beyond the scope of the investigation, since the seized data may include personal information or information that is irrelevant to the investigation. When such a risk materialises, it could significantly delay the investigation and negatively affect the procedural efficiency of enforcement authorities.

A related challenge in criminal cases involves obligations in some OECD countries to make available all relevant information to defendants, particularly that which is exculpatory in nature. Where evidence has been located using AI across large data sets, it could be imperative for defendants to have access to the same data sets and possibly the AI technology itself, particularly where they could not afford this themselves (equality of arms issue). This situation may be less acute for large companies that may well already have lawyers equipped with this technology. Nevertheless, these due process issues raise challenges in ensuring that digital technologies (e.g. search software and algorithms) are used within the limits prescribed by the relevant legal frameworks.

Data location as a legal challlenge

Data location stands as an additional legal challenge for supervisory, competition and law enforcement authorities using digital technologies, and relying on digital evidence, to carry out their investigation. While in certain circumstances, the storage space containing the information relevant to the investigation could be located in another jurisdiction, in such cases, enforcement authorities may find themselves unable to extend their investigative powers to the data located abroad.

In the field of competition law enforcement, the International Competition Network has identified two types of approaches with differing implications (OECD, 2019[22]). The first one, called the "access approach", allows for greater enforcement capabilities regardless of location by permitting the competition authority to search and seize any piece of information which is accessible and can be used or controlled from the premises of the investigated company. Under this approach, the location of the storage is irrelevant. Under the second approach, called the "location approach", if the storage of the data is not at the premises of the investigated company, it would be impossible to have access to that data, unless their location is covered by the authority's order or the judge warrant.

Box 5.4. Access to digital evidence located outside the United States

In the United States, Title II of the Electronic Communications Privacy Act ("ECPA") governs how and when any U.S. law enforcement agency can obtain access to stored digital communications, such as email or phone records, during the course of a criminal investigation.

A recent amendment to ECPA requires providers operating within the U.S. to produce evidence regardless of whether the company stores the evidence in the U.S. This amendment was, in part, a result of a case involving Microsoft's refusal to comply with a search warrant because the data was stored on an overseas server.

In this case, Microsoft challenged a search warrant issued under ECPA by a U.S. magistrate judge. While being a U.S.-based company, Microsoft contended the emails were stored on a server in Ireland, and thus, not subject to the jurisdiction of U.S. courts. The challenge was ultimately appealed to the Supreme Court, but the case was vacated when the above-mentioned amendment was enacted by the U.S. Congress.

Source: (OECD, 2019[22]).

In some jurisdictions, the access approach has been recognised by the law. For example, the United States recently amended Title II of the Electronic Privacy Communications Act to allow law enforcement agencies to access information for enforcement purposes regardless of the location where the data is stored (Box 5.4). In the case of the EU, Article 6(1)(b) of the Directive 2019/1 empowers the competition authorities of the EU Member States to be more effective enforcers provides for the power "*to examine the books and other records related to the business irrespective of the medium on which they are stored, and to have the right to access any information which is accessible to the entity subject to the inspection*". In other jurisdictions, it may still be controversial whether the access approach is followed.[22]

5.4.3. Algorithmic models and human oversight

In relation to its NLP application, Mexico's CNBV reported that having in place good communication channels between data scientists, NLP algorithms analysts and business units to combine their expertise and obtain better recommendations and continuous improvement of the NLP algorithms was a major challenge. This is linked to wider risks with regards to algorithms and their use by authorities. While algorithms can fail by detecting false positives/negatives rather than meaningful signals, there is also a risk of incorporating human biases in algorithmic models, as well as the risk of not being able to explain the outcomes of machine learning (i.e. a black-box issue that may impede accountability) – all of which are exacerbated when authorities lack adequate skills and expertise. On the other hand, supervisors must also deal with the countervailing concern that if they are too transparent about the models used, regulated entities may be able to more easily game the system to avoid detection (Dias and Staschen, 2017[13]; Broeders and Prenio, 2018[35]; di Castri et al., 2019[5]).

In considering such challenges, SC Malaysia has highlighted the importance of ensuring that data scientists have a general understanding of corporate governance principles, practices and disclosures given that a basic understanding of corporate governance concepts is critical to ensure that the data scientists are able to formulate the logic that will be applied by the AI in analysing the adoption of corporate governance practices and the quality of disclosures. As such, building AI capability requires not just more data but also better data. In this case, insightful and reliable corporate governance disclosures. In the developmental stage, a set of good disclosures by listed companies in Malaysia and other markets were selected and used to build the base of the AI.

Importantly, human intervention is required to identify and validate these disclosures in order to feed the development of the AI. Therefore, in order to yield benefits, SupTech tools require skilled human oversight – as technology should not be leveraged to substitute, but rather to complement and support human judgment. This has crucial financial stability implications, as tools built upon historical data associated with past instances of instability may not remain valid for predicting future crises (FSB, 2020[6]).

In addition, from a corporate governance enforcement perspective, as final decisions on whether to pursue enforcement actions are still necessarily taken by humans and based on human judgements, appeals mechanisms also provide a potential lever for considering and addressing potential biases that may be introduced through algorithmic or AI-based supervisory mechanisms. For instance, Germany's BaFin reports that defining the patterns and types of anomalies ALMA should look for represents a challenge, as the assessment of which incidents ALMA should identify as abuse is based on experience and should therefore be verifiable by analysts.

This resonates with a challenge identified by competition authorities in relation to projects seeking to automate the monitoring of remedies (highlighted, for example, in the earlier mentioned description of the UK CMA's automated monitoring of remedies in the payday lending market). In particular, cooperation between case teams and digital specialists with respect to remedies is paramount, so that the possibility of automated monitoring is considered during the design of remedies.

Likewise, for those currently employed by law enforcement or corruption agencies, a comprehensive training is often required to enable a full understanding and acceptance of AI capabilities and results. Where investigative authorities are using this technology, prosecutorial authorities and courts will be required to understand and accept its use as well. Before adopting this technology, law enforcement authorities will need to consult with their investigators and prosecutors to ensure a smooth uptake. Importantly, the need for human oversight will clearly still be required to ensure that AI technology complements and supports existing investigative techniques.

5.4.4. Third-party dependencies, digital security and privacy concerns

Increased dependencies on third parties can stand as a risk – especially with regards to cloud service providers. Although cloud-based services hold the potential to foster information sharing between authorities – in turn improving regulatory co-operation, "public cloud" solutions raise operational, governance and oversight considerations. Such considerations have particular relevance in a cross-border contect, where authorities may be unable to assess whether legal and regulatory obligations around the delivery of a service are being met.[23] Further, interoperability limitations could create lock-in effects and over-reliance on specific platforms and providers (FSB, 2019[36]; FSB, 2017[2]). As such, implementing vetting and auditing processes may be required as a means to ensure adequate safeguards. In addition, greater reliance on outsourced data storage may also increase cyber-vulnerabilities for authorities, which may in turn magnify financial stability risks. At present, most authorities store most of their data in-house for security reasons, and their use of cloud storage is reportedly limited to non-core activities (FSB, 2020[6]; FSB, 2019[37]).

While digital security vulnerabilities can be emphasised by the increased granularity of data and increased data-sharing between government agencies and across public-private partnerships, this can also generate concerns over individual privacy (OECD, 2019[7]). In particular, concerns are raised that the absence of common principles for trusted government access to personal data may lead to undue restrictions on data flows resulting in detrimental economic impacts (OECD, 2020[38]). As such, the processing of data by third parties in the context of public-private partnerships should be transparent, and comply on practices with data management supporting the ethical use of data in the public sector (OECD, 2021[39]).

Conversely, it should be noted that concerns around compliance with data protection regulations and standards (i.e. the EU General Data Protection Regulation, also knows as "GDPR") also arise when contemplating certain SupTech tools. For instance, as distributed ledger technology offers transparency and immutability, this could create challenges in meeting GDPR standards around the ability to anonymise and erase personal data and around storage limitations (Denis and Blume, 2021[40]).

5.4.5. Legacy systems

Legacy systems, along with data formats that are not compatible with SupTech, can also impede Suptech adoption. Implementing changes to such systems may require significant organisational changes at the same time to support their effective implementation.

For example, Germany's BaFin reports the setup of the technical infrastructure behind ALMA as a major challenge, as it requires integrating different databases, AI methods, a visualisation for the supervisors, a feedback mechanism and a consistent data flow through all the stages. Additionally, in order to work with large quantities of data, hardware needs to be updated permanently in order to guarantee a high performance. These obstacles entail that valuable product increments might be difficult to deliver even in several sprints, which might result in stakeholders being potentially dissatisfied over a longer period. This challenge also includes the need for a cultural change in the organisation to enable the whole team to work in an agile framework.

In the case of Mexico, CNBV reports that the main obstacle to the implementation of its cloud computing project is the variety of technological infrastructure amongst the Mexican financial institutions. In the same vein, challenges can also arise upon the integration of SupTech tools into existing processes and procedures. For instance, Australia's ASIC reports that the rewrite of frameworks and dashboards may slightly alter legacy procedures.

5.4.6. Financial and human resources, procurement rules, and barriers to change

Other challenges may be encountered when developing, deploying and maintaining SupTech solutions – including authorities' lack of adequate skills such as with respect to technology, software and hardware expertise, along with budget constraints, rigid procurement rules and obsolete regulatory frameworks. Resistance to change and organisational silos may also hinder the development of SupTech projects.

Regarding budget constraints, a common challenge identified is the cost of implementing AI systems, even though the benefits of doing so are clearly articulated. The cost of the software and user licences, along with the costs of any hardware upgrades often required, are of particular concern. As many enforcement authorities are facing budget restrictions, making an efficient use of their limited resources when designing their use of digital technologies is important. This requires adequate planning and design of the most cost-effective use of digital technologies. In practical terms, this translates for example in carefully managing the number of software licenses and data provider subscriptions to balance analytical capacity with costs (OECD, 2019[22]).

Beyond planning, there are a range of resource challenges that competition authorities have identified when building up their SupTech capacity. First, government policy restrictions may affect their approach. For example, competition authorities may be prohibited from placing data and processing functions on the public cloud, which requires them to invest in onsite capacity that can be relatively more expensive and time-consuming to establish. Second, there may be a lack of tools and products available that are designed for competition authority purposes, which may require them to develop their own such tools, although open source software may help in this process. Third, smaller competition authorities may face challenges given that there is a minimum efficient scale for some SupTech applications, meaning that the associated costs may risk occupying a relatively larger share of their budget. Co-operation and resource sharing among authorities in different jurisdictions may help alleviate this.

Authorities' procurement rules may also render the design and implementation of technology solutions difficult, as evidence suggests that supervisors' procurement offices are often unfamiliar with these new technologies, and conversely, service providers are often unfamiliar with procurement processes and requirements (di Castri et al., 2019[5]).

Further, the integration of SupTech expertise and tools may give rise to certain additional organisational challenges. For example, in the case of competition authorities, it may be difficult to fit data science processes within the compressed timelines of enforcement cases, meaning that more sophisticated tools may need to be pre-prepared (which can be difficult given variations across markets), or focused on advanced screening methods. Digital teams may also face cultural challenges within an authority, such as resistance to changing ways of working, or incorporating SupTech analysis at each stage of a case (including information requests and remedy design). Cultural challenges have also been identified by other law enforcement authorities in their efforts to apply SupTech tools. For example, different institutions involved in enforcement processes may have different levels of data-driven culture and familiarity with Suptech or AI applications. In the absence of sufficient training to understand how AI-driven analyses and conclusions are reached, there may be a lack of trust in relying upon their findings.

5.5. Considerations for devising adequate SupTech strategies

Recognising the potential of SupTech to transform data processes – in turn improving the timeliness and quality of decisions and actions – the use of SupTech tools by supervisory and public enforcement authorities has been gaining momentum in recent years. According to a recent FSB survey (2020[6]), the use of SupTech strategies has grown significantly since 2016, with a vast majority of surveyed financial authorities having a SupTech or innovation or data strategy in place. In addition, several competition authorities have reinforced their digital capabilities in order to take advantage of digital tools, and some competition authorities have created separate forensic IT and strategic data analysis units.[24]

SupTech strategies are hereby defined as seeking to develop tools to support authorities' functions, whereas innovation/data strategies refer to institution-wide digital transformation/data-driven innovation (DT&DI) programmes that encompass the development of SupTech tools. They are not necessarily pursued in isolation (FSB, 2020[6]). SupTech applications can either be initiated by management, or originate as research questions. Evidence also suggests that SupTech applications can be explored through the use of accelerators, tech sprints, and innovation labs, regardless of whether an authority has an explicit SupTech strategy (Broeders and Prenio, 2018[35]; di Castri et al., 2019[5]).

5.5.1. Leadership, budget and skills

Overall, it is important that SupTech strategies be devised in consideration of authorities' needs, regulatory frameworks and technological capacities. Although there is no "one-size-fits-all" approach, authorities have identified several important considerations underpinning successful SupTech strategies, ranging from the design to the implementation stage, and covering leadership, budget and skills concerns.

A well-defined SupTech strategy requires effective leadership – such as through established Chief Data Officers (CDOs) – and management buy-in, as well as early engagement with end-users (i.e. 'front-line' supervisors) – which allows to overcome resistance to change. Evidence also suggests that adopting 'fast fails' approaches can enable authorities to quickly evaluate which applications merit further progress, and which ones are not fit for purpose (FSB, 2017[2]). Securing sufficient budget is also paramount for developing SupTech projects, along with adequate procurement systems.

Having technologically skilled professionals in place with the right data expertise better enables the implementation of a flexible SupTech platform, and the adoption of a data-driven culture by organisations as a whole (Bank of England, 2019[41]; FCA, 2020[42]). Several authorities have implemented a strategy for attracting and retaining adequate skills and talent – such as through employee engagement frameworks, or by offering online or other training programmes to existing staff to enhance their skills. Knowledge-based transfers between departments are also observed. In order to attain a skilled SupTech workforce, some financial services authorities have started tailoring their recruitment strategies to focus on candidates' data analysis skills (FSB, 2020[6]).

It should be noted that a "late mover" advantage applies to authorities that have recently initiated – or are considering to initiate – the development of their data infrastructure. Indeed, integrating advanced analytics tools to a data architecture designed from scratch might prove an easier task than building new tools upon legacy systems (Coelho, De Simoni and Prenio, 2019[14]).

5.5.2. Collaboration between authorities, regulated entities and technology service providers within and across jurisdictions

While data analysis applications are developed to facilitate internal workflows, data collection tools require some involvement from market participants. For the latter category, it is important to consult with regulated entities going forward in order to ensure that solutions adopted on both ends are aligned and compatible. As some supervisors have piloted and adopted SupTech frameworks on an ad-hoc and unco-ordinated basis, this can in turn create negative externalities for regulated entities. In particular, according to one report reviewing the experience of select firms, a lack of common standards – along with differing levels of technological progress within authorities – could lead to inconsistencies in SupTech approaches across jurisdictions (European Commission, 2020[32]).

A recent study found that in terms of automated reporting for instance, certain firms with subsidiaries in more than one jurisdiction are currently unable to implement the same reporting solution for all subsidiary companies, due to cross-country variations in supervisory expectations and technological capacities (European Commission, 2020[32]). Co-ordination between authorities and regulated entities in their respective efforts to adopt innovative technologies is important to aligning their systems where appropriate and in line with their domestic regulatory remit, in order to mitigate potential challenges and adverse effects down the line, as well as to allow both parties to reap maximum benefits from their use (Bank of England, 2020[43]). An important caveat is that SupTech might induce market participants to adjust their behaviour accordingly. A recent study finds that authorities' adoption of SupTech solutions has a feedback effect on companies' corporate disclosure decisions, implying that companies adjust their filings when they anticipate that such disclosure will be processed by machines (Cao et al., 2020[44]). Other evidence suggests that market participants may seek to gain sufficient knowledge of SupTech applications to game the technology to their benefit (di Castri et al., 2019[5]).

Going forward, co-ordination and collaboration between authorities, regulated entities and technology service providers within and across jurisdictions is crucial to: 1) ensure the compatibility of innovative systems adopted by regulators and regulated entities; 2) foster peer learning with regards to the successes and failures of SupTech uses; and 3) consider the possibility of devising common standards and taxonomies for relevant regulatory areas in order to ensure the scalability and interoperability of SupTech tools, especially with regards to reporting solutions. By convening and fostering exchanges among a wide range of stakeholders, international organisations and standard-setting bodies can play an important role in that respect.

References

Autoridade da Concorrência (2018), *BOS1: Unannounced Inspections in the Digital Age, AdC dawn raids: A new (Digital) model*, https://www.oecd.org/competition/globalforum/investigative-powers-in-practice.htm. [29]

BaFin (2017), *BaFin's 2017 Annual Report*, https://www.bafin.de/EN/PublikationenDaten/Jahresbericht/Jahresbericht2017/jahresbericht_node_en.html. [16]

Bank of England (2020), *Transforming data collection from the UK financial sector*, https://www.bankofengland.co.uk/paper/2020/transforming-data-collection-from-the-uk-financial-sector. [43]

Bank of England (2019), *The Future of Finance Report*, https://www.bankofengland.co.uk/-/media/boe/files/report/2019/future-of-finance-report.pdf. [41]

BCBS (2018), *Sound Practices: implications of fintech developments for banks and bank supervisors*, https://www.bis.org/bcbs/publ/d431.htm. [3]

Broeders, D. and J. Prenio (2018), *Innovative Technology in Financial Supervision (Suptech)-the Experience of Early Users*, https://www.bis.org/fsi/publ/insights9.htm. [35]

Cao, S. et al. (2020), *How to Talk When a Machine is Listening: Corporate Disclosure in the Age of AI*, https://dx.doi.org/10.2139/ssrn.3683802. [44]

Casalini, F. and J. López González (2019), "Trade and Cross-Border Data Flows", *OECD Trade Policy Papers* 220, http://dx.doi.org/doi.org/10.1787/b2023a47-en. [51]

CNBV/R2A (2018), *An AML SupTech Solution for the Mexican National Banking and Securities Commission (CNBV): R2A Project Retrospective and Lessons Learned*, http://dx.doi.org/10.2139/ssrn.3592564. [15]

Coelho, R., M. De Simoni and J. Prenio (2019), "Suptech applications for anti-money laundering", Vol. FSI Insights on policy implementation, no 18, August, https://www.bis.org/fsi/publ/insights18.htm. [14]

CSA (2018), *Canadian securities regulators announce agreement with Kx to deliver advanced post-trade analysis*, https://www.securities-administrators.ca/news/canadian-securities-regulators-announce-agreement-with-kx-to-deliver-advanced-post-trade-analysis/. [17]

Denis, E. and D. Blume (2021), *Using digital technologies to strengthen shareholder participations*, Going Digital Toolkit Note, No. 9, https://goingdigital.oecd.org/data/notes/No9_ToolkitNote_ShareholdersTech.pdf. [40]

di Castri, S. et al. (2019), *The Suptech Generations*, https://www.bis.org/fsi/publ/insights19.htm. [5]

Dias, D. and S. Staschen (2017), *Data Collection by Supervisors of Digital Financial Services*, https://www.cgap.org/sites/default/files/researches/documents/Working-Paper-Data-Collection-by-Supervisors-of-DFS-Dec-2017.pdf. [13]

ECB (2021), *The ESCB's long-term approach to banks' data reporting*, https://www.ecb.europa.eu/stats/ecb_statistics/co-operation_and_standards/reporting/html/index.en.html. [45]

ESMA (2019), *Report on Trends, Risks and Vulnerabilities*, https://www.esma.europa.eu/sites/default/files/library/esma50-report_on_trends_risks_and_vulnerabilities_no1_2019.pdf. [8]

European Commission (2020), *Digital Finance Strategy for the EU*, https://eur-lex.europa.eu/legal-content/EN/TXT/?uri=CELEX:52020DC0591. [32]

European Commission (2018), *Summary Report of the Public Consultation on the Fitness Check on Supervisory Reporting*, https://ec.europa.eu/info/sites/info/files/2017-supervisory-reporting-requirements-summary-report_en.pdf. [33]

FCA (2020), *Data Strategy*, https://www.fca.org.uk/publications/corporate-documents/data-strategy. [42]

FCA (2020), *Digital Regulatory Reporting: Phase 2 Viability Assessment*, https://www.fca.org.uk/publication/discussion/digital-regulatory-reporting-pilot-phase-2-viability-assessment.pdf. [31]

FinCoNet (2020), *SupTech Tools for Market Conduct Supervisors*, http://www.finconet.org/FinCoNet-Report-SupTech-Tools_Final.pdf. [12]

FSB (2020), *The Use of Supervisory and Regulatory Technology by Authorities and Regulated Institutions*, https://www.fsb.org/wp-content/uploads/P091020.pdf. [6]

FSB (2019), *FinTech and market structure in financial services*, https://www.fsb.org/wp-content/uploads/P140219.pdf. [37]

FSB (2019), *Third-party dependencies in cloud services: Considerations on financial stability implications*, https://www.fsb.org/2019/12/third-party-dependencies-in-cloud-services-considerations-on-financial-stability-implications/. [36]

FSB (2017), *Artificial Intelligence and Machine Learning in Financial Services: Market Developments and Financial Stability Implications*, https://www.fsb.org/wp-content/uploads/P011117.pdf. [2]

Hodges, C. (2019), "Collective Redress: The Need for New Technologies", *Journal of Consumer Policy* 42, pp. 59-90, https://link.springer.com/article/10.1007/s10603-018-9388-x#citeas. [50]

IBM (2018), *The Four V's of Big Data*, http://www.ibmbigdatahub.com/infographic/four-vs-big-data. [9]

IDC (2012), *Digital Universe Study: Big Data, Bigger Digital Shadows and Biggest Growth in the Far East*. [53]

Jones, A. (2020), *Concurrentialiste: Journal of Antitrust Law*, https://leconcurrentialiste.com/jones-bid-rigging/. [48]

MAS (2019), *Enforcement report 2017-2018*, https://www.mas.gov.sg/-/media/MAS/News-and-Publications/Monographs-and-Information-Papers/MAS-Enforcement-Report.pdf. [27]

Mohun, J. and A. Roberts (2020), "Cracking the code: Rulemaking for humans and machines", *OECD Working Papers on Public Governance*, No. 42, OECD Publishing, Paris, https://dx.doi.org/10.1787/3afe6ba5-en. [34]

OECD (2021), *Good Practice Principles for Data Ethics in the Public Sector*, https://www.oecd.org/gov/digital-government/good-practice-principles-for-data-ethics-in-the-public-sector.htm. [39]

OECD (2020), *Government access to personal data held by the private sector: Statement by the OECD Committee on Digital Economy Policy*, https://www.oecd.org/sti/ieconomy/trusted-government-access-personal-data-private-sector.htm. [38]

OECD (2020), *Latin American and Caribbean Competition Forum - Digital Evidence Gathering in Cartel Investigations*, https://www.oecd.org/competition/latinamerica/. [25]

OECD (2020), *Latin American and Caribbean Competition Forum - Session I: Digital Evidence Gathering In Cartel Investigations - Contribution from Spain*. [20]

OECD (2020), *Latin American and Caribbean Competition Forum - Session I: Digital Evidence Gathering In Cartel Investigations - Issues Note*. [23]

OECD (2020), *Latin American and Caribbean Competition Forum on Digital Evidence Gathering in Cartel Investigations- Contribution from UNCTAD*. [21]

OECD (2020), *Using market studies to tackle emerging competition issues*, http://www.oecd.org/daf/competition/using-market-studies-to-tackle-emerging-competition-issues-2020.pdf. [47]

OECD (2019), *Going Digital: Shaping Policies, Improving Lives*, OECD Publishing, Paris, https://doi.org/10.1787/9789264312012-en. [1]

OECD (2019), *Recommendation of the Council concerning Effective Action against Hard Core Cartels*, https://legalinstruments.oecd.org/en/instruments/OECD-LEGAL-0452. [19]

OECD (2019), *Resolving Foreign Bribery Cases with Non-Trial Resolutions: Settlements and Non-Trial Agreements by Parties to the Anti-Bribery Convention*, http://www.oecd.org/corruption/Resolving-Foreign-Bribery-Cases-with-Non-Trial-Resolutions.htm. [11]

OECD (2019), *The Path to Becoming a Data-Driven Public Sector*, OECD Publishing, Paris, https://dx.doi.org/10.1787/059814a7-en. [22]

OECD (2019), "Using digital technologies to improve the design and enforcement of public policies", *OECD Digital Economy Papers*, No. 274, OECD Publishing, Paris, https://dx.doi.org/10.1787/99b9ba70-en. [7]

OECD (2018), *Investigative powers in practice - Break-out session 1: Unannounced inspections in the digital age - Issues Note by the Secretariat*. [28]

OECD (2018), *Market Study Guide for Competition Authorities*, https://www.oecd.org/daf/competition/market-studies-guide-for-competition-authorities.htm. [46]

OECD (2017), *The Detection of Foreign Bribery*, http://www.oecd.org/corruption/the-detection-of-foreign-bribery.htm. [18]

OECD (2015), *Data-Driven Innovation: Big Data for Growth and Well-Being*, OECD Publishing, Paris, https://dx.doi.org/10.1787/9789264229358-en. [52]

OECD (2014), *OECD Foreign Bribery Report: An Analysis of the Crime of Bribery of Foreign Public Officials*, OECD Publishing, Paris, https://dx.doi.org/10.1787/9789264226616-en. [24]

OECD (2013), *Supervision and Enforcement in Corporate Governance*, OECD Publishing, http://dx.doi.org/10.1787/9789264203334-en. [54]

Porter, R. and J. Zona (1993), "Detection of Bid Rigging in Procurement Auctions", *Journal of Political Economy*, Vol. 101/3, pp. 518-538, https://www.jstor.org/stable/2138774?seq=1#metadata_info_tab_contents. [49]

R²A (2019), *The State of RegTech: The Rising Demand for "Superpowers"*, https://bfaglobal.com/r2a/insights/the-state-of-regtech-the-rising-demand-for-superpowers/. [10]

SC Malaysia (2020), *Corporate Governance Monitor 2020*, https://www.sc.com.my/api/documentms/download.ashx?id=ff69ce0d-a35e-44d4-996a-c591529c56c7. [26]

UK CMA (2015), *Payday Lending Market Investigation Order*, https://assets.publishing.service.gov.uk/media/55cc691e40f0b6137400001f/Payday_Lending_Market_Investigation_Order_2015.pdf. [30]

World Bank (2018), *From Spreadsheets to Suptech : Technology Solutions for Market Conduct Supervision*, https://openknowledge.worldbank.org/handle/10986/29952. [4]

Notes

[1] Suptech is defined by Dias and Staschen (2017[13]) as "technological solutions focused on improving the processes and effectiveness of financial supervision and regulation", and by the World Bank (2018[4]) as "the use of technology to facilitate and enhance supervisory processes from the perspective of supervisory authorities". Castri et al. (2019[5]) define SupTech as "the use of innovative technology by financial authorities to support their work", restricting "innovative technology" to big data and artificial intelligence (AI) tools, and "financial authorities" to supervisory and non-supervisory authorities but excluding authorities in charge of monetary and macroeconomic policies.

[2] Including the Financial Stability Board, World Bank, International Organization of Securities Commissions, European Securities and Markets Authority, FinCoNet, etc.

[3] In March 2021, the OECD Anti-Corruption Division carried out a survey of members of the OECD WGB containing six open-ended questions covering the purposes, benefits, challenges, cases, and plans for the future on the use of AI tools in the fight against corruption and foreign bribery. Sixteen WGB countries responded to the survey. Among the 16 respondents, supervisory and law enforcement authorities in nine countries reported already using AI tools to detect allegations and/or enforce anti-corruption laws and regulations. Five other countries are considering the adoption of AI tools to fight corruption. Two countries reported not having plans yet.

[4] In the recent Airbus SE settlement, the largest non-trial resolution of a foreign bribery case to date and involving three WGB jurisdictions, the French *Parquet National Financier* granted a 50% reduction in the penalty imposed due to the cooperation and internal investigation conducted by Airbus SE.

[5] It was reported in the Airbus SE case that the company made more than 30 million documents available for review by the authorities.

[6] **Structured data** are data based on a predefined data model (i.e. an abstract representation of "real world" objects and phenomenon). Such models can be explicit, as in the case of a structured query language (SQL) database, where the data model is reflected in the structure of the database's tables. The data model can also be implicit, as in the case of **semi-structured data** (e.g. structured web content), where the underlying model can be made explicit at relatively low cost. In contrast, **unstructured data** are data that have no predefined data model and where such a model cannot be cost-effectively extracted. Typical examples include text-heavy data sets such as text documents, emails, social media posts as well as multimedia content such as videos, images and audio streams. A study by IDC (IDC, 2012[53]) estimates that not even 5% of the "digital universe" is tagged, and thus can be considered structured or semi-structured data. However, the difference between structured, semi-structured, and unstructured data is becoming less important, since with rising computing capacities, data analytics are increasingly able to automatically extract some structures embedded in unstructured data, including multimedia content. (OECD, 2015[52])

[7] Digitisation refers to the conversion of analogue data and processes into a machine-readable format (OECD, 2019[1]).

[8] Big data architectures require two key design features: i) internal coherence of each of its layers so they can all process the speed, size and complexity of big data, and ii) built-in quality assurance and security procedures to ensure the validity and integrity of the data from the point of collection to the point of consumption by end users, thus enabling seamless end-to-end data flow without lags of size constraints (di Castri et al., 2019[5]).

[9] Digital technologies can allow policy makers to be more pro-active and reactive in tracking and responding to fast-changing phenomena, whether they be risks or opportunities. At the same, advanced analytics can help to "predict" responses to policy interventions in a more robust manner than was the case previously (OECD, 2019[7]).

[10] In particular, analysis of past supervision data, now made far more efficient and effective through the use of machine learning techniques, has been used by many regulators in many regulatory fields to improve risk-based targeting of supervision. Likewise, while research has shown how much regulators can benefit from using more effectively the complaints from consumers (Hodges, 2019[50]), most regulators remain quite "lagging" on this. SupTech offers very interesting opportunities to more easily aggregate and analyse consumer complaints, and subsequently use them to target supervision.

[11] (Jones, 2020[48]) noted that in 2017, almost half of the KFTC's sanctioned cartels were bid-rigging cases.

[12] It should be noted that the use of statistical and econometric techniques to detect anti-competitive behaviours is not new. For instance, a 1993 paper (Porter and Zona[49]) proposed econometric test procedures designed to detect the presence of bid rigging in procurement auctions.

[13] The UNCTAD contribution to the OECD's 2020 *Latin American and Caribbean Competition Forum on Digital Evidence Gathering in Cartel Investigations*, noted the KFTC's successful detection of bid rigging

in a metro construction project worth USD 5 billion and CADE's successful detection of bid rigging in the supply of cardiac pacemakers (OECD, 2020, p. 6[21])..

[14] As part of remedies, firms' may be required to disclose data or algorithms to allow authorities to monitor their activities. For instance, following the investigation of the retail banking market in theUnited Kingdom, the UK CMA imposed a series of remedies, including the requirement on banks to release and make available certain data (e.g. product and service information and customer transaction data) through open APIs (OECD, 2019[22]).

[15] The Phase 4 monitoring process was launched at the OECD Anti-Bribery Ministerial Meeting held in Paris on 18 March 2016. All the reports are available at: https://www.oecd.org/daf/anti-bribery/countryreportsontheimplementationoftheoecdanti-briberyconvention.htm

[16] See speech by Camilla de Silva, SFO Joint Head of Bribery and Corruption, speaking at the Herbert Smith Freehills Corporate Crime Conference 2018 (https://www.sfo.gov.uk/2018/06/21/corporate-criminal-liability-ai-and-dpas/).

[17] For example, in its investigation of the acquisition of Monsanto by Bayer, the European Commission had to examine over 2.7 million internal documents submitted by Monsanto and Bayer (European Commission, 2018[33]).

[18] Market studies allow competition authorities to assess whether competition in a market or sector is working effectively and to identify measures to address any issues detected (OECD, 2018[46]). They are a useful ex-ante tool and can help competition authorities understand a market resulting in more effective enforcement and can be especially useful in addressing emerging competition issues where enforcement action is limited (OECD, 2020[47]).

[19] Several reasons can explain the increasing costs for supplying regulatory reports, including the challenge for firms to populate reports with the correct data; the spread of instructions across different pieces of interlinking regulation; unclear wording of rules; and firms subjected to multiple regulatory regimes having to submit differing reports containing similar underlying data (European Commission, 2018[33]; FCA, 2020[31]).

[20] The European Commission is aiming to ensure that key parts of EU regulation are accessible to natural language processing, are machine readable and executable, and more broadly facilitate the design and implementation of reporting requirements. It will also encourage the use of modern IT tools for information sharing among national and EU authorities. As a first step in the domain of machine readable and executable reporting, the Commission has launched a pilot project for a limited set of reporting requirements (European Commission, 2020[32]). The digitisation of reporting instructions was also explored by the UK Financial Conduct Authority (UK FCA) and the Bank of England (BoE) during a TechSprint in late 2016, during which it was found that a small set of reporting instructions could be converted into machine-executable code, in turn enabling machines to use this code to automatically find and return regulatory reporting directly from a simulated version of a company's systems. Since then, work has progressed into a first and second phase involving the UK FCA, BoE and regulated banks (FSB, 2020[0]; FCA, 2020[31]; FCA, 2020[42]).

[21] In Europe, some industry attempts to improve and standardise the reporting process have already been made through initiatives likes the Banks Integrated Reporting Dictionary (BIRD), Integrated Reporting Framework (IReF) and the European Banking Authority's Data (DPM) (ECB, 2021[45]).

[22] See, for instance, Canada, where "Bureau investigators have downloaded data stored outside Canada in the course of searches of computer systems located in Canada, although there continues to be some controversy as to the precise limits of the authority granted by a warrant authorising a search of computer systems in a cross-border context.", https://www.lexology.com/gtdt/tool/workareas/report/617528c4-0e23-4678-a460-9333ed458dc0.

[23] In particular regarding compliance with different conditions on cross-border data transfers involving personal information (Casalini and López González, 2019[51]).

[24] For instance, in 2018, the UK Competition and Markets Authority (UK CMA) launched a Data, Technology and Analytics (DaTA) unit, which according to the UK CMA is the largest team of data and technology experts in any competition or consumer agency worldwide (OECD, 2019[22]). The unit includes team members with data engineering, data science, and data and technology market intelligence expertise. It aims to provide the UK CMA with technical capacity for working with data and using algorithms (OECD, 2019[22]). The French Competition Authority has also established a Digital Economy Unit, which will be responsible for, among other things, developing new digital investigation tools, based in particular on algorithmic technology, big data and artificial intelligence (OECD, 2019[22]). The Spanish Competition Authority's Economic Intelligence Unit is made up of a group of experts in mathematics, statistics, and computer science, as well as economists and lawyers and uses algorithms and big data analysis techniques to carry out its investigations (OECD, 2019[22]). Competition agencies from other jurisdictions, such as Canada and EU, have noted their plans to establish a specialist team that will facilitate the use of AI in their investigations (OECD, 2019[22]).

6 Managing access to AI advances to safeguard countries' essential security interests

Artificial Intelligence (AI) has potential to resolve many challenges that our societies face, but as with all innovations, foreign acquisitions of some AI applications may raise security concerns.
International investment in established companies is an important vector for diffusion of AI-related technologies across borders. Concerns about implications for essential security interests have led to tighter government control over such acquisitions, with AI-related technologies often explicitly included in the scope of investment screening mechanisms.
Financing of research abroad is a parallel legal avenue to acquire know-how that is unavailable domestically. It can substitute for acquisitions of established companies. Governments have now begun to set out policies to control such transfers, specifically for AI-related areas. As for foreign investment in equity, such policies need to be carefully devised to avoid forgoing the benefits of international research cooperation. Policy principles agreed at the OECD to strike this balance could offer inspiration.

6.1. Managing risk without stifling opportunities: new challenges require new solutions

While the full scope of future applications of Artificial Intelligence (AI) remains unknown, it is certain that these applications will bring transformational change to all aspects of societies. As with many technological innovations, defence and security applications are likely to be early adopters of AI. To avoid that adversaries or hostile states obtain the technology and the associated military edge, governments seek to establish mechanisms that allow them to manage the proliferation of AI applications and the underlying know-how.

International investment is among the most important channels for technology diffusion. To safeguard their essential security interests, governments have consequently placed great emphasis on managing AI diffusion through international investment. Investment screening mechanisms are the main instrument employed for this purpose: They allow governments to review foreign investment proposals in sensitive sectors for potential threats to essential security interests and to impose conditions, or, as a last resort, to block or unwind related acquisitions of established firms that possess or produce sensitive technology.

Significant efforts to establish, strengthen and refine investment screening mechanisms that began around 2017 are continuing in many advanced economies. Most jurisdictions now operate review mechanisms that allow them to assess whether inward investment proposals may be injurious to their essential security interests and take corresponding action, especially and increasingly transactions that involve the acquisition of advanced technologies or related assets. The first section of this chapter describes how these efforts cover specifically companies that develop advanced technology and AI technology or related applications.

Investment screening mechanisms are only one among several instruments at governments' disposal to manage essential security risks associated with advanced technologies. While reforms, introduction of new investment screening mechanisms in an ever greater number of jurisdictions, and expansion of scopes of existing mechanisms are reducing these actors' access to advanced technology by way of acquiring established companies, foreign financing of research in advanced economies and inward or outward exchange of researchers emerge as a popular avenue for some emerging economies to acquire such know-how.[1]

Governments begin to take the resulting risk of undesirable technology transfer seriously. Some have responded with specific policies or proposals to close gaps that screening mechanisms may have left, while many others are still assessing needs, options and the balance of costs and benefits of any regulatory intervention.[2] The second section of this chapter sets out the traits of these approaches that apply specifically to research into AI and similar advanced technology. These pioneering policies may foreshadow future and broader regulation to manage the proliferation of knowledge, rather than merely the transfer of firms that encapsulate such knowledge.

While investment screening mechanisms and related interventions can be effective in preventing the proliferation of advanced technology such as AI to malicious acquirers, they may, if not designed and implemented carefully, disturb the ecosystem that enables the development of such technology in the first place. This ecosystem thrives on openness, not least on openness to foreign capital, and it thrives on opportunities, entrepreneurship and market forces that drive innovation.[3] While government intervention in this ecosystem is legitimate to safeguard essential security interests, policies and administrative practices need to strike a fine balance to minimise the repercussions on the economic environment for the development of technology – ultimately the foundation on which the potential of AI is built.

This quest to balance openness with imperatives to protect essential security interests has characterised investment policies for decades. Governments at the OECD developed policy principles to achieve this balance in 2009: the Guidelines for Recipient Country Investment Policies relating to National Security

(2009 OECD Guidelines). These Guidelines have stood the test of time well, despite significant changes in the geopolitical and geo-economic environment since their adoption and the strong growth of investment from less-than-transparent jurisdictions and state-controlled entities as well as the more assertive stance of some economies. The third section concludes by setting out how these policies could inspire policy principles beyond screening of acquisitions of established enterprises in order to manage risk without stifling opportunities.

Key messages

Governments are managing risk for their essential security interests that may result from transfer of advanced technology to potentially malicious actors or hostile governments. Recent reforms in many advanced economies have focussed on screening of foreign investment in companies as one of the most prominent transmission channel for technology and knowledge transfer. Almost all advanced economies now cover advanced technology, including AI, by the scope of investment screening mechanisms.

As this avenue for technology acquisition is perceived to get narrower at least for some acquirers, foreign research funding and researcher exchanges are increasingly used to gain access to know-how that is not available domestically. Governments begin to take measures to address this gap in their defences but have to balance interests carefully to avoid stifling the conditions and the openness in which advanced technology development thrives.

Policy guidance developed at the OECD for investment policies related to national security in 2009 is an important reference point for policy-making for international investment in established enterprises. While there are important structural differences between international investment in established enterprises and research funding and cooperation, this policy guidance may provide some inspiration for policy principles for this latter area.

6.2. Managing essential security interests related to foreign acquisitions of AI assets in context

Policies that seek to safeguard essential security interests through screening of foreign acquisitions of sensitive assets have developed with a diverse and growing set of exposures in mind. When such mechanisms were first established in the context of the world wars of the first half of the 20th century, predominant concerns related to espionage, sabotage and the intentional withholding of supply of defence goods.

The design of related policies and sectoral coverage of these early mechanisms – typically single-sector mechanisms enshrined in legislation governing the respective sector such as defence – testify to this focus of concerns. Where such policies were in place in the first half of the 20th century, they typically focused on sensitive real estate and defence industries. Both sectors have retained their relative dominance on governments' priority lists in this policy area until the present day (Figure 6.1).

With the privatisation of infrastructure, which many OECD Member countries started in the 1970s, and with foreign investment in this sector becoming possible, critical infrastructure was progressively included under the scope of investment review mechanisms to manage the risks associated with such foreign ownership. The concerns associated with foreign ownership of these assets were still centred on the risk of sabotage or intentional withholding of such sensitive assets.

Figure 6.1. Sector coverage of acquisition- and ownership-related policies to safeguard essential security interests in OECD Member countries (1960-2021)

Evolution of relative importance of individual sectors

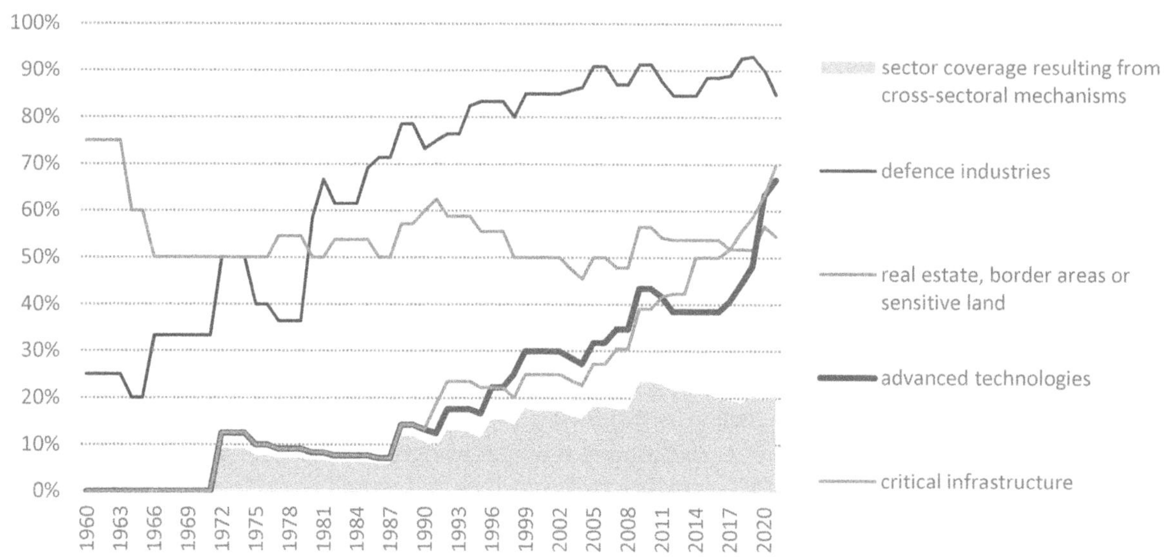

Note: Coloured lines in the graph indicate the proportion of OECD Member countries whose investment review mechanisms in force in any given year cover the indicated sector, thus showing the relative importance attached to individual sectors in the context of investment screening for essential security interests. The basis for calculating 100% reflects only those of today's 38 OECD Members that operated at least one review mechanism in that year.

6.2.1. New vulnerabilities emerge from international investment in advanced technology

An additional set of risks for essential security interests emerged around the same time. They include concerns about dependency on foreign-controlled suppliers, especially for defence procurement, and that the acquisition of advanced technology could level a technological edge, especially in defence applications. In the earlier decades of the Cold War period, export controls were used to limit access to advanced defence technology, but with the expansion of international investment, the role of acquisitions for technology proliferation across borders grew. Technological advances, specifically Japan's success in the development of semiconductors in the 1970s and 1980s, among other developments, sparked concerns in the United States that its advantage in this field would shrink and that the United States would become dependent on foreign-owned suppliers of semiconductors and other technology with military applications. In response, the United States in 1975 laid the foundations of what would become the first modern investment review mechanism specifically established to manage national security risk (Graham and Marchick, 2006, p. 1[1]; Jackson, 2018[2]; United States Government Accountability Office, 2018[3]; Jackson, 2020[4])).

That technology transfer through international investment could undercut technological advantages and thus jeopardise essential security interests initially remained a concern essentially for defence applications proper. They led additional governments to introduce investment review mechanisms, most of which were initially focused on and limited to defence industries.

That focus on traditional defence industries began to fade only very recently, and it has only been in the past few years that advanced technology more broadly was included into the scope of investment review mechanisms.[4] As documented in Figure 6.1, the inclusion of advanced technologies like AI into the scope of investment screening mechanisms only accelerated markedly in 2017, and only since 2019, more than half of OECD Members that screen foreign investment for essential security risks consider the implications of advanced technologies for such security interests.

The recognition of the role of AI as a foundational technology with dual-use applications – civil and military – plays an important part in this change of attitudes and policy: In 2021, twelve OECD Members had explicitly included AI in the definition of scope of their investment screening rules; not a single OECD Member had explicitly mentioned AI in this context before 2017 (Box 6.1).

Box 6.1. Inclusion of AI in the scope of investment screening mechanisms

The inclusion of AI in the scope and context of investment screening mechanisms first appeared in the United States legislation that reformed their earlier investment review mechanisms. This legislation is administered by the interagency Committee on Foreign Investment in the United States, better known under its acronym CFIUS. The reform legislation, the Foreign Investment Risk Review Modernization Act (FIRRMA), was enacted in 2018 and implemented over the subsequent two years, established particular procedures applicable to non-controlling investments in United States businesses that produce, design, test, manufacture, fabricate, or develop one or more critical technologies. Critical technologies includes, but is not limited to, emerging and foundational technologies controlled under section 1758 of the Export Control Reform Act of 2018 (50 U.S.C. 4817).

In Europe, AI was explicitly mentioned in the initial proposal of 2017 to establish EU-wide rules on investment screening which were later adopted as the Regulation 2019/452 of the European Parliament and of the Council of 19 March 2019 establishing a framework for the screening of foreign direct investments into the Union. Several EU Member States added AI to the scope of their screening mechanisms since (France in 2018, Italy 2020, Austria 2020, Slovenia 2020, Spain 2020, Germany 2021) or have planned its inclusion in ongoing reform efforts (e.g. Romania and Czech Republic). AI is also included in the list of 'key enabling technologies' of European Union interest under the Regulation 2019/452.

Other countries have taken action as well. Canada, in its 2021 update of the Guidelines on the National Security Review of Investments, includes AI in the list of sensitive technology areas. Australia introduced notification obligations in 2021 for foreign investments into businesses that develop, manufacture or supply critical technologies (including AI) for, or intended for, military or intelligence use; and encourages voluntary notification of similar investments in technologies with a civilian or dual use purpose. The United Kingdom included AI in the proposed list of critical technologies on which it consulted in late 2020.

OECD Members are not alone in their concerns about AI technology being acquired by foreign firms through international investment and acquisitions: As part of the update of its Catalogue of Technologies whose export is prohibited or restricted in August 2020, P.R. China included AI into the catalogue.

Source: (OECD, 2020[5]; OECD, 2021[6]).

Further changes to investment screening rules and policies have been made, if not specifically for AI acquisitions, but at least with regard to some of the specificities of AI acquisitions. Traditional designs of investment screening mechanisms were made with larger, publicly-listed companies in mind; only acquisitions of larger target companies, so the underlying rationale, could present meaningful risks for essential national security.

Companies that develop AI applications or related advanced technologies do not necessarily fit these criteria: In these sectors, many advances are made by small companies that may be held in private equity, that are not household names and that are not particularly visible to authorities.

In recognition that acquisitions of such smaller, non-listed companies may not come to the attention of investment screening authorities, several countries have adjusted their screening criteria and procedures to better capture such acquisitions of companies that develop advanced technology. For example, monetary or similar thresholds were abolished where these applied to investment screening on essential security grounds (United Kingdom in 2020, Australia in 2021, New Zealand in 2021), and notification requirements were introduced for sectors such as advanced technology where transactions might otherwise escape governments' attention. Most recently, governments have also addressed loopholes of corporate governance arrangements that would give minority shareholders disproportionate rights to access of sensitive information or decision making, issues that are more likely to be observed in small companies that hold sensitive information (OECD, 2021[6]).

Enabling technologies for AI applications, such as semiconductors and quantum computing, have likewise been explicitly included into the scope of investment screening mechanisms in the past few years. Greater control over acquisitions of these technologies through international investments complement policies specifically focused on AI.

6.2.2. Greater scrutiny has not ended the international investment boom in AI

The inclusion of advanced technology and specifically AI under the scope of investment screening mechanisms in recent years has not left a mark in investment flow data in these areas or led to a significant number of visible government interventions against proposed transactions – at least not yet. Data availability is lagged, so trends and effects of most recent policy measures may only show in the future.

Inward investment into advanced economies in AI-related companies grew very significantly in aggregate value and, to a lesser extent, in numbers of transactions between 2015 and 2019 (Arnold, Rahkovsky and Huang, 2020, p. 14[7]) – against the trend of declining FDI flow volumes in that period overall (OECD, 2021[8]).

Caseloads under investment screening mechanisms also increased significantly in several countries over past years (Figure 6.2). However, few transactions are known to have been prohibited or unwound in OECD countries in recent years overall, and where such measures were taken, AI as such did not appear to have played a major role. Naturally, these data have to be used with caution: Investors may have withdrawn or not envisaged specific transactions where they sensed potential regulatory obstacles, hence this data may underestimate the effect on policy. However, the fact that transactions with specific other characteristics experienced increased and public scrutiny, it would appear that foreign investment in companies that develop AI or AI-applications suggests that new policies related to AI have been implemented with restraint.

Figure 6.2. Caseload under investment screening mechanisms in selected countries (2009-2021)

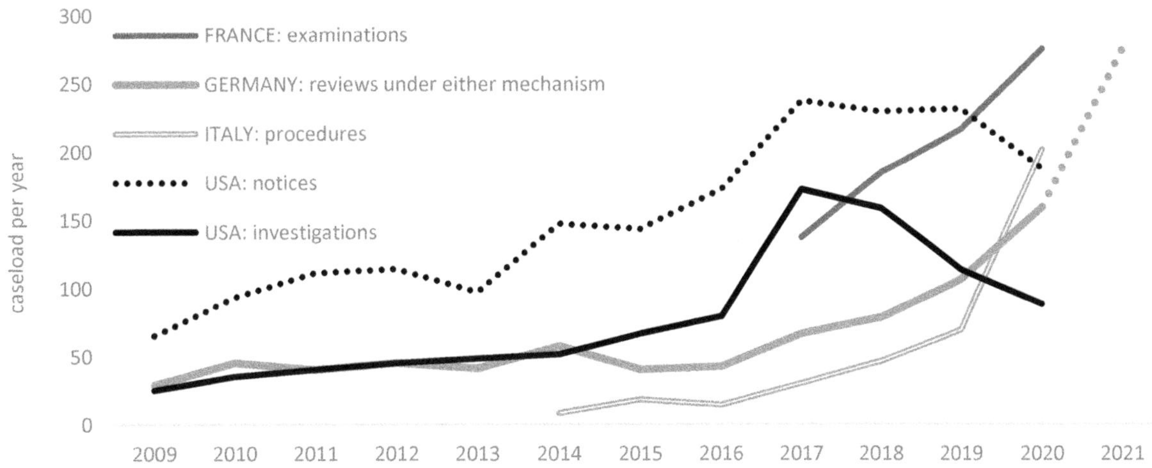

Note: Time-series shown where official data is made available by governments by late August 2021. The indicators shown depend on data availability and are not comparable across jurisdictions. Data for 2021 for Germany represents cases recorded by May 2021.
Source: OECD Secretariat calculations based on data reported by governments.

Judging by these preliminary metrics, investment screening mechanisms have likely had at most a minor impact on AI-related international investment.

Effects on a third potential outcome of more stringent investment screening cannot be assessed at this stage: To what extent will *new* investment, in particular greenfield investment in mobile, research-intensive sectors with security implications be allocated in jurisdictions that refrain from implementing controls over foreign investment. Investors in these areas may engage in regulatory arbitrage to avoid later security-related restrictions on their divestments (Pohl and Rosselot, 2020, p. 100[9]). Whether and to what extent such considerations influence the allocation of capital has not been subject to economic analysis.

6.3. Foreign investment in research: a new challenge calling for an adequate solution

While international investment in equity remains a very significant transmission channel for technology transfer, other avenues exist and develop in parallel. Funding of research in foreign countries, and inward and outward researcher exchanges specifically, are a significant legal[5] avenue through which such transfer of know-how across borders can take place (Hannas and Chang, 2019[10]).

Joint research work in universities or research institutions, or research financed by foreign governments or foreign enterprises, or inward or outward researcher exchanges allow these researchers and their principals or funders to tap into knowledge, know-how and networks to acquire capabilities that are not available domestically.

These forms of allocation of resources to acquire know-how rather than investing in enterprises can substitute for equity investments in the foreign market, especially where and when such equity acquisitions raise suspicion with local authorities or are difficult to execute. Investment in know-how acquisitions may become more attractive as perceptions about more stringent investment screening specifically for AI and related advanced technologies may dampen the appetite for equity acquisitions.

International research funding and researcher exchanges are regulated under rules that are different from investment screening. Some aspects of technology transfer are subject to export control regimes,[6] but these rules do not cover all means of carrying know-how across borders and, especially for foundational research with broad, yet to define applications, they may not always be a suitable instrument to address certain aspects of technology transfers.[7]

International collaboration and cooperation in research is widely recognised as critically important for advancing science and technology as well as solving global challenges.[8] In many OECD countries, independence of research institutions, and, especially in federal states, split competencies to regulate the fields of research and national security, further complicate government action in this area. Furthermore, the implantation of foreign-funded research in one's territory and the attraction of foreign talent and university fees are perceived as an opportunity to generate high-paying employment, advance research in one's institution, and is correspondingly generally welcome.

The implications of legal technology transfer through cross-border research funding and researcher exchanges have come under greater scrutiny lately,[9] in particular where this cooperation concerns advanced technology and specifically AI.[10] It has been suggested that some of the research funding and researcher exchanges are systematic attempts to extract know-how for subsequent use in defence applications developed abroad (Brown and Singh, 2018[11]; Joske, 2018[12]; Silcoff et al., 2018[13]; Segal and Gerstel, 2019[14]; National Science Foundation, 2019[15]; United States Senate Permanent Subcommittee on Investigations, 2019[16]; Hannas and Chang, 2019[10]; Lloyd-Damnjanovic and Bowe, 2020[17]) and have argued that a policy responses are warranted (JASON, 2019[18]; Kratz et al., 2020[19]).

As governments became more suspicious of foreign research involvement in sensitive areas, and as the volume of exchanges grew, especially in these areas, some began to recognise the issue[11] and to consider restrictions on foreign researchers (Edwards, 2016[20]) or on foreign funding of research and the transfer of results abroad. The United States complemented its export control rules in 2018 to manage technology transfer,[12] put in place a targeted limitation of entry for certain students,[13] and legislation was under consideration in June 2021 that aims at managing national security implications of foreign research funding and researcher exchanges.[14] Australia has passed legislation in 2020[15] that requires notifications about non-commercial arrangements that any subnational entities, including research institutions, have concluded or plan to conclude with foreign governments. Canada issued a Research Security Policy Statement[16] in March 2021 that aims at managing the risk of foreign funding arrangements for its national security. Japan is reported to have announced in April 2021 that it would require universities to disclosure foreign financial contributions when applying to government funds in order to avoid transfer of research that could be used for military purposes (Oikawa, 2021[21]).

By June 2021, the issue of transfer of advanced technology and AI-related technologies through foreign research funding and international researcher exchanges had become a broadly shared policy priority among advanced economies as documented by its inclusion in the EU-US Summit of 15 June 2021.[17]

6.4. Managing the implied risks of openness without forgoing benefits

There are parallels between international investment in enterprises and foreign funding of the generation of knowledge:

- Openness brings benefits to home and host societies and fosters prosperity and innovation, and both are keenly needed to address today's and tomorrow's challenges;
- Openness may, in both areas, occasionally bring risk for essential security interests that warrant policy intervention; and
- Diligent calibration of such policy intervention is crucial to avoid damages to the ecosystem in which international investment and international research cooperation thrive and that are required to generate the associated benefits.

In the area of international investment, advanced economies took guidance from time-tested policy principles when designing policies to manage security risks without forgoing the benefits of openness: the 2009 OECD Guidelines for Recipient Country Investment Policies relating to National Security. These Guidelines establish specific standards regarding non-discrimination, transparency, predictability, regulatory proportionality and accountability to allow societies to benefit from open investment environments while managing occasional risks that this openness can bring.

As governments are beginning to address security implications associated with international research cooperation and researcher exchanges, they may wish to consider which of these principles, if not all, could usefully inspire the design of rules in this area.

For example, the section of the 2009 OECD Guidelines on "proportionality" calls on governments to design investment policies so that "restrictions on investment, or conditions on transaction, should not be greater than needed to protect national security and they should be avoided when other existing measures are adequate and appropriate to address a national security concern". Very similar aspects have been identified for research cooperation, especially in areas of emerging technologies and AI: Broad prohibitions are identified as too blunt, risk stifling innovation and progress altogether, or push research and development abroad to more permissive countries with even greater detriment for essential security interests and innovation at home (United States Intelligence, National Security Commission on Artificial Intelligence, 2021, p. 176[22]; Williams, 2018[23]; National Research Council, 2007, p. 27[24]).

The 2009 OECD Guidelines also call for transparency and predictability of policies designed to safeguard essential security interests. They specifically emphasise the need to make regulatory objectives and practices as transparent as possible so as to increase the predictability of outcomes. Research and innovation often require significant upfront investment and personal commitments of researchers; also, many projects run over longer periods, findings may lead them into directions that were not initially anticipated, and produce results or applications that were not planned. This is all the more the case in a resource intensive, fast-moving and foundational field like AI, for which human ingenuity may find applications that we cannot foresee today. Understanding rules, policies and concerns are crucial conditions to create trust that certain research can be successfully carried out in a given jurisdiction – much like in the field of long term commitment of assets in foreign investment.

Finally, the 2009 OECD Guidelines call for accountability of policy actions to citizens on whose behalf these measures are taken, achieved through oversight, public reporting, regulatory impact assessment and the like. Again here, the parallel between international investment in equity and foreign funding of knowledge generation is striking: Accountability generates trust, avoids overreach, and is the foundation for legitimacy that is needed as much for international investment in enterprises as it is for the allocation of resources to research.[18]

Most advances in science are achieved on the basis of or in analogy to preceding findings of others that are assessed, further developed and refined. Policy makers could take inspiration from this incremental approach and look at the advances their peer policy makers have made in related fields. Addressing the risks that international research cooperation in AI and other advanced technology may occasionally generate, be it through foreign funding or inward and outward researcher exchanges, could take inspiration from what makes research so frighteningly successful. The time-tested principles developed for international investment may have some insights in store for international research cooperation, too.

References

Arnold, Z., I. Rahkovsky and T. Huang (2020), *Tracking AI Investment: Initial Findings From the Private Market*, Center for Security and Emerging Technology, http://dx.doi.org/10.51593/20190011. [7]

Brown, M. and P. Singh (2018), *China's Technology Transfer Strategy:How Chinese Investments in Emerging Technology Enable A Strategic Competitor to Access the Crown Jewels of U.S. Innovation*, Defence Innivation Unit Experimental, https://admin.govexec.com/media/diux_chinatechnologytransferstudy_jan_2018_(1).pdf. [11]

d'Hooghe, I. and J. Lammertink (2020), *Towards Sustainable Europe-China Collaborationin Higher Education in Research*, https://leidenasiacentre.nl/wp-content/uploads/2020/10/Towards-Sustainable-Europe-China-Collaboration-in-Higher-Education-and-Research.pdf. [27]

Edwards, J. (2016), *U.S. targets spying threat on campus with proposed research clampdown*, Reuters, https://www.reuters.com/article/us-usa-security-students-idUSKCN0YB1QT. [20]

Federal Office for Economic Affairs and Export Control (BAFA) (2019), *Export Control and Academia Manual*, https://www.bafa.de/SharedDocs/Downloads/EN/Foreign_Trade/ec_academia.pdf. [25]

Graham, E. and D. Marchick (2006), *U.S. National Security and Foreign Direct Investment*, Economics, Peterson Institute for International Economics, https://www.piie.com/bookstore/us-national-security-and-foreign-direct-investment. [1]

Hannas, W. and H. Chang (2019), *China's Access to Foreign AI Technology*, https://cset.georgetown.edu/wp-content/uploads/CSET_China_Access_To_Foreign_AI_Technology.pdf. [10]

Jackson, J. (2020), *The Committee on Foreign Investment in the United States (CFIUS)*, https://crsreports.congress.gov/product/pdf/RL/RL33388/93. [4]

Jackson, J. (2018), *The Committee on Foreign Investment in the United States (CFIUS)*, Congressional Research Service, https://crsreports.congress.gov/product/pdf/RL/RL33388/68. [2]

JASON (2019), *Fundamental Research Security*, https://nsf.gov/news/special_reports/jasonsecurity/JSR-19-2IFundamentalResearchSecurity_12062019FINAL.pdf. [18]

Joske, A. (2018), *Picking flowers, making honey – The Chinese military's collaboration with foreign universities*, Australian Strategic Policy Institute, https://s3-ap-southeast-2.amazonaws.com/ad-aspi/2018-10/Picking flowers%2C making honey_0.pdf. [12]

Kratz, A. et al. (2020), *Chinese FDI in Europe: 2019 Update – Special Topic: Research Collaborations*, Rhodium Group; Merics, https://rhg.com/wp-content/uploads/2020/04/MERICS-Rhodium-Group_COFDI-Update-2020-2.pdf. [19]

Lloyd-Damnjanovic, A. and A. Bowe (2020), *Overseas Chinese Students and Scholars in China's Drive for Innovation*, https://www.uscc.gov/sites/default/files/2020-10/Overseas_Chinese_Students_and_Scholars_in_Chinas_Drive_for_Innovation.pdf. [17]

National Academy of Engineering (1982), *Scientific Communication and National Security*, National Academies Press, Washington, D.C., http://dx.doi.org/10.17226/253. [26]

National Research Council (2007), *Science and Security in a Post 9/11 World: A Report Based on Regional Discussions Between the Science and Security Communities*, National Academies Press, Washington, D.C., http://dx.doi.org/10.17226/12013. [24]

National Science Foundation (2019), *Personnel Policy on Foreign Government Talent Recruitment Programs*, https://www.nsf.gov/bfa/dias/policy/researchprotection/PersonnelPolicyForeignGovTalentRecruitment Programs07_11_2019.pdf. [15]

OECD (2021), *FDI in Figures*, https://www.oecd.org/investment/FDI-in-Figures-April-2021.pdf. [8]

OECD (2021), *Investment policy developments in 62 economies between 16 October 2020 and 15 March 2021*, https://www.oecd.org/daf/inv/investment-policy/Investment-policy-monitoring-March-2021-ENG.pdf. [6]

OECD (2021), *Transparency, Predictability and Accountability for investment screening mechanisms, Research note by the OECD Secretariat*, https://www.oecd.org/daf/inv/investment-policy/2009-Guidelines-webinar-May-2021-background-note.pdf. [28]

OECD (2020), *Inventory of investment measures taken between 16 September 2019 and 15 October 2020*, https://www.oecd.org/daf/inv/investment-policy/FOI-investment-measure-monitoring-October-2020.pdf. [5]

Oikawa, A. (2021), *Japan tightens rules on tech theft*, https://asia.nikkei.com/Business/Technology/Japan-tightens-rules-on-tech-theft-to-safeguard-research-with-US. [21]

Pohl, J. and N. Rosselot (2020), *Acquisition-and ownership-related policies to safeguard essential security interests - Current and emerging trends, observed designs, and policy practice in 62 economies*, https://www.oecd.org/investment/OECD-Acquisition-ownership-policies-security-May2020.pdf. [9]

Segal, S. and D. Gerstel (2019), *Research Collaboration in an Era of Strategic Competition*, Center for Strategic and International Studies, https://csis-website-prod.s3.amazonaws.com/s3fs-public/publication/190925_Segal%26Gerstel_ResearchCollaboration.pdf. [14]

Silcoff, S. et al. (2018), *How Canadian money and research are helping China become a global telecom superpower*, https://www.theglobeandmail.com/canada/article-how-canadian-money-and-research-are-helping-china-become-a-global/. [13]

United States Government Accountability Office (2018), *Committee on Foreign Investment in the United States - Treasury Should Coordinate Assessments of Resources Needed to Address Increased Workload*, https://www.gao.gov/assets/gao-18-249.pdf. [3]

United States Intelligence, National Security Commission on Artificial Intelligence (2021), *Final Report*, https://www.nscai.gov/wp-content/uploads/2021/03/Full-Report-Digital-1.pdf. [22]

United States Senate Permanent Subcommittee on Investigations (2019), *Threats to the U.S. Research Enterprise: China's Talent Recruitment Plans*, https://www.hsgac.senate.gov/imo/media/doc/2019-11-18%20PSI%20Staff%20Report%20-%20China%27s%20Talent%20Recruitment%20Plans.pdf. [16]

Williams, R. (2018), "In the Balance: The Future of America's National Security and Innovation Ecosystem", *Lawfare*, https://www.lawfareblog.com/balance-future-americas-national-security-and-innovation-ecosystem. [23]

Notes

[1] This chapter does not deal with non-commercial forms of technology acquisition, such as theft of intellectual property or espionage.

[2] The OECD Recommendation of the Council on International Co-operation in Science and Technology, initially adopted in 1988 but revised in 2021, calls on Adherents to remove barriers to mutually beneficial international co-operation in science and technology and offers recommendations to expand such cooperation with a view to contribute to sustainable development, inclusive economic growth and social well-being.

[3] The OECD Recommendation of the Council on Artificial Intelligence (2019) emphasises the various aspects that governments wish to keep in mind to provide an enabling ecosystem.

[4] See on the rationale specifically for AI (United States Intelligence, National Security Commission on Artificial Intelligence, 2021, p. 12[22]).

[5] Illegal means to transfer technology, in particular theft and espionage are not considered in the context of this note.

[6] Corresponding guidance is in place for example in Japan (Ministry of Economy, Trade and Industry, Trade Control Department: "*Guidance for the Control of Sensitive Technologies for Security Export for Academic and Research Institutions*", 3rd Edition, October 2017) and Germany (Federal Office for Economic Affairs and Export Control (BAFA), 2019[25]).

[7] The German government states that "basic scientific research is not subject to export controls". (Federal Office for Economic Affairs and Export Control (BAFA), 2019, p. 54[25]).

[8] See the Preamble of the Revised Recommendation of the Council on International Co-operation in Science and Technology, adopted on 23 June 2021.

[9] Similar concerns had been raised in the 1980s in the United States, then in relation to technology acquisition by Eastern Bloc nations (National Academy of Engineering, 1982[26]). They led, among others to the adoption of the National Security Decision Directive 189 (NSDD-189) on 21 September 1985.

[10] A vivid debate about potential foreign interference and intimidation in research institutions is taking place contemporaneously in several countries, often the same that have expressed greatest concern about the implications of researcher exchanges and foreign research funding. Alleged censorship of certain social media content has also been cited in relation to foreign investment reviews. These issues raise other aspects than those related to transfer of technology and are thus not further discussed here. Context and other contemporaneous concerns are summarised in (d'Hooghe and Lammertink, 2020, p. 59[27]).

[11] E.g. *Government bill 2020/21:60 Research, freedom, future – Knowledge and innovation for Sweden*, 17 December 2020, in particular section 17.3 of the explanatory memorandum.

[12] Export Control Reform Act of 2018 (ECRA; P.L. 115-232, Subtitle B, Part I)

[13] "Suspension of Entry as Nonimmigrants of Certain Students and Researchers From the People's Republic of China", Proclamation by the President of the United States of America 10043 of May 29, 2020, Federal Register Vol. 85, No. 108, June 4, 2020. "Technology Alert Lists" (TAL), of which older, publicly available versions specifically mention AI, are used by consular officers to screen applicants for United States visa.

[14] Bill S.1260 — 117th Congress (2021-2022).

[15] Australia's Foreign Relations (State and Territory Arrangements) Act 2020.

[16] Research Security Policy Statement – Spring 2021, 24 March 2021.

[17] EU-US Summit Statement, "Towards a renewed Transatlantic partnership", 15 June 2021.

[18] More details on the implementation of the 2009 OECD Guidelines is available in (OECD, 2021[28])

www.ingramcontent.com/pod-product-compliance
Ingram Content Group UK Ltd.
Pitfield, Milton Keynes, MK11 3LW, UK
UKHW051503290926
15471UKWH00008B/1384